h

Mexican and Mexican-American Agricultural Labor in the United States

An International Bibliography

Mexican and Mexican-American Agricultural Labor in the United States

An International Bibliography

Martin H. Sable

The Haworth Press
New York • London

Mexican and Mexican-American Agricultural Labor in the United States: An International Bibliography is monographic supplement #1 to the journal *Behavioral & Social Sciences Librarian*, Volume 5, 1986. It is not supplied as part of the subscription to the journal, but is available from the publisher at an additional charge.

The Haworth Press, Inc., 12 West 32 Street, New York NY 10001
EUROSPAN/Haworth, 3 Henrietta Street, London WC2E 8LU England

Library of Congress Cataloging in Publication Data

Sable, Martin Howard.
    Mexican and Mexican-American agricultural labor in the United States.

    Includes indexes.
    1. Mexican American agricultural laborers—United States—Bibliography.
I. Title.
Z7164.L1S2   1986   016.3316'2'72073   85-27346
[HD8081.M6]
ISBN 0-86656-542-6

CONTENTS

THIS BOOK IS DEDICATED TO
MY SON
CHARLES DAVID SABLE, A.B., M.A.

Introduction

Mexican and Mexican-American Agricultural Labor in the United States is a combination bibliography and directory that fills a major gap in the reference literature of this topic. While attempts have been made over the years to treat this topic, the results have appeared as segments of bibliographies dealing with a variety of aspects of Mexican-American culture. The purpose of the present work is to provide university students and faculty, as well as researchers and librarians (whether employed in universities, research centers, government agencies, professional organizations or social service agencies), a research guide of breadth and depth, that reflects the literature, both popular and scholarly, of the major topic and its subtopics. A secondary purpose is to make available directories of relevant organizations, labor unions, government agencies and research centers.

KINDS OF MATERIALS INCLUDED

The main section of this work, the bibliography, contains print-format materials, both popular and scholarly: books, monographs, pamphlets, government publications (issued not only by the United States and Mexican governments, but in addition by states and counties), masters' theses, doctoral dissertations, conference papers and proceedings, chapters from books, journal and newspaper articles. It should be noted that previously-compiled bibliographies precede each section of the bibliography in the *Scholarly Materials* segment.

Appendix A contains audiovisual materials: films and filmstrips, transparencies, audio- and videotapes, cassettes and phonorecords. In Appendix B are included print-format materials of a type found in archives: autobiographies, diaries and memoirs, oral histories, business and personal records, collections of newspaper clippings, and government and labor union documents. The author located many of these items in the Bancroft Library of the University of California, Berkeley; and others in archival collections at UCLA, the University of Texas, the Walter P. Reuther Library's Archive of Labor and Urban Affairs of Wayne States University in Detroit, and the National Archives in Washington, D.C. English- and Spanish-language newspapers as well as scholarly journals are listed in Appendix C. Appendix D comprises a directory, arranged in ten sections: associations concerned with Mexican-Americans; associations concerned with migrant agricultural workers; social science research centers that have treated any of the groups or topics covered; Mexican-American research centers; research centers treating the topic of immigration; agricultural labor unions and concerned organizations; United States Government agencies, commissions and departments; and agencies, commissions and programs of the State of California. The ultimate aim of this conglomeration of print and nonprint of materials, in combination with the directories listed above, is to place at the disposal of those concerned with the major topic and any of its subdivisions a research/resource guide that makes readily available required bibliographic data or, alternatively, the names and addresses of entities to which they might submit their inquiries. In other words, the present work can be considered a "one-stop" reference tool.

ARRANGEMENT

The various segments of the bibliography section are arranged, in accordance with the preference of researchers, *chronologically,* and each subtopic is divided into *Popular Materials* and *Scholarly Materials,* i.e., each subtopic in the bibliography section is repeated in the "Popular Materials" section and in the "Scholarly Materials" section.

The subtopics are:

Agricultural Labor, General. This serves as a preface to the major theme of the bibliography. Incidental subtopics here include statistics on farmworkers' wages (retrospective into the nineteenth century), agricultural mechanization, and significant historical materials.

Immigration of Mexican Agricultural Labor. This largest segment of the bibliography includes entries in both popular and scholarly sections concerning *braceros,* whether in the form of articles (many from the dissident and alternative press), masters' theses and dissertations, or government publications. Many of the articles were published in the first two decades of the twentieth century.

Mexican-American Farm Labor. The third segment contains entries on this topic in general and others on the history of individual western and southwestern states, land-holding, living standards and social conditions of the rural Mexican-American population.

Migrant Agricultural Labor. It is inevitable that some entries refer to both white and Black migrant farmworkers. In cases in which this occurs, Mexican-American migrants are represented in each entry, either in whole or in part. State and federal government documents are prominent here. Included are publications of the various agencies of the executive branch (e.g., the Departments of Agriculture and Labor) and Congressional hearings on living and working conditions and civil rights. Included also are items issued by the states on these matters.

Agricultural Labor Unions. Articles from the alternative and dissident press (as well as from the *Los Angeles Times*) comprise a significant cross-section of the entries here. The history of the agricultural labor movement is highlighted by entries not only for the I.W.W. (Industrial Workers of the World) and the Agricultural Workers Industrial Union but also for additional defunct groups such as the National Agricultural Workers Union and the National Farm Labor Union. Currently there are two farmworkers' labor unions: Cesar Chavez's United Farm Workers of America, located in Keene, California, and the Farm Labor Organizing Committee in Toledo, Ohio. Articles by and about Cesar Chavez and several complete books about him are included.

Farm Labor Strikes. This final section of the bibliography contains references to articles from the alternative and standard press and to books and masters' theses concerning farm labor problems and strikes. The earliest entry dates from the year 1896. Much of the unrest is well-documented, including the berry pickers' strike in El Monte, California, in 1933, the DiGiorgio Farm strike in 1947, the grape strike in Delano, California, and the subsequent march by Chavez and his followers to Sacramento in 1967, current work stoppages and the controversy concerning *el cortito* (the short-handled hoe), still legal in Arizona but outlawed in California.

For descriptions of the type of materials found in the four appendices and the subsections of the directory, please refer to *Kinds of Materials Included.*

As regards *arrangement* of periodical article entries, it should be noted that (as for books, masters' theses and doctoral dissertations, conference papers and proceedings and similar "book type" items) each item is entered chronologically by year of publication, and subsequently by month and date. Where two or more items are published in the same month and/or on the same date of the same month, the arrangement then is alphabetical by author surname. Where no author is present, the arrangement is alphabetical by the title of the article.

INDEX

Given the subject-approach arrangement of the body of the bibliography and appendices, there is no need for a subject index. There are, however, in-depth author and title indexes for all of the bibliographical materials. For entries without an author (and especially in the case of periodical articles), the title is entered as author.

SPECIAL FEATURES

An effort was made to include the addresses of the producers and/ or distributors of the audiovisual materials identified and described in Appendix A. Likewise, investigations were undertaken to identify and describe the manuscripts in their respective archives, as set forth in Appendix B. The newspapers and journal titles and the names of the associations, organizations and governmental agencies, presented respectively in Appendices C and D, supplement the materials in the bibliography section and provide access to information not readily available but often needed by researchers.

SCOPE

All aspects of the topic and its various ramifications have been treated. With respect to the employment of *braceros,* for example, there are English-language entries (mainly articles and pamphlets) by noted Mexicans such as the economist, Edmundo Flores, and the government officials, Ezequiél Padilla and José Vasconcelos.

Of the total of the entries, some 150 were published in the Spanish language (whether in Mexico, Spain, Latin America or the United States; one journal article was published in Barranquilla, Colombia; and two were issued in Spain with the balance in Mexico and the USA); one book was issued in Norwegian, while four conference papers were published in French. English is the language of all other entries. A few items were issued in England.

The oldest materials, located at the Bancroft Library of the University of California, Berkeley, represent the inventory of the San Diego de Alcalá Mission, and were recorded during the years 1777-1784. The cutoff date is 1984. Hence the time span covered exceeds 200 years.

In addition to the several Mexican authors previously mentioned, others who wrote on some aspect of the topic, whether in the early decades of the twentieth century or currently, are represented. A current Mexican author is Dr. Jorge A. Bustamante, Director of the Center for North American Border Studies of the Universidad Autonoma de Baja California in Tijuana. North American scholars giving attention to the topic as of 1984 include Wayne C. Cornelius, Director of the Center for U.S. Mexican Studies at the University of California at San Diego, and others at the Center: Ann L. Craig, Ina R. Dinerman, Richard Mines, and David S. North. Additional U.S. scholars are Vernon M. Briggs, Jr., Robert Coles, William H. Friedland, Joan W. Moore, Dorothy Nelkin, Alejandro Portes, and Robert D. Tomasek. Writings, spanning the period from the 1920s to the 1970s, by the following are noted: Louis Bloch, Emory S. Bogardus, Frank J. Bruno, Anne Draper, Louis J. Ducoff, Ernesto Galarza, Manuel Gamio, Leo Grebler, Pauline R. Kibbe, Carey McWilliams, Lowry Nelson, Robert Refield, Paul S. Taylor, and Thorstein Veblen. Works by two noted authors, the first a Latinamericanist, Erna Fergusson, and Eric Hoffer are given entries; and articles by labor leaders and U.S. Secretaries of Labor William Green, Ray Marshall and George Meany are represented.

ACKNOWLEDGEMENT

The author thanks two of his students in the School of Library and Information Science of the University of Wisconsin-Milwaukee who assisted in the physical preparation of this work. Judy Wojcik arranged half of the bibliography chronologically, and James Ramseyer set up the program for the computerization of the author index.

ABBREVIATIONS

a.—annual
bim.—bimonthly
ed.—editor, edition; *Ed.*—Editorial (publisher, publishing house)
enl.—enlarged
G.P.O.—U.S. Government Printing Office
Impr.—Imprenta (printing shop)
m.—monthly
n.d.—no date given
n.p.—no place given
p., pp.—pages
q.—quarterly
rev.—revised
s.a.—semi-annual
s.m.—semi-monthly
v.—volume(s)
v.p.—variously paged
w.—weekly

The letters "ED," followed by six digits, signify a publication which may be ordered (utilizing the "ED" number), from the ERIC Document Reproduction Service, P.O. Box 190, Alexandria, VA 22210.

Popular Materials

A. AGRICULTURAL LABOR, GENERAL

1
California. Dept. of Human Resources Development. Rural Manpower
   Services Division. *California Guide for Farm Workers; a Handbook.*
   Sacramento [n.d.] 22p.

2
Good, Paul
   Breaking new Ground. Rural Advancement Fund of the National Share-
   croppers Fund, Inc., 112 E. 19th St., New York, N.Y. 10003.

3
Texas State Federation of Labor.
   Monthly Roundup. Austin? [n.d.] (monthly).

4
Hayes, J.
   "Skilled Farming in Los Angeles." *Overland Monthly* 7, 1871, p. 448.

5
"The Rural Labor Problem." *Independent* 55, September 17, 1903, pp.
   2244-2245.

6
Holmes, George K.
   "Supply and Wages of Farm Labor." *U.S. Dept. of Agriculture Year-
   book 1910.* Washington, 1910, pp. 189-220.

7
"Distribution of Agricultural Immigrants." *Survey* 27, October 7, 1911,
   pp. 927-928.

8
"Wages of Farm Labor." *Farmers' Bulletin* 665, March 20, 1915, pp.
   8-9.

9
U.S. Dept. of Agriculture.
   Plan for Handling the Farm-Labor Problem. Washington, June 5, 1917,
   31p.

10
Lasker, Bruno
"Swords and Plowshares: who Shall Grow Crops to win the War and Feed a Hungry World?" *Survey* 39, February 9, 1918, pp. 513-516.

11
"Wages of Farm Labor in the United States." *Monthly Review* 6, June 1918, pp. 1484-1485.

12
Wallace, H. C.
"Farm Wages Compared With Others . . ." *American Industries,* January 1923, pp. 19-20.

13
Crissey, Forrest
"The Farmer and a 'Living Wage' . . ." *American Bankers Association Journal* 15, February 1923, pp. 538-540.

14
Sherman, C. B.
"The Farm Labor Problem." *American Bankers Association Journal,* July 1925, pp. 21-22.

15
"Average Wages Paid to Hired Farm Labor by States, October 1923-1925; Average Prevailing Farm Wage Rates, by Geographic Divisions; Farm Wage Rates and Index Numbers, 1866-1925." *Crops and Markets Monthly Supplement* 2, October 1925, pp. 327-328.

16
"The Farm Laborer as a Human Being." *Monthly Labor Review* 25, July 1927, pp. 27-30.

17
"Farmers Covered by California Workmen's Compensation Law." *Monthly Labor Review* 25, December 1927, p. 1269.

18
Munson, Edward L.
"Solving the Farm Labor Problem in California." *Overland Monthly* (new series), 87, May 1929, pp. 147-148.

19
"Perquisites and Wages of Hired Farm Labor." *Monthly Labor Review* 29, August 1929, pp. 418-422.

20
Sakolski, Aaron M.
The Great American Land Bubble: the Amazing Story of Land Grabbing,

Speculations and Booms From Colonial Days to the Present Time. New York, Harper, 1932, 373p.

21
Rak, Mary (Kidder)
A Cowman's Wife. Boston, Houghton, Mifflin, 1934, 292p.

22
"The Wage Earner in Agriculture." *Monthly Labor Review* 42, February 1936, pp. 339-346.

23
Vasey, Tom, & Folsom, J. C.
"Farm Laborers: Their Economic and Social Status." *Agricultural Situation* (U.S. Dept. of Agriculture), October 1937, pp. 14-15.

24
Johnson, Elizabeth
"Wages, Employment Conditions and Welfare of Sugar-Beet Laborers." *Monthly Labor Review* 46, February 1938, pp. 322-340.

25
Wendzel, J. T.
"Distribution of Hired Farm Labor in the United States." *Monthly Labor Review* 47, August 1938, pp. 395-396.

26
"Wages in Cotton Picking, 1937 and 1938." *Monthly Labor Review* 47, December 1938, pp. 1239-1249.

27
Conner, Palmer
The Romance of the Ranchos. 6th ed. Los Angeles, Title Insurance & Trust Co., 1939, 40p.

28
Bowden, Witt
"Farm Employment 1909 to 1938." *Monthly Labor Review* 48, June 1939, pp. 1241-1257.

29
"Farm Wage Hearings; California Group Aims to fix pay Rates for Each Major Crop." *Business Week,* October 21, 1939, p. 42.

30
Ham, W. T.
"Farm Labor in an era of Change." (In U.S. Dept. of Agriculture. *Yearbook of Agriculture 1940.* Washington, GPO, 1940, pp. 907-921).

31
Plenn, Jaime H.
Saddle in the sky. Indianapolis, Bobbs-Merrill, 1940, 287p.

32
"Minimum Wages for Sugar-Beet and Sugar-Cane Workers." *Monthly Labor Review* 53, July 1941, pp. 167-169.

33
Rusinow, Irving
A Camera Report on El Cerrito, a Typical Spanish-American Community in New Mexico. Washington, U.S. Dept. of Agriculture, Bureau of Agricultural Economics, Miscellaneous Publication #479, 1942.

34
Brown, Agnes E.
"Ho, for a Tall Glass of Lemonade! California Women Help Save Lemon Crop." *Christian Science Monitor Weekly Magazine Section,* January 9, 1943, p. 12.

35
"Wartime Relaxation of California's Woman and Child Labor Laws in 1943." *Monthly Labor Review* 59, July 1944, pp. 121-122.

36
Hill, George W.
"The Farm Labor Situation Today and Tomorrow." *Agricultural Situation* (U.S. Dept. of Agriculture), August 1944, pp. 15-18.

37
"Wages on Farms." *Business Week,* November 11, 1944, pp. 103-104.

38
"Farm Labor: Who's who in Farm Labor; Wages; Productivity; Price and Progress." *Borden's Economic Digest,* November 1946, pp. 1-6.

39
U.S. Dept. of Agriculture, Federal Extension Service
A Guide to Farm Jobs From Gulf to Great Lakes. Extension Farm Labor Program. (U.S. Dept. of Agriculture PA-32). Washington, GPO, 1947, 31p.

40
U.S. Dept. of Agriculture. Extension Farm Labor Program *A Guide to Farm Jobs From Gulf to Great Lakes.* (PA-32). Washington, May 1947, 31p.

41
Birch, John J.
"The Fields are White." *Extension* (43: 4), September 1948, pp. 12-13, 44-45.

42

Myers, David
"More Reports of California Farm Labor." *The American Child* 32, May 1950, pp. 1-4.

43

Myers, David, & Hill, Gladwin
"More Reports on California Farm Labor." *American Child,* May 1950, p. 1.

44

"The Farm Placement Program, 1955". *Employment Security Review,* March 1955- (entire issue).

45

Bennett, Fay
"How the Farm Worker Fares: the Forgotten man of the Boom." *Socialist Call,* April/May 1957, pp. 10-13.

46

Hale, Will (pseud.)
24 Years a Cowboy and Ranchman in Southern Texas and old Mexico; Desperate Fights With the Indians and Mexicans. New ed. Norman, University of Oklahoma Press, 1959, 183p.

47

Rush, Philip S.
The Californias, 1846-1957. San Diego? 1959, 167p.

48

Bailey, Linwood K., & Vernoff, Samuel
"American Wage Policy Developments During 1958." *Employment Security Review* 26, February 1959, pp. 12-14.

49

Mitchell, J. P.
"Farm Worker in America; Excerpt from Address, February 23, 1959." *Monthly Labor Review* 82, April 1959, pp. 396-398.

50

Fuller, Varden
"Farm Labor: Supply, Policies, and Practices: Pacific Coast States." *Monthly Labor Review* 82, May 1959, pp. 518-523.

51

Seabrook, J. M.
"Farm Labor: Address, February 5, 1959." *Vital Speeches* 25, July 1, 1959, pp. 556-559.

52
Farinholt, Mary K.
"Farm Wages and Food Prices." *Progressive* 24, May 1960, pp. 34-36.

53
Ogle, Alice
"California Farm Labor." *America* 3, December 19-26, 1964, pp. 799, 802.

54
Rush, Philip S.
Some old Ranches and Adobes. San Diego, Philip S. Rush, 1965, 121p.

55
"Stoop Labor; California Farm Workers." *Commonweal* 81, February 5, 1965, pp. 596-597.

56
"These Hired Hands Want to Stay: California Dairies." *Farm Journal* 89, September 1965, p. 40.

57
Koch, William H., Jr.
Dignity of Their own; Helping the Disadvantaged Become First-Class Citizens. New York, Friendship Press, 1966, 190p.

58
"Crusade Against Gringos: Federal Alliance of Land Grants Claims Original Spanish Land." *Newsweek* 67, January 3, 1966, pp. 17-18.

59
"Stooping to Conquer; Wirtz Report." *Newsweek* 67, February 7, 1966, pp. 61-62.

60
Groom, Phyllis
"Today's Farm jobs and Farmworkers." *Monthly Labor Review* 90, April 1967, pp. 1-5.

61
"Halting the Flight From the Land." *Christian Century* 84, June 14, 1967, pp. 773-774.

62
Hanson, D.
"How Will you Hire Farm Labor?" *Successful Farming* 65, July 1967, p. 22.

63

Scott, Wayne S.

"Spanish Land Grant Problems Were Here Before the Anglos." *New Mexico Business* (20: 7), July 1967, pp. 1-9.

64

Kentfield, C.

"Incident in Rio Arriba; Attempt by Small Band of Spanish Americans to Seize Land in New Mexico." *New York Times Magazine,* July 16, 1967, pp. 20-21.

65

King, L. T.

"Unjolly Green Giant; Unemployment in Imperial Valley." *Commonweal* 86, July 28, 1967, p. 461.

66

Koziara, Karen (Shallcross)

"The Agricultural Minimum Wage: a Preliminary Look." *Monthly Labor Review* 90, September 1967, pp. 26-29.

67

Ballis, George

New Housing by Poor Farm Workers. Photographed and Produced by George Ballis. Visalia, CA, Self-Help Enterprises, 1968, 50p.

68

Vanderbilt, Cornelius

Ranches and Ranch Life in America. New York, Crown, 1968, 280p.

69

"Labor Problem." *Successful Farming* 66, January 1968, pp. 35-37.

70

Jones, E. W.

"Farm Labor and Public Policy." *Monthly Labor Review* 91, March 1968, pp. 12-15.

71

Taylor, Paul S.

"Water, Land and People in the Great Valley." *American West* (5: 2), March 1968, pp. 24-29.

72

Booth, Philip

"Sickness Insurance and California Farm Workers." *Social Security Bulletin* 31, May 1968, pp. 3-13.

73
"The Rural Worker in America." *Monthly Labor Review* 91, June 1968, pp. 1-32.

74
Fowler, R. G.
"Incentive Plan That Makes Workers try Harder." *Farm Journal* 92, October 1968, pp. 46L-46N.

75
Bennett, Fay
The Condition of Farm Workers and Small Farmers in 1969; Report. National Board of the National Sharecroppers Fund, 112 E. 19th St., New York, N.Y. 10003, 1969, 5p.

76
Hastings, Lansford W. (1819- ca. 1870)
The Immigrant's Guide to Oregon and California. New York, Da Capo Press, 1969, 152p.

77
Nabokov, Peter
Tijerina and the Courthouse Raid. Albuquerque, University of New Mexico Press, 1969.

78
"Nixon Plan for Farm Workers." *U.S. News & World Report* 66, May 19, 1969, p. 110.

79
Becker, James W.
"A Career Ladder for Farmworkers." *Farm Labor Developments,* December 1969, pp. 7-11.

80
Nabokov, Peter
"After Tijerina: La Raza, the Land and the Hippies." *The Nation* 210, April 20, 1970, pp. 464-468.

81
Reno, Lee P.
Pieces and Scraps: Farm Labor Housing in the United States. Rural Housing Alliance (1346 Connecticut Ave., NW, Suite 500, Washington, D.C., 20036), September 1970, 141p.

82
Gordon, Alvin, & De Grazia, Ted
Of Vines and Missions. Flagstaff, AZ, Northland Press, 1971.

83

Palmer, Kenyon T.
For Land's Sake; the Autobiography of a Carefree Arizonian. Flagstaff,
AZ, Northland Press, 1971, 354p.

84

California. Dept. of Human Resources Development.
Employment Data and Research Division
Agricultural Employment by Type of Worker for California and the Major Agricultural Counties. Sacramento, 1973, unpaged. (Report 881M,
#11).

85

California. Employment Development Dept.
Agricultural Orientation, Recruitment. Sacramento, 1974?

86

"Farm Workers Communiqúe." *La Raza* (2: 1), February 1974, pp.
10-11.

87

Klein, D. P., & Whipple, D. S.
"Employment in Agriculture: a Profile." *Monthly Labor Review* 97,
April 1974, pp. 28-32.

88

"Editorial on California Court Ruling on Short-Handled Hoe." *Los Angeles Times,* January 20, 1975, sec. II, p. 7, c. 1.

89

"California Bans use of Short-Handled Hoe by Farm Workers." *Los Angeles Times,* April 8, 1975, sec. I, p. 20, c. 4.

90

"History of the Short-Handled Hoe Recently Outlawed in California."
Los Angeles Times, April 14, 1975, sec. II, p. 1, c. 1.

91

"California Senate Panel Okays Governor's Farm Labor Bill." *Los Angeles Times,* May 8, 1975, sec. II, p. 1, c. 5.

92

"California; Farmer Brown." *The Economist* 255, May 17, 1975, p. 63.

93

"California Senate Passes Farm Labor Bill." *Los Angeles Times,* May 27,
1975, sec. I, p. 3, c. 1.

94

"The Farmworker Journal." *The Workbook* (4: 3), June 1975, p. 107- .

95
"California Passes Farm Labor Law." *Monthly Labor Review* 98, August 1975, p. 47.

96
"Farm Workers Salad Bowl Law." *The Economist* 257, November 8, 1975, pp. 73-74.

97
"California Supreme Court Rules vs. Employee Eviction From Company Housing." *Los Angeles Times,* August 12, 1976, sec. I, p. 2, c. 5.

98
"U.S. Labor Dept. Investigates Violations of Farm Labor Act." *Los Angeles Times,* August 15, 1976, sec. I, p. 2, c. 5.

99
"California Governor Brown and Senator Tunney Endorse Proposition 14." *Los Angeles Times,* September 4, 1976, sec. II, p. 1, c. 4.

100
"U.S. Senate Committee Refuses to Extend Jobless pay for Farm Workers." *Los Angeles Times,* September 16, 1976, sec. I, p. 3, c. 4.

101
"Editorial Opposition to California Proposition 14 on Farm Labor Law." *Los Angeles Times,* October 29, 1976, sec. II, p. 6, c. 1.

102
"Governor Brown Claims oil Companies Play Large Role vs. Proposition 14." *Los Angeles Times,* October 30, 1976, sec. II, p. 1, c. 5.

103
"Governor Brown Urges 'Yes' Vote on Proposition 14 in ad." *Los Angeles Times,* November 2, 1976, sec. I, p. 12, c. 1.

104
Tichy, George J., & Meyers, James J., Jr.
Growers' Handbook to the California Agricultural Labor Relations Act.
[Stockton, California] San Joaquin Nisei Farmers League, 1977, 85p.

105
"Effect of Lettuce Picking Machine on California Farm Workers Viewed." *Los Angeles Times,* August 22, 1977, sec. III, p. 9, c. 5.

106
Weisbord, A.
"Report Knocks Agribusiness." *Guardian* (29: 49), September 28, 1977, p. 6- .

107

Marable, M.
"The new South has Some Old Problems." *Moving on* (1: 7), October 1977, p. 20- .

108

"California Assembly Subcommittee Hears Testimony on Farm Unemployment." *Los Angeles Times,* November 8, 1977, sec. I, p. 13, c. 3.

109

California. Dept. of Human Resources Development.
Employment Data and Research Division.
Agricultural Employment Estimates, Annual Averages, 1950-1977. Sacramento, Employment Development Dept., Employment Data and Research Division, 1978, 44p.

110

Winter, M.
"I am Confident we Will win." *Militant* (42: 1), January 13, 1978, p. 6- .

111

"Cesar Chavez Cites Peril to Farm Laborers From Mechanization." *Los Angeles Times,* February 12, 1978, sec. I, p. 32, c. 1.

112

"Cesar Chavez Addresses University of California Regents Commission on Displaced Farm Workers." *Los Angeles Times,* February 17, 1978, sec. II, p. 1, c. 5.

113

"U.S. Officials Questioned in Withholding Funds From Texas Group." *Los Angeles Times,* March 16, 1978, sec. I, p. 19, c. 1.

114

Elterich, G. J.
"Estimating the Cost of Extending Jobless Insurance to Farmworkers." *Monthly Labor Review* 101, May 1978, pp. 18-24.

115

Martinez, Douglas R.
"A Chance for the Tillers to own the Soil." *Agenda* (8: 3), May/June 1978, pp. 27-29.

116

Foster, D.
"Weeding Workers." *In These Times* (2: 25), May 10, 1978, p. 12- .

117
"California Assembly Panel Defeats 2 key Grower-Sponsored Farm Bills." *Los Angeles Times,* May 18, 1978, sec. I, p. 29, c. 4.

118
"Government Farmworker Policies." *Ms.* 6, June 1978, p. 68.

119
Halsell, Grace
   "With Farm Workers. Part I: California." *Agenda* (8: 4), July/August 1978, pp. 18-21.

120
"The Life of a Farm Worker (Photo Essay)." *Agenda* (8: 4), July/August 1978, pp. 11-13.

121
Saavedra-Vela, Pilar
   "A Community Returns to Agriculture." *Agenda* (8: 4), July/August 1978, pp. 7-9.

122
"Governor Brown Addresses UFW Convention on Farm Labor law Issue." *Los Angeles Times,* August 8, 1978, sec. I, p. 3, c. 5.

123
"Farming the Garden State." *Food Monitor* 6, September 1978, p. 4- .

124
"Editorial on Controversy Over UC Research on Farm Mechanization." *Los Angeles Times,* January 24, 1979, sec. II, p. 4, c. 1-E.

125
Remer, L.
   "Square Tomatoes Bring Round Figures." *In These Times* March 7, 1979, p. 4- .

126
"University Picks off Farm Workers' Jobs." *Rochester Patriot* (7: 7), April 13, 1979, p. 6- .

127
Werner, M.
   "Senate Hears Farmworkers." *In These Times* (3: 26), May 16, 1979, p. 4- .

128
Cianci, L.
   "Machines Will put Farm Workers out." *In These Times* (3: 38), August 22, 1979, p. 4- .

129
Fleming, Robert
"The South's Sugar Plantations: one Step From Slavery." *Encore* 8, September 4, 1979, pp. 12-15.

130
"Lost in the Stream." *Southern Exposure* (8: 4), Winter 1980, p. 67-

131
Petrow, S.
"Sugar Cane Slavery." *Southern Exposure* (8: 4), Winter 1980, p. 72- .

132
"Community Owned by Farm Workers in Ventury County Featured." *Los Angeles Times,* April 27, 1980, sec. VII, p. 1, c. 2.

133
"Ventura Court Orders Improvements for Farm Workers Near Fillmore." *Los Angeles Times,* Junc 25, 1980, sec. I, p. 28, c. 6.

134
Haig, S.
"The new Slavery in America." *Militant* (44: 42), November 14, 1980, p. 20- .

135
"Working Under the Spray gun." *Industrial Worker* (72: 12), November 16, 1980, p. 1- .

136
Howard, R.
"Besieged OSHA Regulators." *In These Times* (5: 3), November 19, 1980, p. 6- .

137
"California Appeal Court Backs ALRB on Farm Workers' Rights." *Los Angeles Times,* December 28, 1980, sec. I, p. 22, c. 1.

138
"Rural Workers, key to the Economy." *Dollars & Sense* 64, February 1981, p. 9.

139
Mulligan, J.
"Slave Labor in the Cane Fields." *The Progressive* 45, May 1981, pp. 36-37.

140
"In-Depth Feature on Child Labor in California Counties' Fields." *Los Angeles Times,* August 26, 1981, sec. I, p. 1, c. 1.

141
Daly, P. A.
"Agricultural Employment: has the Decline Ended?" *Monthly Labor Review* 104, November 1981, pp. 11-17.

142
Ekers, V.
"OSHA Delays Sanitation Rule." *In These Times* (6: 8), January 13, 1982, p. 5- .

143
"Editorial on Controversy Over Study of California's Farm Labor Law." *Los Angeles Times,* April 16, 1982, sec. II, p. 6, c. 1-E.

144
Krass, A.
"Ohio Tomato Farmers . . . Corporate Greed." *Food Monitor* 27, May 1982, p. 20- .

145
Mulligan, J.
"Sugar in Okechobee." *Win Magazine* (18: 9), May 1, 1982, p. 13- .

146
Lange, Dorothea, & Moore, T.
"On the Land, Then . . . on the Land, now." *Living Wilderness* 46, Summer 1982, pp. 17-23.

147
Gilroy, C. L.
"The Effects of the Minimum Wage on Farm Employment: a new Model." *Monthly Labor Review* 105, June 1982, pp. 47-51.

148
Thomas, R.
"Sharecroppers Being Cheated on Wages." *Labor Notes* 42, July 21, 1982, p. 1- .

149
"Always With us, Always us." *Progressive* (46: 8), August 1982, p. 12- .

150
"Deukmejian and Bradley Discuss Farm Labor Laws During Mini-Debate." *Los Angeles Times,* October 12, 1982, sec. I, p. 3, c. 5.

151
Spady, P.
"Compromise Farmworker Bill Adopted." *Rural America* (8: 1), Winter 1983, p. 19- .

152
Harkin, T.
"Crumbs for the Poor." *Rural America* (8: 2), March 1983, p. 7- .

153
Carson, C.
"The Trouble With Farming." *The Freeman* (33: 5), May 1983, pp. 286-298.

154
Harris, J.
"Women Farm Workers Meet." *Intercontinental Press* (21: 9), May 16, 1983, p. 257- .

155
Yoerger, Y.
"We're Putting the Food on Your Table." *Big Mama* (11: 6), June 1983, p. 4- .

156
Critser, G.
"Agribusiness Gets the Upper Hand." *Nation* (37: 1), July 2, 1983, p. 10- .

157
Johnston, G., & Martin, Philip L.
"Employment and Wages Reported by California Farmers in 1982." *Monthly Labor Review* 106, September 1983, pp. 27-31.

158
"Pesticide Adviser Teaches of Hazards in Spanish for Farm Workers." *Los Angeles Times,* September 19, 1983, section I, p. 17, c. 1.

159
Yañez, A.
"Farm Workers Weigh Grower . . . Government Attack." *Militant* (47: 35), September 30, 1983, p. 10- .

160
"Del Olmo Column on Death of Farm Worker in California." *Los Angeles Times,* October 6, 1983, section II, p. 7, c. 1.

161
"The Ten Most-Asked Questions About Managing Employees." *Successful Farming* 81, December 1983, p. 22L.

162
"Questions Farm job Seekers ask Most Often." *Successful Farming* (82: 4), March 1984, p. 14N.

163
Fibich, Linda
"Professors Fear Research Suit." *Milwaukee Journal,* "Accent" Section, April 22, 1984, p. 4.

B. IMMIGRATION OF MEXICAN AGRICULTURAL LABOR

164
McLaughlin, Allan
"Italian and Other Latin Immigrants." *Popular Science Monthly* 65, August 1904, pp. 341-349.

165
"The South and Immigration." *Outlook* 83, August 4, 1906, pp. 778-779; 84, November 24, 1906, p. 691.

166
"Southern Peonage and Immigration." *Nation* 85, December 19, 1907, p. 557.

167
Mashek, Nan
"The Immigrant and the Farm." *World To-day* 20, February 1911, pp. 206-209.

168
Bryan, Samuel
"Mexican Immigrants in the United States." *Survey* 28, September 7, 1912, pp. 726-730.

169
Johnson, Alvin S.
"Mexico in San Antonio." *New Republic* 7, June 24, 1916, pp. 190-191.

170
"Mexican Invaders of El Paso." *Survey* 36, July 8, 1916, pp. 380-382.

171
"Importation of Mexican Labor." *American Industries* 19, August 1918, pp. 14-15.

172
Gwin, J. B.
"New Mexican Immigration." *Survey* 40, August 3, 1918, pp. 491-493.

173

"Regulations by U.S. Dept. of Labor for Admission of Mexican Laborers." *Monthly Labor Review* 7, November 1918, pp. 1416-1421.

174

Heald, J. H.
"Mexicans in the Southwest." *Missionary Review of the World* 42, 1919, pp. 860-865.

175

Murray, J.
"Labor's Call Across the Border." *Survey* 42, April 5, 1919, pp. 46-47.

176

"Mexican-American Friendship." *Pan American Magazine,* August 1919, pp. 24-29.

177

Stowell, Jay S.
A Study of Mexicans and Spanish Americans in the United States. New York, Home Missions Council 1920, 78p.

178

Esquivel, Servando I.
"Immigrant From Mexico." *Outlook* 125, May 19, 1920, p. 131.

179

Calcott, Frank
"The Mexican Peon in Texas." *Survey,* June 26, 1920, pp. 437-438.

180

Simpich, Frederick
"Along our Side of the Border." *National Geographic Magazine* 38, July 1920, pp. 61-80.

181

"Mexican Invaders Relieving our Farm Labor Shortage." *Literary Digest* 66, July 17, 1920, pp. 53-54.

182

"Results of Admission of Mexican Laborers Under Departmental Orders for Employment in Agricultural Pursuits." *Monthly Labor Review* 11, November 1920, pp. 1095-1097.

183

Roundy, R. W.
"The Mexican in our Midst, III." *Missionary Review of the World* 44, May 1921, pp. 371-377.

184
Sturgess, Vera L.
"Mexican Immigrants." *Survey* 46, July 2, 1921, pp. 470-471.

185
"Our Restrictive Immigration law and the Shortage of Common Labor."
The Commercial and Financial Chronicle 116, February 10, 1923, pp.
557-558.

186
Clark, Elmer T.
The Latin Immigrant in the South. Dallas, Cokesbury Press, 1924, 57p.

187
McLean, Robert N.
"Rubbing Shoulders on the Border." *Survey* 52, May 1, 1924, pp.
184-185.

188
"Without Quota." *Survey* 52, May 15, 1924, pp. 219-220.

189
Airman, D.
"Hell Along the Border." *American Mercury* 5, May 1925, pp. 17-23.

190
Thomson, Charles A.
"What of the Bracero? The Forgotten Alternative in our Immigration
Policy." *Survey* 54, June 1, 1925, pp. 291-292.

191
Thomson, Charles A.
"The man From Next Door." *Century Magazine,* January 1926, pp.
275-282.

192
Simpich, Frederick
"Little Brother Treks North." *Independent* 116, February 27, 1926,
pp. 237-239.

193
Brown, Edwin R.
"The Challenge of Mexican Immigration." *Missionary Review of the
World* 49, March 1926, pp. 192-196.

194
"The Mexican in the United States." *Bloomfield's Labor Digest* 20, March
27, 1926, pp. 3424-3425.

195
Carver, T. N.
"We now Face the Problem of Mexican Immigration." *American Bankers Association Journal* 18, April 1926, p. 692.

196
Hayne, Coe
"Study Mexican Relations at El Paso." *Missionary Review of the World* 50, February 1927, pp. 110-112.

197
"Shall we Apply the Quote to our Nearest Neighbors?" *Literary Digest* 94, August 27, 1927, p. 12.

198
Burgess, T.
"On the American Side of the Rio Grande." *Missionary Review of the World* 50, September 1927, pp. 689-692.

199
Dawson, J. M.
"Among the Mexicans in Texas." *Missionary Review of the World* 50, October 1927, p. 757.

200
Bremer, E. T.
"Up From the Border: From Mexico is Coming a new Immigration." *Woman's Press* 21, November 1927, pp. 762-764.

201
"Mexican Immigration and the Farm." *Outlook* 147, December 7, 1927, p. 423.

202
McLean, Robert N.
That Mexican! As he Really is, North and South of the Rio Grande. New York, Revell, 1928, 184p.

203
Roberts, Kenneth L.
"Mexicans or Ruin." *Saturday Evening Post* 200, February 4, 1928, pp. 14-15.

204
Roberts, Kenneth L.
"Wet and Other Mexicans." *Saturday Evening Post* 200, February 4, 1928, pp. 10-11.

205
Roberts, Kenneth L.
"The Docile Mexican." *Saturday Evening Post* 200, March 10, 1928, pp. 39-41.

206
Teague, Charles C.
"Statement on Mexican Immigration." *Saturday Evening Post* 200, March 10, 1928, pp. 169-170.

207
"Should Quota law be Applied to Mexico?" *Congressional Digest* 7, May 1928, pp. 155-164.

208
Strout, Richard L.
"A Fence for the Rio Grande." *Independent* 120, June 2, 1928, pp. 518-520.

209
"The Mexicans of Imperial Valley." *Foreign Language Information Service* 6, May 15, 1929, pp. 85-91.

210
McLean, Robert N.
"Dyke Against Mexicans." *New Republic* 59, August 14, 1929, pp. 334-337.

211
Winslow, Mary I.
"Mexican Laborers in the United States." *Commonweal* 10, September 11, 1929, pp. 476-477.

212
Taylor, Paul S.
"More Bars Against Mexicans." *Survey* XLIV, April 1930, pp. 26-27.

213
McLean, Robert N.
"Tightening the Mexican Border." *Survey* 64, April 1, 1930, pp. 28-29.

214
Woehlke, Walter V.
"Don't Drive out the Mexicans." *Review of Reviews* 81, May 1930, pp. 66-68.

215
Beals, Carleton
"Mexico and the Harris Bill." *The Nation* 131, July 9, 1930, pp. 51-52.

216
"Mexican Immigrants in El Paso." *Foreign Language Information Service* 7, July 18, 1930, pp. 44-46.

217
de Laittre, Karl
"The Mexican Laborer and you." *Nation's Business,* November 1930, p. 44.

218
Goethe, C. M.
"Peons Need not Apply." *World's Work* 59, November 1930, pp. 47-48.

219
"Mexican Exclusion: a Problem of Method." *National Sphere,* December 1930, pp. 41-43.

220
"Labor and Social Conditions of Mexicans in California." *Monthly Labor Review* 32, January 1931, pp. 83-89.

221
Austin, Mary H.
"Mexicans and New Mexico." *Survey Graphic* LXVI, May 1931, pp. 141-144, 187-190.

222
Galarza, Ernesto
"Without Benefit of Lobby." *Survey* 66, May 1, 1931, p. 181.] *seen?*

223
Gamio, Manuel
"Migration and Planning." *Survey Graphic* 66, May 1, 1931, pp. 174-175.

224
McLean, Robert N.
"Goodbye, Vicente." *Survey Graphic,* May 1, 1931, pp. 182-183.

225
Rowell, Chester H.
"Why Make Mexico an Exception?" *Survey* 66, May 1, 1931, p. 180.

226
Deering, Ivah (Everett)
"Los Pastores." *Survey* 67, December 1, 1931, pp. 264-265.

227
McLean, Robert N.
"Mexican Return." *The Nation* 135, August 24, 1932, pp. 165-166.

228
Colcord, Joanna (Carver), & Kurtz, Russell H., ed.
"Back to the Homeland." *Survey* 69, January 1933, p. 39.

229
McWilliams, Carey
"Getting rid of the Mexican." *American Mercury* 28, March 1933, pp. 322-324.

230
"Occupational Trends in Immigration to the United States, 1928 to 1932." *Monthly Labor Review* 36, March 1933, pp. 704-707.

231
"Increase of Mexican Population in the United States, 1920-1930." *Monthly Labor Review* 27, July 1933, pp. 46-48.

232
"Is Mexican Labor Cheap?" *Saturday Evening Post* 207, July 21, 1934, p. 22.

233
Carver, T. N.
"Where we Need Planning the Most; Population Planning." *Nation's Business* 23, March 1935, pp. 18-20.

234
Rorty, James W.
"Lettuce With American Dressing." *The Nation* 140, May 15, 1935, pp. 575-576.

235
Saroyan, William
"Good Year; Mexicans Work in the Vineyard; Story." *New Republic* 86, April 1, 1936, pp. 217-218.

236
Stevenson, Philip
"Deporting Jesús." *The Nation* 143, July 18, 1936, pp. 67-69.

237
"Mexican Migrants." *Survey* 73, March 1937, p. 82.

238
Dawber, Mark A.
"The Mexican Immigrant" (In his, *Frontiers of American Populations, Our Shifting Population,* #2, Chapter 11. New York, Joint Committee on Publicity of the Home Missions Council and Council of Women for Home Missions, 1939-   ).

239
"Mexican Exodus." *Newsweek* 14, July 31, 1939, p. 11.

240
Davis, Edward E.
"Peons." (In his, *The White Scourge.* San Antonio, Naylor Co., 1940, pp. 166-175).

241
McWilliams, Carey
"Mexicans to Michigan." *Common Ground,* September 1941, pp. 5-18.

242
"Back to Tortillas." *Commonweal* 37, April 2, 1943, pp. 579-580.

243
Garaza, George J.
"Good Neighbors—Texas Version?" *Texas Outlook* 27, June 1943, p. 39.

244
Smith, Charles M.
"Farm Workers from Mexico." *The Agricultural Situation* (U.S. Dept. of Agriculture, Bureau of Agricultural Economics), June 1943, pp. 12-14.

245
"Admission of Alien Farm Workers into United States." *Monthly Labor Review,* July 1943, pp. 124-125.

246
"Foreign Workers for American Agriculture." *U.S. Immigration and Naturalization Service Monthly Review* 1, July 1943, pp. 6-10.

247
"Across the Border: Southern California Citrus Growers see 100% Harvest with Mexican Workers Helping." *Business Week,* July 31, 1943, p. 85.

248
McWilliams, Carey
"They Saved the Crops." *Inter-American Monthly,* August 1943, pp. 10-14.

249
"Plan set up for Mexican Workers." *National Underwriter* 47, August 26, 1943, pp. 32-33.

250
"No Mexicans Allowed; Mexico Will Send no More Contract Laborers to Texas." *Inter-American* 2, September 1943, p. 8.

251
"Borrowed Help." *Business Week,* September 11, 1943, p. 19.

252
Davidson, Cecilia (Ragovsky)
"Mexican Laborers Imported into the United States." *Interpreter Releases* 20, October 1943, pp. 298-300.

253
Issler, A. R.
"Good Neighbors Lend a Hand: our Mexican Workers." *Survey Graphic* 32, October 1943, pp. 389-391.

254
"Immigration and Emigration in 1942-43." *Monthly Labor Review,* December 1943, pp. 1203-1204.

255
Tercero, D. M.
"The Views of a Mexican Worker on his Return From the United States." *Inter-American* 3, February 1944, p. 37.

256
"Farmers get Lift: Helpers From Bahamas, Mexico and Jamaica." *Business Week,* February 12, 1944, pp. 104-105.

257
Williams, Florence
"What's Happening on the West Coast?" *Recreation* 37, March-May 1944, pp. 674-676.

258
"Works on Paper; Law to Facilitate Importation of Foreign Farm Workers Fails, in Mexico, it Backfires." *Business Week,* April 29, 1944, p. 21.

259
Padilla, Ezequiel
"Conferencias Mexico-Norteamericanas para Impedir la Inmigración Ilegal de Braceros." México, *Desde México,* June 15, 1944, p. 4.

260
Beal, E. H.
"Good Fences Make Good Neighbors." *Southwest Review,* Autumn 1944, pp. 42-47.

261
Tercero, D. M.
"Workers from Mexico." *Pan American Union Bulletin* 78, September 1944, pp. 500-506.

262
Tercero, D. M.
" 'Braceros' for the United States: Mexico has Sent More Than 110,500 Braceros or Laborers to Work in the Fields and on the Railways of the United States." Mexico, *Mexican-American Review*, October 1944, pp. 15-16.

263
Castellano, Pablo
"El Problema del 'Bracerismo'." México, *Carta Semanal*, November 6, 1944, pp. 5-6.

264
Stegner, Wallace
"Okies in Sombreros: Migrant Mexican Cropworkers" (In *One Nation.* Boston, Houghton, Mifflin, 1945, pp. 95-116).

265
Cooper, Elizabeth A.
"Good Neighbors in Boxcars; Needlessly Bungled job." *Commonweal* 43, November 2, 1945, pp. 65-68.

266
Sansep, A.
"Miles de Braceros Mexicanos Abandonados en los Estados Unidos por las Autoridades del Trabajo." México, *La Nación*, December 22, 1945, p. 12.

267
Gutierrcz Reynoso, Miguel
"Triste Regreso de un Bracero." México, *Todo*, February 14, 1946, pp. 24-25, 58.

268
Hopkins, John A.
"Mexico and the United States Report on Agricultural Progress." *Agriculture in the Americas*, March 1946, pp. 54-56.

269
Vazquez Humasque, Adolfo
"La Técnica en la Agricultura." México, *Hoy*, March 2, 1946, pp. 50-51.

270
Del Guercio, Albert
"Some Mexican Border Problems." *U.S. Immigration and Naturalization Service Monthly Review* 3, April 1946, pp. 289-293.

271
Hinga, D.
"Rio Grande, River of Death." *Collier's* 118, August 17, 1946, pp. 24-26.

272
Gutierrez Reynoso, Miguel
"El Río Bravo, el Río de la Muerte." México, *Todo,* November 14, 1946, pp. 36-37, 41.

273
Wyatt, James L.
"U.S.A.—School for Braceros." Mexico, *Mexican-American Review,* December 1946, pp. 55-56, 106-107.

274
McWilliams, Carey
"Is Your Name Gonzalez?" *The Nation* 164, March 15, 1947, pp. 302-304.

275
"Importing Farm Laborers." *Commonweal* 47, January 23, 1948, p. 364.

276
Flores Magón, Enrique
"Enviamos Braceros, pero no Esquiroles." México, *Todo,* March 4, 1948, p. 24.

277
Gonzalez Marquez, Benjamín
"Lo que Exigirse a los 'Braceros'." México, *Todo,* April 29, 1948, p. 43.

278
Sanchez Septién, Salvador
"Habla el ex-Diputado Madrazo Sobre el Fraude a los Braceros." Mexico, *La Nación,* June 12, 1948, pp. 8-9.

279
"Mexico-United States Farm Labor Agreement." *Bulletin of the Pan American Union* 82, July 1948, pp. 411-412.

280
"Summer Brings the Mexicans; Statement From the National Farm Labor Union." *Commonweal* 48, July 2, 1948, pp. 275-278.

281
Sotomayor, Arturo
"325.867 Braceros Lanzó México a una de las más Crueles Aventuras que Registra la Historia!" México, *Hoy,* October 9, 1948, pp. 22-25, 66.

282
Guisa y Azevedo, Jesús
"Por qué los Estados Unidos Dejan Pasar Ilegalmente a los Braceros?"
México, *Carta Semanal,* October 23, 1948, p. 10.

283
"Mexican Wetbacks." *Newsweek* 32, October 25, 1948, p. 80.

284
Madrigal, Carlos
"Braceros; Obra Social Entre los Mexicanos Residentes en el Estado de Michigan, Estados Unidos." México, *La Nación* (8: 368), November 1, 1948, pp. 19, 22.

285
"North From the Border." *Time* 52, November 1, 1948, p. 38.

286
Kibbe, Pauline (Rochester)
"American Standard—for all Americans." *Common Ground* (10: 1), 1949, pp. 19-27.

287
Topete, Jesús
Aventuras de un Bracero. México, Editorial AmeXica, 1949, 143p.

288
Fergusson, Erna
"The new New Mexican." *New Mexico Quarterly Review* 19, Winter 1949, pp. 417-426.

289
"Braceros." *Americas* 1, March 1949, pp. 14-17.

290
Stilwell, Hart
"The Wetback Tide." *Common Ground* 9, Summer 1949, pp. 3-14.

291
Leibson, Art
"The Wetback Invasion." *Common Ground,* Autumn 1949, pp. 11-19.

292
Lester, Olive P.
"The Wetback Invasion." *Common Ground* 10, Autumn 1949, pp. 11-19.

293
"Changes in Population Law Affecting Immigration." *Foreign Commerce Weekly* 39, April 24, 1950, pp. 23-24.

294
Alvarez   Dávalos, Rafael
"Mr. Truman y los Braceros." México, *Todo,* June 15, 1950, p. 26.

295
Whalen, William A.
"The Wetback Problem in Southeast Texas." *Monthly Review* (8: 8), February 1951, pp. 103-105.

296
Esparza, Javier
"Un Grave Problema Social: el Éxodo de Braceros Mexicanos." México, *Lectura* (79/80: 4), February 15, 1951, pp. 2041-2111.

297
Martínez de la Vega, Francisco
"Dolor y Vergüenza de México: Los Braceros." México, *Hoy* 739, April 21, 1951, pp. 18-19.

298
"Hiring Mexican Farm Hands." *Commonweal* 54, May 4, 1951, p. 76.

299
"Wetbacks Swarm in." *Life* 30, May 21, 1951, pp. 33-37.

300
Korcik, William
"Wetback Story." *Commonweal* 54, July 13, 1951, pp. 327-329.

301
"Boon for the Braceros." *Newsweek* 38, July 23, 1951, p. 46.

302
Begeman, J.
"Sweatshops on the Farm; Mexican Wetbacks." *New Republic* 125, July 30, 1951, pp. 16-17.

303
Truman, Harry S.
"Congress Asked for Further Measures on Illegal Entry of Migrant Workers; Message to Congress, July 13, 1951." *U.S. Dept. of State Bulletin* 25, July 30, 1951, pp. 197-199.

304
"Importation of Mexican Farm Labor Authorized by Public Law 78 (82nd Congress, S. 984): Includes Text of Law, and President's Message to Congress, July 13, 1951). *Interpreter Releases* 28, August 1, 1951, pp. 215-222.

305
"The Wetback Invasion." *Co-op Grain Quarterly,* September 1951, pp. 29-34.

306
"AFL vs. Wetback Labor." *New Republic* 125, September 24, 1951, p. 7.

307
Begeman, J.
"Wetbacks, Slaves of Today; Report of Commission on Migratory Labor." *New Republic* 126, March 10, 1952, pp. 15-16.

308
"Recommendations on Immigration Policy." *Monthly Labor Review* 76, January 1953, pp. 45-47.

309
Hill, Gladwin
"Wetbacks: McCarran's Immigrants." *The Nation* 177, August 22, 1953, pp. 151-152.

310
"Fresh Approach to the Wetbacks." *America* 89, August 29, 1953, p. 510.

311
Baker, Verne A.
"Braceros Farm for Mexico." *Americas* 5, September 1953, pp. 3-5.

312
Thunders, J. A.
"Feature X: System of Mexican Contract Laborers." *America* 89, September 19, 1953, pp. 599-600.

313
"Wetbacks in the Middle of Border War." *Business Week,* October 24, 1953, pp. 62-64.

314
"Wetbacks and American Farm Labor." *Information Service* (National Council of Churches of Christ in the USA), November 21, 1953, pp. 1-4.

315
Kelly, Willard F.
"The Wetback Issue." *The Immigration and Naturalization Reporter* (2: 3), January 1954, pp. 37-39.

316
Larin, Don
"Mexican Contract Fees and the Revolving Fund." *Employment Security Review* (21: 1), January 1954, pp. 17-18, 29.

317
Mitchell, H. L.
"Unions of Two Countries Act on Wetback Influx." *American Federationist* 61, January 1954, pp. 28-29.

318
Lucey, Robert E.
"Migratory Workers." *Commonweal* 59, January 14, 1954, pp. 370-373.

319
Hill, Gladwin
"Two Every Minute Across the Border." *New York Times Magazine*, January 31, 1954, p. 13.

320
"Bulge of Braceros at the Border." *Life* 36, February 15, 1954, pp. 26-29.

321
Carrillo, Alejandro
"Dos Conductas Frente a los Braceros." México, *Mañana* (54: 547), February 20, 1954, pp. 22-23.

322
"Why Not Agree With Mexico?" *Christian Century* 71, February 24, 1954, p. 227.

323
Alexander, R. J.
"What to do About Wetbacks: a 3-Point Program of Action." *Socialist Call,* March 1954, pp. 15-17.

324
Banco Nacional de Comercio Exterior, S.A.
"Convenio Sobre Braceros. Protección a Nuestros Trabajadores Agrícolas." México, *Comercio Exterior* (4: 3), March 1954, pp. 86-87.

325
"Venta de Esclavos en la Bolsa de los Mercados Diplomáticos. Los Campesinos Quedaron a Merced de los Granjeros, por Adoptar una Actitud Digna." México, *Hoy* 889, March 6, 1954, pp. 22-23.

326
Eckels, R. P.
"Hungry Workers, Ripe Crops and the Non-Existent Mexican Border."
The Reporter 10, April 1954, pp. 28-32.

327
"War With the Wetbacks." *Newsweek* 43, June 28, 1954, p. 22.

328
"Wetback Drive Hurts Pocketbooks." *America* 91, August 14, 1954, p. 469.

329
Kelley, J. B., & Collett, W.
"The Deportation of Mexican Aliens and its Impact on Family Life."
Catholic Charities Review 37, October 1954, pp. 169-171.

330
Lopez, Henry
"Here They Come Again." *Frontier* 6, May 1955, pp. 13-14.

331
McLellan, Andrew C.
"Thirty Cents an Hour." *American Federationist* 62, May 1955, pp. 23-24.

332
Smith, G. A.
"Non-Occupational Life and A. & H. Plan Offered on Mexican Migrant Workers, Texas (Abstracts)." *Eastern Underwriter* 56, July 8, 1955, p. 31.

333
Swing, J. M.
"A Workable Labor Program." *I & N Reporter* 4, November 1955, pp. 15-16.

334
Maisel, Albert Q.
"The Mexicans Among us." *Readers' Digest* 68, March 1956, pp. 177-178.

335
García Treviño, Rodrigo
"The Wetback: a Mexican View of a Mexican Problem." *Central America & Mexico* (IV: 2), October 1956, pp. 21-24.

336
"Importing Farm Workers." *America* 96, November 10, 1956, p. 144.

337
Eldridge, Fred
"Helping Hands From Mexico." *Saturday Evening Post* 230, August 10, 1957, pp. 28-29.

338
Cunningham, Robert R.
"North and South of the Border." *America* 97, August 17, 1957, pp. 500-502.

339
LeBerthon, T.
"At the Prevailing Rate." *Commonweal* 66, November 1, 1957, pp. 122-125.

340
"Farm Dogs in the Manger." *The Economist* 186, February 15, 1958, p. 567.

341
Mendoza Rivera, Ignacio
"El Trágico Destino del Bracero. Un Problema que no se Resuelve." México, *Mañana* (80: 773), June 21, 1958, pp. 56-59.

342
Cameron, Frank
"Braceros' Weird Nightmare of Death." *Coronet* 44, July 1958, pp. 341-342.

343
"New Deal for the Mexican Worker." *Look* 23, September 29, 1959, pp. 54-56.

344
Soto, Anthony
"The Bracero Story." *Commonweal* 71, November 27, 1959, pp. 258-260.

345
"Limitation of Mexican Farm Labor Urgent." *Interchurch News* 1, July 1960, p. 1.

346
"Churches and Braceros." *America* 104, March 25, 1961, pp. 810-811.

347
"Discussion of the Mexican Farm Labor Program: Legislative Bulletin #4." *Interpreter Releases* 38, June 15, 1961, pp. 156-157.

348

"Migrants and Machines; Braceros." *New Republic* 145, July 24, 1961, pp. 7-8.

349

Garza, Daniel
   "Saturday Belongs to the Palomia." *Harper's Magazine* 225, July 1962, pp. 42-44.

350

"End of Bracero Program." *America* 108, June 22, 1963, pp. 878-879.

351

"Other Texans; Mexicanos." *Look* 27, October 1963, pp. 68-70.

352

Coombs, S. W.
   "Bracero's Journey." *Americas* 15, December 1963, pp. 7-11.

353

"Congress Extends Braceros Program." *Christian Century* 81, January 1, 1964, p. 5.

354

Graves, J.
   "Overlap Land, Gringo and Mexican Meet in the Rio Grande Country." *Holiday* 35, March 1964, pp. 74-75.

355

"Employment of Foreign Workers in 1964 (U.S.)." *Employment Service Review* 1, May 1964, pp. 47-48.

356

"Growers Face Loss of Braceros." *Business Week,* August 22, 1964, p. 120.

357

"Should the Gates be Open Wider?" *Business Week,* October 17, 1964, p. 114.

358

"Churches Oppose Braceros Program." *Christian Century* 81, December 23, 1964, p. 1580.

359

Moore, Truman E.
   The Slaves we Rent. New York, Random House, 1965, 171p.

360

"Battle Over the Braceros." *Business Week,* January 9, 1965, p. 24.

361
"Where Braceros Once Worked: Jobless Californians Replacing Foreign Stoop Laborers now cut off by law Find the Work Hard and Many Soon Quit." *Business Week,* January 16, 1965, pp. 32-33.

362
"Job Problems for 2 Countries: U.S. and Mexico." *U.S. News & World Report* 58, January 18, 1965, p. 74.

363
Leary, Mary E.
"As the Braceros Leave." *The Reporter* 32, January 28, 1965, pp. 43-45.

364
"Bring Back the Braceros; Shortage of Domestic Farm Workers in California." *Newsweek* 65, March 8, 1965, p. 78.

365
"Will Growers get Mexican Labor? Bracero Program." *U.S. News & World Report* 58, April 4, 1965, pp. 93-94.

366
"Wirtz Helps Growers a Little (Yields Slightly on ban on Foreign Farm Labor)." *Business Week,* April 17, 1965, pp. 45-46.

367
Benedict, Robert W.
"Bracero Battle: Farmers Dispute Labor, Government on Impact of Foreign Worker Ban." *Wall Street Journal* 165, April 26, 1965, p. 1.

368
"How a Government Policy Conflicts: Problems From Keeping Braceros." *Nation's Business* 53, May 1965, p. 33.

369
"When U.S. Barred Foreign Workers From Farms . . ." *U.S. News & World Report* 58, May 31, 1965, pp. 73-75.

370
"Who Pays for the Celery?" *Social Service Review* 39, June 1965, pp. 234-235.

371
"Who'll Pick the Strawberries? Problem of Braceros, Minimum Wage, and Immigration Laws." *Time* 85, June 4, 1965, p. 19.

372
"Recent Immigration to the United States." *Metropolitan Life Insurance Company Statistical Bulletin* 46, July 1965, pp. 4-6.

373
Moley, Raymond
"Bracero Blunder." *Newsweek* 66, July 19, 1965, p. 88.

374
"Old Myth Fadcs; Braccro Program's end in California." *The Nation* 201, July 19, 1965, p. 31.

375
Turner, William, & Beecher, John
"Bracero Politics: a Special Report; No Dice for Braceros", by William Turner; "To the Rear, March! -1965-1940", by John Beecher. *Ramparts* 4, September 1965, pp. 14-32.

376
"Machines Take Over Bracero job." *Business Week,* January 8, 1966, pp. 108-110.

377
Maverick, Maury, Jr.
"Marching for a Ghastly Recompense in Texas; Mexican Farm Workers." *New Republic* 155, September 24, 1966, p. 11.

378
Lopez, Enrique H.
"Back to Bachimba." *Horizon* 9, Winter 1967, pp. 80-83.

379
Bliss, Peggy A.
"The Streets of Laredo." *Vista Volunteer* 3, February 1967, pp. 14-18.

380
Bylin, James E.
"Bracero Boomerang: all the Predictions About Ending the Program Were Wrong." *Wall Street Journal* 169, March 9, 1967, p. 16.

381
Kline, Harriet H.
"Bravo Silvestre." *Texas Outlook,* August 1968, pp. 18-19.

382
Recent Immigration to the United States." *Metropolitan Life Insurance Company Statistical Bulletin* 49, September 1968, pp. 2-3.

383
"Deathtrap for Wetbacks; Trade in Illegal Immigrants." *Time* 92, October 11, 1968, pp. 24-25.

384
Miller, Paul B., & Glasgow, John M.
"Job Crisis Along the Rio Grande." *Monthly Labor Review* 91, December 1968, pp. 18-23.

385
Turner, William
"No Dice for Braceros." *Ramparts* 7, January 25, 1969, pp. 37-40.

386
Logsdon, Gene
"Wrath of Grapes: Unions Want to Organize all Hired Farm Labor." *Farm Journal* 93, February 1969, p. 33.

387
McNamara, P. H.
"Rumbles Along the Rio: U.S. Civil Rights Commission Hearings in San Antonio." *Commonweal* 89, March 14, 1969, pp. 730-732.

388
MacGregor, James
"Boss men; Migrant Workers Find Their Lives Controlled by Farm Crew Leaders; Some Overseers get $50,000 a Year; Keeping Workers in Debt a Common Tactic." *Wall Street Journal* 174, September 15, 1969, p. 1- .

389
Greene, Sheldon L.
"Operation Sisyphus, Wetbacks, Growers, and Poverty." *The Nation* 209, October 20, 1969, pp. 403-406.

390
Wollenberg, Charles
"Mexican Workers in California Agribusiness" (In his, *Ethnic Conflict in California History.* Los Angeles, Tinnon-Brown, Inc., 1970, 215p.).

391
Ericson, A. S.
"Impact of Commuters on the Mexican-American Border Areas." *Monthly Labor Review* 93, August 1970, pp. 18-27.

392
Velie, L.
"Poverty at the Border; Mexican Labor Brought in by Greedy U.S. Employers." *Readers Digest* 97, August 1970, pp. 92-97.

393
Koepplin, Leslie W.
A Relationship of Reform: Immigrants and Progressions in the Far West. Los Angeles, 1971, 229p. (Ph.D. Dissertation, UCLA)

394
Phillips, N. D.
"Chicano Workers, Rio Grande Farmers Agree to Meet." *Christian Century* 88, January 20, 1971, pp. 84-86.

395
Austin, Danforth W.
"Leaky Border: Increase of Wetbacks Entering from Mexico Stirs Concern in United States . . ." *Wall Street Journal* 178, September 29, 1971, p. 1.

396
"California Tries to dam the Alien Tide." *Business Week,* February 12, 1972, p. 34.

397
Sanchez, Arturo
"Represión de los Campesinos." *La Raza* (1: 12), 1973, pp. 20-21.

398
Skotzko, E.
"Title VII and U.S. Citizenship." *Monthly Labor Review* 97, February 1974, pp. 68-69.

399
McLellan, Andrew C., & Boggs, Michael D.
"Illegal Aliens: a Story of Human Misery." *American Federationist* 81, August 1974, pp. 17-23.

400
"Mexican Workers are a hot Issue Again." *Business Week,* October 19, 1974, p. 45.

401
Cruz, Pablo
Pablo Cruz and the American Dream; the Experiences of an Undocumented Immigrant From Mexico. Compiled by Eugene Nelson. Introduction by Julian Sanora. Illus. by Carlos Cortez. Salt Lake City, Peregrine Smith, 1975, 171p.

402
"Editorial on the Illegal Alien Problem Facing the U.S." *Los Angeles Times,* February 6, 1975, sec. II, p. 4. c. 1.

403
"Del Olmo Column on Chicano Attitudes on Alien Controversy." *Los Angeles Times,* February 23, 1975, sec. V, p. 5, c. 4.

404
"INS Commissioner Says only 50% of Illegal Aliens are Mexican." *Los Angeles Times,* March 13, 1975, sec. I, p. 1, c. 5.

405
Fogel, Walter A.
"IRRA Conference Papers: Immigrant Mexicans and the U.S. Work Force." *Monthly Labor Review* (98: 5), May 1975, p. 44.

406
Fogel, Walter A.
"Immigrant Mexicans and the U.S. Work Force." *Monthly Labor Review* 98, May 1975, pp. 44-46.

407
Piore, M. J.
"The Impact of Immigration on the Labor Force." *Monthly Labor Review* 98, May 1975, pp. 41-44.

408
"Mexican-American Political Association Urges Amnesty for Aliens." *Los Angeles Times,* May 23, 1975, sec. II, p. 2, c. 1.

409
"Editorial on U.S. Supreme Court Rule on Border Patrol Authority." *Los Angeles Times,* July 2, 1975, sec. II, p. 6, c. 1.

410
"U.S. Senator Tunney to Push Bill on Illegal Aliens' Jobs." *Los Angeles Times,* August 5, 1975, sec. II, p. 1, c. 5.

411
"Plan to Slow the Flood of Illegal Aliens." *Business Week,* August 11, 1975, pp. 67-69.

412
Natanson, George
"Wetbacks." *Texas Monthly* (3:9), September 1975, p. 82.

413
"Chavez Comments on Supreme Court Ruling on Illegal Alien Law." *Los Angeles Times,* February 26, 1976, sec. I, p. 1, c. 1.

414
"Mexico Refuses to Permit Airlift of Aliens by U.S. Agency." *Los Angeles Times,* June 1, 1976, sec. I, p. 3, c. 3.

415
"U.S. Reports on Seizure of Illegal Aliens in Southwest." *Los Angeles Times,* August 6, 1976, sec. I, p. 22, c. 1.

416
"Mexican President Criticizes U.S. on Illegal Aliens." *Los Angeles Times,* August 16, 1976, sec. II, p. 4, c. 1.

417
Griswold, D.
"Immigrants . . . the Question of Jobs." *Workers' World* (19: 1), January 7, 1977, p. 6- .

418
Gomez, Y.
"Drama on the Border." Paris, *Direct From Cuba* 61, January 15, 1977, p. 7- .

419
"Dionisio Morales Column on Illegal Mexican Immigrants." *Los Angeles Times,* January 28, 1977, sec. II, p. 7, c. 3.

420
Helvarg, D.
"Immigrants From Over the Border." *In These Times* (1: 11), February 2, 1977, p. 6- .

421
Pendas, M.
"Carter's Gratitude." *Militant* (41: 7), February 25, 1977, p. 14- .

422
"Aiding Illegal Aliens." *Off our Backs* (7: 2), March 1977, p. 9- .

423
Flanigan, J.
"North of the Border: who Needs Whom?" *Forbes* 119, April 15, 1977, pp. 37-41.

424
Schneider, M.
"Carter Picks La Migra Head." *Militant* (41: 15), April 22, 1977, p. 8- .

425
"Mexican President Lopez Portillo Interviewed on Illegal Aliens." *Los Angeles Times,* April 25, 1977, sec. I, p. 1, c. 2.

426
James, M.
"Jobs on the Line in Texas Border tug of war." *Worklife* 2, May 1977, pp. 2-5.

427
"California Senator Proposes U.S. Military Base Along Mexican Border." *Los Angeles Times,* May 2, 1977, sec. I, p. 2, c. 5.

428
"Carter Attacks . . . Immigrant Workers." *Workers' World* 5, May 2, 1977, p. 8- .

429
"California Assemblyman Alatorre Opposes Reviving Bracero Program." *Los Angeles Times,* May 13, 1977, sec. I, p. 2, c. 5.

430
"Anti-Mexican Hysteria Mounts." *El Gallo* (9: 3), June 1977, p. 11- .

431
Sojourner, K.
"National Antideportation Conference." *Militant* (41:24), June 24, 1977, p. 3- .

432
"California Concerned About U.S. Alien Worker Plan." *Los Angeles Times,* June 29, 1977, sec. II, p. 2, c. 4.

433
"U.S. and Mexican Officials Hold Secret Conference on Illegal Immigrants." *Los Angeles Times,* July 3, 1977, sec. I, p. 25, c. 3.

434
Betries, J.
"Carter to Deny . . . Undocumented Workers." *Workers' World* (19: 30), July 29, 1977, p. 7- .

435
Gutierrez, J.
"Chicano Leaders Speak vs. La Migra." *Militant* (41: 29), July 29, 1977, p. 32- .

436
Hurt, Harry, III
"Cactus Curtain." *Texas Monthly* (5: 8), August 1977, p. 94.

437
"Illegal Immigrants: the Problem That Won't go Away." *The Economist* 264, August 13, 1977, pp. 29-30.

438
"Immigrant Workers . . . Victims." *Workers' Power* 18, August 15, 1977, p. 3- .

439
Brown, M.
"Illegal Immigrants." *In These Times* (1: 38), August 17, 1977, p. 6- .

440
MacLean, J.
"Carter's Plan is Full of Loopholes." *In These Times* (1: 38), August 17, 1977, p. 6- .

441
Ring, H.
"What's at Stake in Fight . . . La Migra." *Militant* (41: 36), September 16, 1977, p. 6- .

442
Warren, R.
"Recent Immigration and Current Data Collection." *Monthly Labor Review* 100, October 1977, pp. 36-41.

443
Rodriquez, O.
"The Fight Against Deportation." *Militant* (41: 27), October 7, 1977, p. 13- .

444
Scheer, R.
"KKK Says it Will Patrol Border." *Militant* (41: 41), November 14, 1977, p. 26- .

445
Peterson, K.
"Contractor Citing . . . Illegal Aliens." *Workers' World* (19: 45), November 25, 1977, p. 12- .

446
Marshall, Ray
"Inside the Country, Outside the law." *Worklife* (2: 12), December 1977, pp. 22-26.

447
North, David S.
"Illegal Aliens: Fictions and Facts." *Worklife* (2: 12), December 1977, pp. 16-21.

448
Camejo, P.
"Human Rights for Immigrants." *Militant* (41: 46), December 9, 1977, p. 20- .

449
"Mexican Immigration and U.S. Reforms." *Kapitalstate* 7, 1978, p. 63- .

450
"From the Other Side." *In These Times* (2: 9), January 18, 1978, p. 8- .

451
Baer, Joshua
"Ilegales; the new Immigrants: Aliens From Mexico." *New Times* 10, January 23, 1978, pp. 26-32.

452
"Editorial on U.S. Dept. of Agriculture Secretary Bergland's Remarks on the Bracero Program." *Los Angeles Times,* February 9, 1978, sec. II, p. 6, c. 1-E.

453
"Immigration Plan . . . Deport Millions." *Guardian* (30: 19), February 15, 1978, p. 2- .

454
"Repression Workshop." *El Gallo* (10: 2), March 1978, p. 1- .

455
"Susan Goldman-Chavez Article on Effort to Cross Border Illegally." *Los Angeles Times,* March 2, 1978, sec. I, p. 5, c. 1-C.

456
"La Raza Looks to its Roots." *The Economist* 266, March 4, 1978, pp. 25-26.

457
Perez, J.
"Guardian Attacks Latino Conference." *Militant* (42: 10), March 17, 1978, p. 19- .

458
Gordon, D.
"Safety Valve." *The Economist* 267, April 22, 1978, pp. 27-28.

459
"Maria Herrera-Sobeck Article on Stereotyped Mexican Immigrants." *Los Angeles Times,* May 21, 1978, sec. VI, p. 3, c. 1-C.

460
"Second Thoughts About Illegal Immigrants." *Fortune* 97, May 22, 1978, pp. 80-82.

461
"Regulating the Undocumented." *Sevendays* (2: 10), June 16, 1978, p. 11- .

462
Riding, Alan
"Silent Invasion: why Mexico is an American Problem." *Saturday Review* 5, July 8, 1978, pp. 14-17.

463
"INS Director Addresses Fourth Annual INS Symposium in Los Angeles." *Los Angeles Times,* July 16, 1978, sec. I, p. 1, c. 1.

464
"Western Grower Authorized to Legally Recruit Foreign Farm Labor." *Los Angeles Times,* August 3, 1978, sec. I, p. 3, c. 4.

465
"Increasing Number of Illegal Mexican Aliens Catch Trains to Los Angeles." *Los Angeles Times,* August 14, 1978, sec. II, p. 1, c. 5.

466
"U.S. Ambassador to Mexico Nava Calls for Accords on Border Immigration." *Los Angeles Times,* September 3, 1978, sec. II, p. 3, c. 3.

467
Lobaco, G.
"Unions Fight Deportation . . . Mexicans." *In These Times* (2: 41), September 6, 1978, p. 7- .

468
Proppe, K.
". . . Challenges Law on Undocumented Workers." *Guardian* (30: 46), September 6, 1978, p. 8- .

469
"INS Director Denies De-Emphasis on Arrests of Aliens in Southland." *Los Angeles Times,* October 12, 1978, sec. II, p. 5, c. 1.

470
"New Fence Along Mexican Border to Begin Despite Fire From Groups." *Los Angeles Times,* October 24, 1978, sec. I, p. 32, c. 1.

471
Gollobin, I.
"Foreign Born . . . Dragnets and Amnesty." *Right* 11, December 1978, p. 18- .

472
"U.S. House Committee Sees aid to Mexico as Solution to Alien Problem." *Los Angeles Times,* December 21, 1978, sec. I, p. 1, c. 2.

473
"U.S. Imperialism and Migration." *Review of Radical Political Economy* (11: 4), Winter 1979, p. 112- .

474
"It Works With Cattle." *Dollars & Sense* 43, January 1979, p. 11- .

475
"David Weber Article on Mexican Immigrants and Mexican Americans." *Los Angeles Times,* January 14, 1979, sec. V, p. 2, c. 1-C.

476
Gudkov, Yuri
"Illegal Aliens' or Legalized Slavery." Moscow, *New Times* 9, February 1979, pp. 24-27.

477
New INS Study Ties Alien Influx to Growth of Mexican Towns." *Los Angeles Times,* February 3, 1979, sec. I, p. 12, c. 1.

478
"Mexico/U.S. Labor Join Forces." *Guardian* (31: 24), March 21, 1979, p. 24- .

479
"Texas: Wetbacks hit Back." *The Economist* 270, March 24, 1979, p. 52.

480
Morris, R.
"The Phantom Border." *New Republic* 180, March 31, 1979, pp. 17-18.

481
Bollinger, W.
"Carter's Policy, Tortilla Curtain." *Guardian* (31: 26), April 4, 1979, p. 10- .

482
"U.S. Labor Dept. Authorizes California Jobs for Aliens." *Los Angeles Times,* April 8, 1979, sec. IV, p. 5, c. 1.

483
"Commission of California Meets to Discuss Mexican Alien Problem." *Los Angeles Times,* April 29, 1979, sec. I, p. 3, c. 2.

484
"MCOP Criticizes UFW . . . Undocumented." *Guardian* (31: 31), May 9, 1979, p. 9- .

485
"The Hanigan Case." *El Gallo* (11: 4), June 1979, p. 5- .

486
O'Dell, R.
"The Illegal Immigration Bugaboo." *Environmental Action* (11: 1),
June 1979, p. 14- .

487
"Gunfire Exchanged at Mexican Border Between U.S. Agent and Alien."
Los Angeles Times, June 10, 1979, sec. I, p. 17, c. 1.

488
"Prosecute the Hanigans." *Guardian* (31: 36), June 13, 1979, p. 10- .

489
"Mexico to Crack Down on Smuggling of Illegal Aliens Into U.S." *Los
Angeles Times,* June 26, 1979, sec. II, p. 1, c. 5.

490
"U.S. To Probe Mexican Torture." *Guardian* (31: 42), July 25, 1979,
p. 8- .

491
"California Lt. Governor Urges Importing Labor From Mexico." *Los
Angeles Times,* July 26, 1979, sec. I, p. 29, c. 1.

492
"Behind U.S. Immigration Policy." *El Gallo* (11: 5), August 1979, p.
9- .

493
Ehrlichmann, John D.
"Mexican Aliens aren't a Problem . . . They're a Solution: Observations From a Prison Camp in Arizona." *Esquire* 92, August 1979, pp.
54-56.

494
Salinas Ríos, Francisco
"Tinder Along the Border." *Atlas* 26, August 1979, pp. 33-35.

495
"Illegal Mexican Aliens now Flowing to Northeast U.S." *Los Angeles
Times,* August 15, 1979, sec. 1-B, p. 3, c. 1.

496
"U.S. Hispanics Petition Mexican President on Illegal Immigrants."
Los Angeles Times, September 27, 1979, sec. I, p. 12, c. 1.

497
Mann, W.
"Coalition . . . Justice . . . in Arizona." *Workers' World* September
28, 1979, p. 12- .

498
Burnett, R.
"Illegal Aliens Come Cheap." *Progressive* (43: 10), October 1979, p. 44- .

499
Elam, F.
"Castillo Criticizes INS Policy." *Guardian* (32: 2), October 17, 1979, p. 9- .

500
"Editorial on U.S. Immigration Raids in Chicano Areas on Southern California." *Los Angeles Times,* October 30, 1979, sec. II, p. 4, c. 1-E.

501
Bracamonte, J.
"Workers Without Papers." *Keep Strong* (4: 7), November 1979, p. 65- .

502
Marcy, S.
"The World Underground Economy." *Worker's World* (21:44), November 9, 1979, p. 5- .

503
"Need we Fear the Undocumented?" *Industrial Worker* (76: 12), December 1979, p. 3- .

504
"Rights of Immigrant Workers." *Political Affairs* (58: 12), December 1979, p. 35- .

505
"John Ehrlichman Article on Bureaucracy Dilemma of Mexican Aliens." *Los Angeles Times,* December 9, 1979, sec. IV, p. 3, c. 1-C.

506
Ehrlich, Anne H., & Ehrlich, Paul R.
"Immigration in the Future." *Mother Earth News* 61, January 1980, pp. 150-151.

507
"INS, Institutionalized Repression." *Guardian* (32: 13), January 2, 1980, p. 8- .

508
Elam, F.
"INS . . . Riddled With Corruption." *Guardian* (32: 17), January 30, 1980, p. 6- .

509

"Census Bureau Study Shows 6 Million Illegal Aliens in U.S." *Los Angeles Times,* February 8, 1980, sec. I, p. 3, c. 5.

510

"Editorial on Immigration From Mexico." *Los Angeles Times,* February 10, 1980, sec. V, p. 4, c. 1-E.

511

Nelson, E.
"Mean Things Happening." *Industrial Worker* (77: 2), February 16, 1980, p. 6- .

512

"Border Officials . . . Illegal Aliens." *Berkeley Barb* (30: 11), February 21, 1980, p. 4- .

513

"Appalachian Roundup." *Mountain Life* (56: 3), March 1980, p. 36- .

514

"A Call for Action." *El Gallo* (12: 2), March 1980, p. 4- .

515

"One-time Smuggler of Aliens From Mexico Relates Experiences." *Los Angeles Times,* March 16, 1980, sec. II, p. 1, c. 1.

516

Elam, F.
"Hispanic News." *Guardian* (32: 25), March 26, 1980, p. 10- .

517

"Ricardo Chaviria Column on Aliens Crossing U.S.-Mexican Border." *Los Angeles Times,* April 28, 1980, sec. II, p. 5, c. 1.

518

Preston, J.
"Foreign Workers Pull Their Weight." *In These Times* (4: 23), May 7, 1980, p. 8- .

519

McFarland, P.
"California Undocumented Meet Brutality." *Workers' World* (22: 21), May 23, 1980, p. 10- .

520

Calderon, C.
"Meeting on Immigrants." *Guardian* (32: 34), May 28, 1980, p. 16- .

521
"The new Immigration." *Dissent* (27: 3), Summer 1980, p. 341- .

522
"Mexican President Lopez Portillo Favors 'Guest Worker' Plan in U.S."
Los Angeles Times, June 10, 1980, sec. I, p. 3, c. 2.

523
Barry, T.
"Racist Arizona Ranchers Indicted." *Guardian* (32: 38), June 25, 1980, p. 8- .

524
"Bunco Scams Aimed at Illegal Mexican Aliens Discussed." *Los Angeles Times,* June 29, 1980, sec. II, p. 1, c. 1.

525
"Plight of the Undocumented." *Workers' World* (22: 28), July 11, 1980, p. 12- .

526
"Michael Maggio Article on Flaws in U.S. Immigration Policy." *Los Angeles Times,* July 13, 1980, sec. V, p. 1, c. 1-C.

527
"INS Guilty in Arizona Desert Tragedy." *Militant* (44: 27), July 18, 1980, p. 3- .

528
Kingsolver, B.
"Mexican Torture Victims Face Trial." *Militant* (44: 28), July 25, 1980, p. 5- .

529
" 'Guest Worker' may be Answer to U.S. Illegal Immigration Problem."
Los Angeles Times, July 31, 1980, sec. I, p. 1, c. 1.

530
Waldinger, R.
"Undocumented Workers." *Democratic Left* (8: 7), September 1980, p. 16- .

531
"Undocumented Setback." *Guardian* (32: 46), September 3, 1980, p. 7- .

532
Calderon, C.
"To be Young, Undocumented and Scared." *Guardian* (32: 48), September 17, 1980, p. 4- .

533
"Reagan Endorses Plan to Legalize Mexican Aliens in U.S." *Los Angeles Times,* September 17, 1980, sec. I, p. 20, c. 1.

534
"U.S. Senate Committee Votes to Forbid Counting Aliens in House Issue." *Los Angeles Times,* September 17, 1980, sec. I, p. 12, c. 1.

535
Calderon, C.
"Undocumented Workers." *Guardian* (32: 50), October 1, 1980, p. 9- .

536
"Los Undocumenteds." *Industrial Worker* (77: 11), October 16, 1980, p. 5- .

537
"Editorial on U.S. Court Ruling on Treatment of Illegal Aliens." *Los Angeles Times,* November 10, 1980, sec. II, p. 8, c. 1-E.

538
Gonzalez, R.
"INS Cops . . . Brutalize Mexican Immigrants." *Militant* (44: 45), December 5, 1980, p. 10- .

539
Ring, H.
"Exploitation of Undocumented Workers." *Militant* (44: 45), December 5, 1980, p. 10- .

540
"Life of Mexican Farm Workers on California Avocado Farms Viewed." *Los Angeles Times,* December 15, 1980, sec. I, p. 1, c. 1.

541
Adams, J.
"Sexual Abuse of Undocumented Women." *Guardian* (33: 11), December 17, 1980, p. 10- .

542
"Two Riverside Growers to pay $33,000 in Back Wages to 12 Aliens." *Los Angeles Times,* December 17, 1980, sec. II, p. 1, c. 1.

543
Mack, T.
"Bring Back Braceros." *Forbes* 126, December 22, 1980, pp. 30-31.

544
Jaech, R.
"Undocumented Women . . . Stories." *Lucha* (5: 6), 1981, p. 4- .

545
Blum, B.
"Undocumented Workers." *Socialist Revolution* 55, January 1981, p. 139.

546
Johnstone, D.
"But Nobody Wants Them as Neighbors." *In These Times* 5, January 14, 1981, p. 9.

547
Ralph, L.
"Slamming the Golden Doors." *Lucha* 5, February 1981, p. 14.

548
Otero, J.
"Justice Demanded for Mexicanos." *Militant* 45, February 13, 1981, p. 6.

549
"Film, 'Mojado Power', Gives Insight into Plight of Illegal Alien." *Los Angeles Times*, February 22, 1981, sec. California, p. 41, c. 1.

550
"Letter to the Editor on 'Open Border' for Mexican Neighbors." *Los Angeles Times*, March 2, 1981, sec. II, p. 4, c. 4-L.

551
Jencson, L.
"Wetbacks in the Woods." *Industrial Worker* (78: 5), April 1981, p. 6-   .

552
Fones, M.
"2 Worlds Together: Towns Along the U.S.-Mexican Border Could Provide Marketing Edge." *Advertising Age* (52: 2), April 6, 1981, 22.

553
"Reynaldo Baca and Dexter Bryan Article on Mexican Immigrants." *Los Angeles Times*, April 12, 1981, sec. V, p. 3, c. 1-C.

554
"Immigration Recognition for the Reserve Labour Army." *The Economist* 279, June 6, 1981, pp. 32-33.

555
Calderon, C.
"Latinos/Labor Slam Guestworker Proposal." *Guardian* (33: 38), June 24, 1981, p. 4-   .

556

"California Governor Brown Discusses 'Guest Worker Plan' With Mexican President." *Los Angeles Times,* July 5, 1981, sec. I, p. 24, c. 3.

557

"When Guest Workers Last Came to the United States (Bracero Plan)." *U.S. News & World Report* 91, August 3, 1981, p. 38.

558

Guerrero, V.
"Texas Meet Defends Undocumented." *Workers World* (23: 32), August 7, 1981, p. 12- .

559

"Ins and Outs of Immigration Policy." *The Economist* 280, August 8-14, 1981, pp. 17-18.

560

"Mexican Leader Denounces Reagan Plan for Undocumented Workers." *Los Angeles Times,* August 19, 1981, sec. I, p. 20, c. 1.

561

"Art Torres Column on Reagan Administration's Immigration Policy." *Los Angeles Times,* September 3, 1981, sec. II, p. 11, c. 3-C.

562

Gonzalez, R.
"Reagan Takes aim at Latino Workers." *Militant* (45: 32), September 4, 1981, p. 17- .

563

Fox, G.
"Inferior Status." *The Nation* (233: 6), September 5, 1981, p. 165- .

564

"An American Caste System." *Inquiry* (4: 16), September 14, 1981, p. 3- .

565

Dotson, K.
"Attack on Undocumented Workers." *Militant* (45: 35), September 25, 1981, p. 4- .

566

Jaech, R.
"Undocumented Women . . . Strength, Courage." *Lucha,* (5: 5), October 1981, p. 9- .

567

"Those Alien Hordes." *Progressive* (45: 10), October 1981, p. 12- .

568
"Allow Mexican Guest Workers? Yes, Interview with David D. Hiller, Special Assistant to the Attorney General; No, Interview with Philip L. Martin, Associate Professor of Agricultural Economics, University of California, Davis." *U.S. News & World Report* 91, October 5, 1981, pp. 85-86.

569
Hiller, David D., & Martin, Philip L.
"Allow Mexican Guest Workers?" *U.S. News & World Report* 91, October 5, 1981, pp. 85-86.

570
Dyson, D.
"Bringing Back Braceros." *Win Magazine* (17: 19), November 1, 1981, p. 13- .

571
Allen, Gina
"Across the River to the Farm." *Humanist* 41, November/ December 1981, pp. 18-23.

572
Bracamonte, L.
"Reagan Immigration Proposals." *Labor Today* (20: 11), December 1981, p. 7- .

573
Howard, D.
"For 'Illegals' Migration Goes Both Ways." *R & D Mexico* (2: 3/4), December 1981-January 1982, pp. 14-17.

574
Brom, T.
"Good Fence Makes Unrealistic Policy." *In These Times* (6: 5), December 9, 1981, p. 6- .

575
Kalke, D.
"Forces Migration, but Where to?" *Lucha* (6: 6), 1982, p. 4- .

576
Kalke, D.
"Open Season on Immigrants." *Lucha* (6: 2), 1982, p. 8.

577
"Mexican Farmworkers, California Field." *Antipode* (14: 3), 1982, p. 51- .

578
"U.S. Ambassador Denies Plan to Deport Mexican Citizens Living in U.S." *Los Angeles Times,* January 8, 1982, sec. I, p. 6, c. 4.

579
"Bustamante Column on U.S. INS Plan to Deport Illegal Aliens." *Los Angeles Times,* January 12, 1982, sec. II, p. 5, c. 3.

580
"Editorial on U.S. Immigration Quotas for Mexico and Canada." *Los Angeles Times,* January 27, 1982, sec. II, p. 4, c. 1-E.

581
Ridgeway, J.
"U.S. to Scrap Welcome mat." *In These Times* (6: 10), January 27, 1982, p. 4- .

582
Martin, Philip L.
"Select Commission Suggests Changes in Immigration Policy—a Review Essay." *Monthly Labor Review* 105, February 1982, pp. 31-37.

583
"Editorial on California Assembly Hearings on Mexican Guest Workers." *Los Angeles Times,* February 3, 1982, sec. II, p. 6, c. 1-E.

584
"Alatorre Column on U.S. INS Guest Worker Program With Mexico." *Los Angeles Times,* February 12, 1982, sec. II, p. 11, c. 1.

585
Semler, H. M.
"The new Immigration law and Guestworkers (H-2 Program)." *The Progressive* 46, March 1982, pp. 42-44.

586
Perez, J.
"Repression vs. Undocumented Workers." *Militant* (46: 8), March 5, 1982, p. 15- .

587
"INS Alien Raid's Impact on Orange County Strawberry Harvest Eyed." *Los Angeles Times,* March 28, 1982, sec. II, p. 1, c. 2-P.

588
"U.S. INS Raids on Illegal Aliens Protested in U.S. and Mexico." *Los Angeles Times,* April. 29, 1982, sec. I, p. 3, c. 4-P.

589
"Transnational Trade Unions." *Win Magazine* (18: 9), May 1, 1982, p. 13- .

590
La Botz, D.
"Immigration Raids Make Latin Worker . . ." *Labor Notes* 40, May 26, 1982, p. 13- .

591
"Imported Farmhands." *Industrial Worker* (79: 6), June 1982, p. 4- .

592
"Invasion of the Body Snatchers." *Inquiry* (5: 11), July 1982, p. 5- .

593
Langemach, Sharon, & Koepplinger, Jessica
Guide for Migrants in the State of Illinois / Guiá para Migrantes en el Estado de Illinois. Chicago, Illinois Migrant Council, July 1982, 21p.

594
Early, S.
"Refugees and Undocumented Workers." *Labor Notes* 42, July 21, 1982, p. 7- .

595
"Official Urges U.S. to Accept Unemployed Mexican Workers." *Los Angeles Times,* August 25, 1982, sec. I, p. 7, c. 1.

596
"Scapegoating the Immigrant." *Guardian* (34: 45), August 25, 1982, p. 19- .

597
Alaniz, Y.
"Campesinas Journey." *Freedom Socialist* (8: 1), Fall 1982, p. 27- .

598
Hornik, P.
"In Search of Cheap, Docile Labor." *Guild Notes* (11: 4), September 1982, p. 14- .

599
Brom, T.
"Mexico . . . More Shock Waves Ripple." *In These Times* (6: 35), September 15, 1982, p. 7- .

600
Gonzalez, N.
"AFL-CIO Backs Bosses' Anti-Immigrant . . ." *Militant* (46: 35), September 24, 1982, p. 13- .

601
Swarthout, K.
"Scapegoats for Reagan Recession." *Changes Socialist Monthly* (4: 9), October 1982, p. 6- .

602
Cockcroft, James D.
"Immigration Bill Threatens Liberty." *Guardian* (35: 2), October 13, 1982, p. 3- .

603
Foster, Douglas
"The Desperate Immigrants of Devil's Canyon." *The Progressive* 46, November 1982, pp. 44-49.

604
"Western Airlines ends Deportation." *Win Magazine* (18: 21), December 1, 1982, p. 22- .

605
"Increase in Illegal Aliens From Mexico Blamed on the Economy." *Los Angeles Times,* December 3, 1982, sec. I, p. 1, c. 4.

606
McConahay, M.
"Undocumented, the Invisible Community." *Guardian* (35: 11), December 15, 1982, p. 11- .

607
"Low Rate of Naturalization of Mexicans Living in U.S. Discussed." *Los Angeles Times,* January 5, 1983, section I, p. 1, c. 1-P.

608
"Spanish Book to Aid Farm Laborers Criticized as Racist." *Los Angeles Times,* January 31, 1983, section IV, p. 5, c. 5.

609
"Editorial on INS Decision on Mexicans and Deportation Immunity." *Los Angeles Times,* February 9, 1983, section II, p. 4, c. 1-E.

610
"Can America get Control of its Borders?" *The Economist* 286, February 26, 1983, pp. 43-44.

611
"Bridling at a U.S. Immigration Bill." *Business Week,* February 28, 1983, pp. 3-4.

612
Guttmacher, S.
"No Golden Door." *Health PAC Bulletin* (14: 2), March 1983, p. 15- .

613
Chaze, W. L.
"Invasion from Mexico: it Just Keeps Growing." *U.S. News & World Report* 94, March 7, 1983, pp. 37-41.

614
"Relief From Immigrants? Perhaps in 50 Years (Interview With Jorge Bustamante)." *U.S. News & World Report* 94, March 7, 1983, p. 44.

615
Coryell, B.
"Liberty, Equality, Austerity." *Guardian* (35: 25), March 23, 1983, p. 1- .

616
Starr, M.
"The Border: a World Apart." *Newsweek* 101, April 11, 1983, pp. 36-40.

617
Duke, D.
"Unions Split on Immigration." *In These Times* (7: 20), April 20, 1983, p. 9.

618
Wang, D.
"Anti-Immigration Bill Discussed." *Militant* (47: 15), April 29, 1983, p. 11- .

619
"U.S. House Committee OK's Bill on Illegal Aliens." *Los Angeles Times,* May 6, 1983, section I, p. 1, c. 3.

620
"Editorial on Immigration—Reform Bill Passed by U.S. House Committee." *Los Angeles Times,* May 8, 1983, section IV, p. 4, c. 1-E.

621
Ring, H.
"Government Pushes Racist Attack on Undocumented." *Militant* (47: 17), May 13, 1983, p. 16- .

622
"U.S. Senate Passes Immigration Bill." *Los Angeles Times,* May 19, 1983, section I, p. 1, c. 5.

623

Kurzban, I.
"Highlights From the NECLC Docket." *Rights & Bill of Rights Journal* (29: 2), June 1983, p. 12- .

624

Ring, H.
"Senate Bill and Rights of Immigrants." *Militant* (47: 20), June 3, 1983, p. 1- .

625

Kenkelen, W.
"Border Patrol Running Wild." *Guardian* (35: 36), June 8, 1983, p. 3- .

626

"Arnoldo Torres Column on U.S. Immigration Reform Bill." *Los Angeles Times,* June 14, 1983, section II, p. 5, c. 3.

627

Arias, R.
"The Rooster That Called me Home." *The Nation* 236, June 18, 1983, pp. 758-761.

628

"Behind Illegal Alien Scare." *Militant* (47: 26), July 15, 1983, p. 18- .

629

"Series on Southern California Latinos—California Poll on Amnesty for Aliens." *Los Angeles Times,* July 25, 1983, section I, p. 3, c. 1.

630

Alexander, N.
"Third World Community Wins Citymood." *Guardian* (35: 40), July 27, 1983, p. 4- .

631

Goehring, M.
"Introduction . . . the Human Tide." *Coyote* (2: 7), August 1983, p. 12- .

632

Chase, Marilyn
"Hired Hands: California Growers Rail vs. Efforts to Stem Flow of Illegal Aliens." *Wall Street Journal* 202, August 5, 1983, p. 1.

633

"Where 2 Worlds Meet." *The Economist* 288, August 20, 1983, pp. 28-31.

634
"Santa Ana Police Chief Opposes U.S. Immigration Raids." *Los Angeles Times,* September 5, 1983, section I, p. 1, c. 1-P.

635
"Editorial on 'Guest Worker' Program Before Congress." *Los Angeles Times,* September 18, 1983, section IV, p. 4, c. 1-E.

636
"U.S. Senator Wilson Calls for aid to Mexico to Stem Flood of Aliens." *Los Angeles Times,* September 20, 1983, section I, p. 6, c. 1.

637
"Two INS Raids at San Luis Rey Downs Stable net 260 Aliens." *Los Angeles Times,* September 23, 1983, section II, p. 5, c. 1.

638
Rips, G.
"Supply-Side Immigration Reform." *The Nation* 237, October 8, 1983, p. 289.

639
Shapiro, W.
"Immigration: Failure of Will." (House Kills Simpson-Mazzoli Bill). *Newsweek* 102, October 17, 1983, p. 32.

640
"Editorial on Ford Foundation's Report on Illegal Migration." *Los Angeles Times,* October 31, 1983, section II, p. 4, c. 1-E.

641
"U.S. House Expected to Pass Immigration Reform Bill in January." *Los Angeles Times,* December 1, 1983, section I, p. 13, c. 1.

642
"U.S. Supreme Court to Review Labor Laws Protecting Illegal Aliens." *Los Angeles Times,* December 7, 1983, section I, p. 8, c. 1.

643
"California Implements new Unemployment pay Policy Involving Aliens." *Los Angeles Times,* December 17, 1983, section I, p. 1, c. 5.

644
"Lungren Column on Renewed Look at U.S. Immigration Bill." *Los Angeles Times,* January 4, 1984, section II, p. 5, c. 1.

645
"Congressional Hispanic Caucus Seeks Weakened Immigration Bill." *Los Angeles Times,* January 17, 1984, section I, p. 1, c. 4.

646
García, Carolina
"Time Will Tell if Migrant Tuition Bill is Just Sympolism." *Milwaukee Journal,* "Ethnic Milwaukee" section, part 2, February 22, 1984, p. 2.

647
Kilpatrick, James J.
"Some Myths Surround Immigrants." *Milwaukee Journal,* part 1, February 22, 1984, p. 11.

648
Griffin, E.
"Help Mexican Workers at Home." *The Nation* 238, March 3, 1984, pp. 250-252.

649
Chaze, W.L.
"America's Third World—the Rio Grande Valley." *U.S. News & World Report* 96, March 26, 1984, pp. 64-65.

650
"Penalize Bosses who Hire Illegal Aliens?" *U.S. News & World Report* 96, April 16, 1984, pp. 45-46.

651
"Plan Would OK Aliens on Farms." *Milwaukee Journal,* June 15, 1984, p. 3.

652
Garcia, Carolina
" 'Guest Workers' in Line for Short end of job Stick." *Milwaukee Journal,* June 20, 1984 (Ethnic Milwaukee section), part 2, p. 2.

653
Ingwerson, Marshall
"Immigration Bill Concerns Farmers; Facing Loss of Illegal Work Force, They Seek new Guest-Worker Program." *Christian Science Monitor,* June 29, 1984, pp. 3-4.

654
Ingwerson, Marshall
"Immigration Reform: the big Challenge Will be Enforcement." *Christian Science Monitor,* July 3, 1984, pp. 3, 6.

655
"U.S. Immigration: Should we Change the Rules?" Donahue Television Program, Produced at Station WBBM-TV, Chicago. Broadcast July 4, 1984, 11 AM-12 Noon, on Television Channel 6, WITI-TV Milwaukee, CBS Television Network. Donahue Transcripts, Box 2111, Cincinnati, Ohio 45201.

C. MEXICAN-AMERICAN FARM LABOR

656
Godkin, E. L.
"Mexicanization." *Nation* 23, 1876, p. 365.

657
Woods, Katharine (Pearson)
"Educational Colony: Mexican Tenant Farmers in Texas." *Outlook* 62, May 27, 1899, pp. 214-216.

658
Callcott, Frank
"Mexican Peons in Texas." *Survey* 44, June 26, 1920, pp. 437-438.

659
"Mexican Rights in the United States." *The Nation* 115, July 12, 1922, pp. 51-53.

660
"Working Conditions of Agricultural Wage Earners, a Survey." *Monthly Labor Review* 15, August 1922, pp. 250-253.

661
Coulter, Clara
"The Little Melting Pot on the Plains." *Normal Instructor and Primary Plans* 32, May 1923, p. 54.

662
"Employment and Welfare of Children in Cotton-Growing Areas of Texas." *Monthly Labor Review* 19, July 1924, pp. 128-130.

663
McGinnis, John H.
"Cities and Towns of the Southwest." *Southwest Review* 13, October 1927, pp. 36-47.

664
Fergusson, Erna
"New Mexico's Mexicans." *Century,* August 1928, pp. 437-444.

665
Graves, Jackson A.
My 70 Years in California, 1857-1927. Los Angeles, Times Mirror Press, 1929, 478p.

666
"Mexican Labor in the Imperial Valley, California." *Monthly Labor Review* 28, March 1929, pp. 868-871.

667
Rembao, Alberto
"Are the Mexicans Here to Stay?" *Interpreter,* January 1930, pp. 6-11.

668
"Labor and Social Conditions of Mexicans in California." *Monthly Labor Review* 32, January 1931, pp. 83-89.

669
Austin, Mary H.
"Mexicans and New Mexico." *Survey Graphic,* May 1, 1931, pp. 141-144.

670
Dobie, J. F.
"Ranch Mexicans." *Survey Graphic,* May 1, 1931, pp. 167-170.

671
Galarza, Ernesto
"Without Benefit of Lobby." *Survey Graphic,* May 1, 1931, p. 181.

672
Handman, Max S.
"San Antonio." *Survey Graphic,* May 1, 1931, pp. 163-166.

673
Taylor, Paul S.
"Mexicans North of the Rio Grande." *Survey Graphic,* May 1, 1931, pp. 135-140.

674
"Increase of Mexican Population in United States, 1920 to 1930." *Monthly Labor Review* 37, July 1933, pp. 46-48.

675
"San Diego Mexicans." *Survey* 69, August 1933, p. 293.

676
Calvin, Ross
Sky Determines. New York, Macmillan, 1934, 354p.

677
Quaife, Milo M., ed.
Narrative of the Adventures of Zenas Leonard: Written by Himself. Chicago, The Lakeside Press, 1934, pp. 160-177.

678
Wynnton, E. A.
"Child Labor and Sweatshops." *Commerce and Finance* 23, July 25, 1934, p. 613.

679
Laughlin, Ruth
Caballeros. New York, Appleton, 1935, 379p.

680
Mini, Norman
"That California Dictatorship." *The Nation* 140, February 20, 1935, pp. 224-226.

681
"Piece Rates in Harvesting of Crops, 1934." *Monthly Labor Review* 40, May 1935, pp. 1306-1308.

682
Otero, Miguel A.
My Life on the Frontier. New York, The Press of the Pioneers, Inc., 1935-1939.

683
Rusinow, Irving
"Spanish Americans in New Mexico." *Survey Graphic* 27, 1938, pp. 95-99.

684
Munz, C. C.
"Awakening in the 'Corral': the 2 Million Mexicans and Spanish-Americans in the Southwest Unite . . ." *New Masses,* April 18, 1939, pp. 10-12.

685
Murphy, L. F.
"Experiment in Americanization." *Texas Outlook* 23, November 1939, pp. 23-24.

686
Fergusson, Erna
Our Southwest. New York, Knopf, 1940, 376p.

687
Wittke, Carl
We who Built America. New York, Prentice-Hall, 1940, pp. 454-458.

688
"Wage Rates and Employment on Farms, 1929 to April 1940." *Monthly Labor Review* 51, July 1940, pp. 183-187.

689
Williams, F. M., et al.
"Money Disbursements of Employed Wage Earners and Clerical Work-

ers in 12 Cities of the South, 1931-36; Mexican Families in Houston."
U.S. Bureau of Labor Statistics Bulletins 640, 1941, pp. 119-140.

690
Fisher, Reginald
"Hispanic People of the Rio Grande: a Statement of a Program of Research Being Planned in the Conservation of Human Resources." *El Palacio* 49, 1942, pp. 157-162.

691
"Women's Emergency Farm Service on the Pacific Coast in 1943." *U.S. Women's Bureau Bulletin* 204, 1943, pp. 1-36.

692
Parker, Zelma
"Strangers in Town." *Survey* 79, June 1943, pp. 170-171.

693
Woods, Betty
"Timeless Town." *New Mexico Magazine* 21, August 1943, pp. 16-17, 38-39.

694
Stilwell, Hart
"Some Spot of Good Will." *Tomorrow* 3, October 1943, pp. 11-14.

695
Muro Asúnsulo, Pedro
"Como Viven y Trabajan los Braceros Mexicanos en Estados Unidos." México, *Desde México,* December 15, 1944, p. 3-4; December 31, 1944, pp. 3-4.

696
Tipton, Elis M.
"What we Want is Action: Relations of Americans and Mexicans in San Dimas, California." *Common Ground* (7:1), 1946, pp. 74-81.

697
McWilliams, Carey
"Is Your Name Gonzalez?" *The Nation,* March 15, 1947, pp. 302-304.

698
Stilwell, Hart
"Portrait of the Magic Valley." *New Republic* 116, April 7, 1947, pp. 14-17.

699
Johnson, Dallas
"They Fenced Tolerance in Mendota, California." *Survey Graphic* 36, July 1947, pp. 398-399.

700
Moncada, Raúl
"Un Gran Amigo de México." Mexico, *Hoy,* December 13, 1947, pp. 14-15.

701
Galarza, Ernesto
"The Mexican American: a National Concern; Program for Action." *Common Ground* (IX: 4), Summer 1949, pp. 27-38.

702
"The Mexican-American: a National Concern." *Common Ground,* Summer 1949, pp. 3-38.

703
"The Mexican-American." London, *The Economist* 156, June 18, 1949, pp. 1139-1140.

704
McCully, John
"The Spanish-Speaking: North From the Rio Grande." *The Reporter* (3: 13), December 26, 1950, pp. 25-28.

705
Winters, Allen
"Peonage in the Southwest." *Fourth International* 14, March 1953, pp. 43-49; May 1953, pp. 74-78.

706
Bloom, Hannah R.
"Vigilantism Plays the Villain, Silver City, New Mexico." *The Nation* 176, May 9, 1953, inside cover.

707
"Timeless Ways of the Earliest Texans." *Life* 46, April 20, 1959, pp. 84-85.

708
"Farmworkers Wage." *The Economist* 193, December 26, 1959, p. 1232.

709
"Fight Brews Over Mexican Worker Law." *Congressional Quarterly Weekly Report* 19, March 31, 1961, pp. 537-540.

710
"Mexican Residents in Southwest Studied by Quaker Oats." *Sponsor* 17, February 25, 1963, p. 54.

711
Panger, Daniel
"The Forgotten Ones." *The Progressive* 27, April 1963, pp. 20-23.

712

Groom, P.

"Report From the National Farm Labor Conference." *Monthly Labor Review* 88, March 1965, pp. 275-278.

713

"Recommendations of the California Farm Labor Panel." *Monthly Labor Review* 88, December 1965, p. 1413.

714

Ballis, George

Basta! La Historia de Nuestra Lucha. Enough! The Tale of our Struggle. Photos: George Ballis. Text From the Plan of Delano. Delano, CA, Farm Workers Press, 1966, 72p.

715

"Minority Groups in California." *Monthly Labor Review* 89, September 1966, pp. 978-983.

716

"Who Owns New Mexico?" *The Economist* 224, July 8, 1967, p. 113.

717

Jenkinson, Michael

Tijerina. Albuquerque, Paisano Press, 1968, 103p.

718

Rey, Tony

"Tierra Amarilla is Dying." *El Grito* (I: 3), Spring 1968, pp. 10-11.

719

Ortego, Philip D.

"The Mexican-Dixon Line." *El Grito* (I: 4), Summer 1968, pp. 29-33.

720

"America's Other Minority." *The Economist* 227, June 8, 1968, pp. 53-60.

721

Miller, Paul B., & Glasgow, John M.

"Job Crisis Along the Rio Grande." *Monthly Labor Review* 91, December 1968, pp. 18-23.

722

Acuña, Rodolfo

The Story of the Mexican-Americans; the men and the Land. New York, American Book Co., 1969, 140p.

723
Egan, Ferol
"Twilight of the Californias." *The American West* (6: 2), March 1969, pp. 34-42.

724
Coles, Robert, & Huge, Henry
"Thorns on the Yellow Rose of Texas." *New Republic* 160, April 19, 1969, pp. 13-17.

725
Vaca, Nick C.
"The Mexican-American in the Social Sciences, 1912-1935." *El Grito* (3: 3), Spring 1970, pp. 3-24.

726
Vaca, Nick C.
"The Mexican-American in the Social Sciences: 1936-1970." *El Grito* (4: 1), Fall 1970, pp. 17-51.

727
Phillips, N. D.
"Chicano Workers, Rio Grande Farmers Agree to Meet." *Christian Century* 88, January 20, 1971, pp. 84-86.

728
Griffith, Beatrice (Winston)
American me. Westport, CT, Greenwood Press, 1973, 341p.

729
Magee, James J.
"The Church and the Farm Workers." *America* (129: 13), October 27, 1973, p. 302.

730
Rocha Alvarado, Arturo
Crónica de Aztlan: a Migrant's Tale. Berkeley, Quinto Sol Publications, 1977, 179p.

731
Fishburn, D.
"North of the Border." *The Economist* 263, May 14, 1977, p. 24 (Survey).

732
"Mexico's President on the Migrants—Interview." *U.S. News & World Report* (83: 1), July 4, 1977, p. 28.

733
"Mexican American Effort to Trace History of Land Grants Viewed." *Los Angeles Times,* April 5, 1978, sec. 1-B, p. 1, c. 1.

734
Farnsworth, G.
"Mexico . . . Chicanos Seek Joint Strategy." *International Bulletin* (5: 10), May 22, 1978, p. 3- .

735
"Luis Valdez Article on Pachucos and the First Mexican-Americans." *Los Angeles Times*, August 13, 1978, sec. V, p. 3, c. 1-C.

736
Roueché, Berton
"Profiles: Zavala County, Texas." *New Yorker* 54, December 4, 1978, pp. 54-56.

737
Williams, D. A., et al.
"Chicanos on the Move." *Newsweek* 93, January 1, 1979, pp. 22-26.

738
"Issue is Brutality Against Latinos." *Keep Strong* (4: 5), September 1979, p. 62- .

739
"El Valle Land Struggle." *El Gallo* (11: 6), October 1979, p. 3- .

740
Elam, F.
"Slavery, Peonage . . . Farmer Accused." *Guardian* (32: 3), October 24, 1979, p. 10- .

741
Cardona, J.
"Behind the Faces." *Keep Strong* (4: 9), February 1980, p. 16- .

742
Langdon, D.
"Lalo Valdez, From the Grapes of Wrath to Champagne at the White House." *People* 13, April 14, 1980, pp. 125-126.

743
"Changes." *Win Magazine* (16: 8), May 15, 1980, p. 22- .

744
"Colorado Land Grants." *Guild Notes* (9: 3), June 1980, p. 1- .

745
Smith, Griffin, Jr.
"Mexican Americans, a People on the Move." *National Geographic Magazine* 157, June 1980, pp. 780-809.

746
"Torture Trial in Tucson." *Time* 116, July 21, 1980, pp. 38-40.

747
Ruth, M.
"Chicanos Reaffirm Struggle." *Guardian* (32: 47), September 10, 1980, p. 5- .

748
"Chicano Organization Protests Film 'Borderline' for Stereotypes." *Los Angeles Times,* October 25, 1980, sec. II, p. 9, c. 1.

749
Aguirre, J. D.
"Mexican." *Advertising Age* (52: 2), April 6, 1981, S6-S7.

750
Diperna, P.
"Lethal Cloud of Indifference." *The Nation* (232: 25), June 27, 1981, p. 786- .

751
Marshall, Ray
"Guest Workers: no Needs, no Justification." *American Federationist* 88, August 1981, pp. 15-19.

752
"Ladder of Success." *U.S. News & World Report* 91, August 17, 1981, pp. 59-60.

753
"PBS TV Series 'Somos' Receives $750,000 Grant." *Los Angeles Times,* August 27, 1981, sec. VI, p. 2, c. 1.

754
Cort, John C.
"Down on the Farm." *Commonweal* 108, August 28, 1981, pp. 455-456.

755
Chavira, R.
"Innocents Innured." *Progressive* (45: 9), September 1981, p. 20- .

756
"Summer Project Exposes Brutality." *Guild Notes* (10: 5), September 1981, p. 5- .

757
"Grand Jury Used vs. Texas Group." *Big Mama* (9: 11), December 1981, p. 12- .

758
Pope, B.
"Down on the Farm . . . Agrarian Revolt." *Radical America* (16: 1),
January 1982, p. 139- .

759
Laws, B.
"Crystal City is hot and Dusty Town." *Southern Exposure* (10: 2),
March 1982, p. 67- .

760
Grimond, J.
"Reconquista Begins." *The Economist* 283, April 3, 1982, p. 12.

761
Klein, Karen E.
"Citizens in all but Name." *Newsweek* 99, May 31, 1982, pp. 12-13.

762
Mulligan, John E.
"Organizing Farm Workers in Arizona." *America* 147, July 24-31,
1982, pp. 51-53.

763
"Through the Revolving Door." *Dollars and Sense* 83, January 1983,
p. 8- .

764
Haner, L. G.
"The new Wave: Strangers in our Land." *Business Horizons* 26, May-
June 1983, pp. 2-6.

765
"Series on Southern California Latinos—History of Four Generations."
Los Angeles Times, July 24, 1983, section I, p. 1, c. 1.

766
"Series on Southern California Latinos—Mexican Descendants in U.S."
Los Angeles Times, August 12, 1983, section I, p. 1, c. 1.

767
" 'Chicano Voices and Visions'. Social and Public Resource Center Review." *Los Angeles Times,* January 2, 1984, section V, p. 1, c. 3-R.

D. MIGRANT AGRICULTURAL LABOR

768
Earthbond. Washington, Migrant Legal Action Program [n.d.] (monthly).

769
Fuller, Varden
No Work Today! The Plight of America's Migrants. New York, Public Affairs Pamphlets #190 [n.d., n.p.]

770
Rosenthal, J. J.
"State-wide Clean-up of Labor Camps in California." *Engineering News* 75, June 8, 1916, pp. 1074-1076.

771
Woehlke, Walter V.
"Labor—the World Problem in the Far West." *Sunset,* volume 38, April 1917, pp. 7-10; May 1917, pp. 10-12; June 1917, pp. 10-12; volume 39, July 1917, pp. 17-18; August 1917, pp. 14-16; September 1917, pp. 20-21; October 1917, pp. 28-29; November 1917, pp. 11-13; December 1917, pp. 14-16; volume 40, January 1918, pp. 14-16; February 1918, pp. 15-16; March 1918, pp. 11-13; April 1918, pp. 14-16; May 1918, pp. 11-13.

772
Wolfson, Theresa
"People who go to Beets." *American Child* 1, November 1919, pp. 217-239.

773
Duke, Emma
"California the Golden; Cotton Picking in the Imperial Valley." *American Child* 2, November 1920, pp. 233-256.

774
Buffington, A. A.
"Automobile Migrants." *Family* 6, July 1925, pp. 149-153.

775
Gage, E. W.
"The Army of the Harvest Fields . . ." *American Elevator and Grain Trade,* July 15, 1925, pp. 21-22.

776
"Survey of Child Labor in Agriculture in California, 1924." *Monthly Labor Review* 21, August 1925, pp. 334-336.

777
Shields, L. F.
"Labor Conditions During the 1926 Apple Harvest in the Wenatchee Valley, Washington." *Monthly Labor Review* 24, April 1927, pp. 667-671.

778

Mangold, George B. & Hill, Lillian B.

Migratory Child Workers. New York, National Child Labor Committee (Publication #354), 1929, 16p.

779

Allen, Ruth A.

"Following the Cotton." *Survey* 62, June 15, 1929, pp. 361-363.

780

Lowry, Edith E.

"Untouched Migrant Field." *Missionary Review of the World* 54, September 1931, pp. 692-693.

781

"Transient Families in Arizona and Florida." *Monthly Labor Review* 33, December 1931, pp. 1363-1365.

782

Makepeace, Laura

"Among Migrant Spanish-Americans." *Missionary Review of the World* 56, November 1933, pp. 536-538.

783

Wilson, Charles M.

"Fruit People." *Commonweal* 20, May 18, 1934, pp. 65-66.

784

Winslow, Mary I.

"Catholic Action in Kansas." *Commonweal* 24, May 15, 1936, pp. 69-71.

785

Taylor, Paul S.

"The Resettlement Administration and Migratory Agricultural Labor in California." *Plan Age,* June 1936, pp. 26-29.

786

Lowry, Edith E.

Migrants of the Crops; They Starve That we May Eat. New York, Council of Women for Home Missions & Missionary Education Movement, 1938, 72p.

787

Taylor, Paul S., & Rowell, Edward J.

Refugee Labor Migration to California. Washington, GPO, 1938, 11p. (U.S. Bureau of Labor Statistics. Serial number R. 794). (Reprinted from *Monthly Labor Review,* August 1938 issue).

788
Krohn, Mildred
"Migratory Home." *Sierra Educational News,* November 1938, p. 22.

789
Taylor, Paul S., & Rowell, E. J.
"Patterns of Agricultural Labor Migration Within California." *Monthly Labor Review* 47, November 1938, pp. 982-990.

790
"Migrant Households in California, 1938." *Monthly Labor Review* 49, September 1939, pp. 622-623.

791
Brown, Malcolm, & Cassmore, Orin
"Earnings of Migratory Cotton Pickers in Arizona." *Labor Information Bulletin,* November 1939, pp. 10-12.

792
Lowry, Edith E., et al.
Tales of Americans on Trek. New York, Friendship Press, 1940, 95p.

793
McWilliams, Carey, & Bishop, Holmes
"To Ease California's Farm Problem." *Christian Science Monitor Weekly Magazine Section,* February 24, 1940, p. 5.

794
Nordyke, L. T.
"Mapping Jobs for Texas Migrants." *Survey Graphic* 29, March 1940, pp. 152-157.

795
Douglas, Katharine
"West Coast Inquiry; Testimony Before the La Follette Committee in California." *Survey Graphic* 29, April 1940, pp. 227-231.

796
"Migratory Strawberry Pickers." *Monthly Labor Review* 50, September 1940, pp. 1416-1417.

797
Meany, George
"Peonage in California." *American Federationist* 48, May 1941, pp. 3-5.

798
McKinley, R. M., & Banks, E. H.
"Texas Gives her Migrants Jobs." *Employment Security Review,* June 1941, pp. 13-16.

799
Janow, Seymour, & Gilmartin, William
"Labor and Agricultural Migration to California, 1935-1940." *Monthly Labor Review* 53, July 1941, pp. 18-34.

800
"California's Crops rot in Fields and on the Vine for Want of Farm Labor." *Life* 12, June 15, 1942, p. 38.

801
"Getting in the Crops." *Commonweal* 36, August 21, 1942, pp. 412-413.

802
Ham, W. T.
"Farm Labor and 1943 Goals." *Agricultural Situation* (U.S. Dept. of Agriculture), January 1943, pp. 12-15.

803
Warburton, Amber (Arthun)
"Children in the Fields: Summary of Children's Bureau Publication, *Work and Welfare of Children of Agricultural Workers in Hidalgo County, Texas.*" *Survey Midmonthly* 80, January 1944, pp. 13-15.

804
McWilliams, Carey
Small Farm and big Farm. New York, Public Affairs Committee, 1945, 31p.

805
Stegner, Wallace
"Okies in Sombreros: Migrant Mexican Crop-Workers" (In his, *One Nation.* Boston, Houghton, Mifflin, 1945, pp. 95-116).

806
White, Helen
"Social Agency Offers Program for Migrant Workers: Growers Find Improved Conditions key to Better Labor Supply." *Food Packer,* April 1945, pp. 40-41.

807
"A 15-Point Program for the Rights of Migrants." *National Consumers League Bulletin,* Fall 1945, p. 3.

808
Amidon, Beulah
What Next for New York's Joads? New York, Consumers League of New York, January 1946, 32p.

809
"Recommendations for Protection of Migrant Workers; Summary of Paul
S. Taylor's Program." *Monthly Labor Review* 62, February 1946, pp.
228-229.

810
McWilliams, Carey
"Poverty Follows the Crops." *The Nation* 162, March 23, 1946, pp.
343-344.

811
Hamman, A. H., et al.
"The Social Consequences of Migratory Labor; a Radio Discussion."
Reviewing Stand, September 22, 1946, pp. 1-12.

812
"Migrant Labor Report Seeks aid for 'Forgotten People': Citizens and
Governments Asked to Improve Conditions." *Labor Information Bulletin* (U.S. Dept. of Labor), April 1947, pp. 10-12.

813
McMillan, George E.
"Pickin' Time." *New York Times Magazine,* August 31, 1947, p.
10-11.

814
Whitman, Howard
"Heartless Harvest." *Collier's* 120, September 13, 1947, pp. 22-23;
September 20, 1947, p. 28.

815
"Migrant Workers in the U.S." Geneva, *International Labour Review* 56,
November-December 1947, pp. 33-36.

816
Casey, R. J.
"Pageant of the Poor" (In Kartman, Ben, & Brown, Leonard, eds.
Disaster! New York, Pellegrini & Cudahy, 1948, pp. 235-239).

817
"Wandering Workers: our Migratory Farm Laborers are in for bad Days
Again if Present Economic and Governmental Trends Continue." *The
Reporter,* June 21, 1949, pp. 14-16.

818
Kibbe, Pauline (Rochester)
"The American Standard for all Americans." *Common Ground,*
Autumn 1949, pp. 19-27.

819

"The People who Harvest our Crops: Grapes of Wrath, 1949-1950," *American Child,* January 1950, p. 1.

820

Wagner, Nancy, & Keehn, T. B.
"Our Robbery of American Migrants." *Social Action,* April 1950, pp. 5-36.

821

McNickle, R. K.
"Migrant Farm Labor." *Editorial Research Reports,* April 19, 1950, pp. 227-292.

822

Gardner, Virginia, & Miller, Mark
"Hunger in the San Joaquin Valley." *Masses and Mainstream,* June 1950, pp. 48-56.

823

"Migratory Workers: a Major Social and Economic Problem." *American Child,* October 1950, p. 1.

824

Green, William
"Our own Forgotten People: Migratory Workers Denied a Square Deal." *American Federationist* 57, December 1950, pp. 20-22.

825

Wunderlich, Frieda
"Migratory Labor." *Labor and Nation,* Spring 1951, pp. 18-20.

826

"The Nation's Task, Help for our Farm Help: Summary of Migrant Recommendations in the Report of the President's Commission on Migratory Labor, as Submitted, April 7, 1951." *Co-op Grain Quarterly,* September 1951, pp. 35-38.

827

National Child Labor Committee
Colorado Tale. (Publication #406). Washington, November 1951, 22p.

828

Fontaine, André
"No Migrant Problem Here." *Nation's Business* 39, December 1951, pp. 39-41.

829

"Exploitation in Tennessee." *Commonweal* 55, December 7, 1951, pp. 213-214.

830
Wood, L. D.
Manual for Summer Workers. San Antonio, Convención Bautista Mexicana de Texas, 1952.

831
Galarza, Ernesto
"They Work for Pennies." *American Federationist* 59, April 1952, pp. 10-13.

832
"National Conference on Labor Legislation. 19th, Washington, December 2-3." *Monthly Labor Review* 76, January 1953, pp. 21-22.

833
"Pablo is a Migrant." *School Life* 35, January 1953, pp. 56-58.

834
Cort, John C.
"In the Factories-in-the-Field." *Commonweal* 58, May 29, 1953, pp. 199-200.

835
"Migrant Workers Welcomed in Wisconsin." *Nation's Business* 41, August 1953, p. 86.

836
"Native Migrants: U.S. Democracy's Shame." *America* 89, September 26, 1953, p. 613.

837
"The Hired Farm Working Force of 1952, With Special Information on Migratory Workers." *Labor Market,* December 1953, pp. 26-28.

838
Lucey, Robert E.
"Migratory Workers." *Commonweal* 59, January 15, 1954, pp. 370-373.

839
Keller, Robert A.
"Feature X." *America* 91, July 24, 1954, pp. 418-419.

840
Richardson, W. W.
"Churches Join to Serve Migrants." *Christian Century* 71, August 18, 1954, pp. 988-990.

841
U.S. Interdepartmental Committee on Children and Youth *When the Migrant Families Come Again; a Guide for Better Community Living.*

Prepared by the Special Committee on Migrants and Their Families. Washington, 1955, 27p.

842

"Short-Changing Migrant Labor." *America* 93, May 7, 1955, pp. 147-148.

843

Clarke, Mary M.
"The Plight of the Migratory Workers." *Catholic World* 81, September 1955, pp. 406-413.

844

Minnesota Council of Churches. Migrant Committee
These are our Migrants: the Summary Report of a Survey of Current Trends and Needs Among Migratory Workers in Minnesota and the Ministry Provided by Churches Working Together, by Albert Z. Mann. [Minneapolis?] 1956, 19p.

845

"Nomads of California." *Look* 20, September 18, 1956, pp. 36-37.

846

Kilday, Francis A.
"A Southwestern Priest Advises his Northern Colleagues." *Central America & Mexico* (LV: 2), October 1956, pp. 10-20.

847

Lucey, Robert E.
"Migratory Labor in American Agriculture." *Central America & Mexico* (IV: 2), October 1956, pp. 1-6.

848

Koos, Earl L.
They Follow the sun. Jacksonville, Bureau of Maternal & Child Health, Florida State Board of Health, 1957, 55p.

849

LeBerthon, T.
"At the Prevailing Rate." *Commonweal* 67, November 1, 1957, pp. 122-125; "Discussion", *Commonweal* 67, July 4, 1957, pp. 353-356.

850

Myers, James
"The Continuing Farm Migrant Scandal; a Program for America's Forgotten Workers." *Socialist Call* 25, August 1957, pp. 7-10.

851

Gorman, Thomas
"They Help Feed America; a Photo Story of the Braceros." *Today's Health* 35, October 1957, pp. 24-27.

852
Seligman, D.
"Enduring Slums." *Fortune* 56, December 1957, pp. 144-149.

853
Plumb, Milton
"Turning Point for the Migrant Worker." *IUD Digest* 3, Spring 1958, pp. 109-117.

854
Talney, M. A.
"Migrant Labor in Oregon." *Christian Century* 76, January 21, 1959, p. 91.

855
Morgan, Edward P.
"Forgotten People." *The Reporter* 20, March 5, 1959, p. 4.

856
"Possible Turning Point." *Commonweal* 70, April 17, 1959, pp. 68-69.

857
"Two Approaches to Problems of Migrant Workers." *Christian Century* 76, June 3, 1959, p. 660.

858
"Legal Umbrella for Farm Workers." *America* 101, June 13, 1959, pp. 426-427.

859
"Migrant Workers' Plight." *Fortune* 60, November 1959, p. 274.

860
Hudson, L. P.
"Children of the Harvest" (In *Essays Today, 4*. Edited by Richard M. Ludwig. New York, Harcourt, Brace & Jovanovich, 1960, pp. 9-16).

861
"The Plight of Migrant Labor." *Social Order,* January 1960, pp. 1-3.

862
Raskin, A. H.
"For 500,000, Still Tobacco Road." *New York Times Magazine,* April 24, 1960, p. 14.

863
"Children of Migrant Workers Pose a Problem for Schools." *Saturday Evening Post* 232, May 28, 1960, p. 10.

864
King, Lawrence T.
"America's Poor." *Commonweal* 72, July 22, 1960, pp. 366-369.

865
Mayer, Arnold
"The Grapes of Wrath, Vintage 1961." *The Reporter* 24, February 2, 1961, pp. 34-37.

866
"Employment and Earnings of New York Migrant Farm Workers." *Monthly Labor Review* 84, April 1961, pp. 393-394.

867
"American Outcasts." *Christian Century* 78, May 3, 1961, p. 548- .

868
Keisker, S.
"Harvest of Shame." *Commonweal* 74, May 19, 1961, pp. 202-205.

869
"Nine Cents an Hour." *Newsweek* 57, June 5, 1961, p. 31.

870
Raskin, A. H.
"Misfortune's Children on the Move." *New York Times Magazine,* August 6, 1961, pp. 8-9.

871
King, Lawrence, T.
"Blight in our Fields." *Commonweal* 75, November 24, 1961, pp. 227-230.

872
America's DP's." *America* 107, April 7, 1962, pp. 9-10.

873
"Our Harvest of Shame." *Social Action,* May 1962- (entire issue).

874
Roberts, Holland
"American Untouchables: how Migrant Children are Exploited by the big Farmers and Neglected by the Government." *Mainstream* 15, May 1962, pp. 29-36.

875
Haltom, Kate
"Migrants: Nobody's People?" *YWCA Monthly* 56, June 1962, pp. 2-4.

876
Jacobs, Paul
"The Forgotten People" (In his, *The State of the Unions.* New York, Atheneum, 1963, pp. 172-191).

877
"Latter-day Serfs." *Commonweal* 77, February 8, 1963, p. 504.

878
"Vagabond Kings." *The Reporter* 28, May 9, 1963, pp. 12-14.

879
"Roots for the Rootless." *Christian Century* 80, May 15, 1963, pp. 635-636.

880
U.S. Dept. of Labor. Bureau of Labor Standards
Welcome, Stranger! Goodbye, Friend. A Guide to Community Efforts to Improve Conditions for Agricultural Migrants, by Thelma H. Harper. Revised. Washington, Bureau of Labor Standards Bulletin #258, 1964, 14p.

881
Cope, Myron
"Minister who Follows the Migrants: Migrant Ministry Program of N.C.C." *Saturday Evening Post* 237, January 4, 1964, pp. 34-36.

882
Bennett, Fay
"Still the Harvest of Shame." *Commonweal* 80, April 10, 1964, pp. 83-86.

883
Hartmire, W. C., Jr.
"Farm Workers on the Fringe." *Christian Century* 81, July 29, 1964, pp. 959-962.

884
"Caravan of Sorrow." *Living Age* 332, September 1964, pp. 870-872.

885
"Harvester Corps?" *New Republic* 152, April 3, 1965, pp. 6-7.

886
Mayer, Arnold, & Kelley, Eugene A.
"The Forgottenest." *IUD Agenda* (I: 4), May 1965, pp. 6-9.

887
Beecher, John
"To the Rear, March! 1965-1940." *Ramparts* 4, September 1965, pp. 27-32.

888
"Remembering the Forgotten People: Credit Unions are Beginning to Reach the Migrant Laborers." *Credit Union Monthly* 30, September 1965, pp. 26-29.

898
Corker, J. L.
"Our Brother the Migrant." *Christian Century* 82, September 29, 1965, pp. 1192-1193.

899
Logsdon, G.
"I Picked Apples With the Unemployed; With Editorial Comment." *Farm Journal* 89, November 1965, pp. 36-37, 118.

900
Allen, Steve
The Ground is our Table. Garden City, N.Y., Doubleday, 1966, 141p.

901
Koch, William H., Jr.
Dignity of Their own; Helping the Disadvantaged Become First-Class Citizens. New York, Friendship Press, 1966, 190p.

902
Scholes, William E.
Next Move for the Migrants. New York, Friendship Press, 1966, 31p.

903
Rogers, John
"Poverty Behind the Cactus Curtain." *Progressive* 30, March 1966, pp. 22-25.

904
"Migrant Labor, a Human Problem: Report and Recommendations." *Newsweek* 67, May 23, 1966, pp. 32-36.

905
Bennett, Fay
"Farm Crisis, City Crisis." *Christian Century* 83, June 22, 1966, p. 793-   .

906
Ogle, Alice
"The Plight of Migrant America." *America* 115, July 9, 1966, pp. 33-34.

907
Conway, James F.
"Migrants in the Promised Land; Farm Workers in Utah." *America* 115, September 10, 1966, pp. 253-255.

908
"Now They Walk With us; Texas Pickers." *Newsweek* 68, September 12, 1966, p. 54.

909
U.S. Office of Economic Opportunity
Traveler/El Viajero. Quarterly Newsletter for Migrant and Seasonal Farm Workers; Published as Information Service by Special Field Programs, Division of Community Action Programs. Washington, (I: 1), November 1966-   (quarterly).

910
MacNabb, Betty L.
"Texas Migrants Program; From Tax-Eaters to Tax-Payers." *Communities in Action* 2, March 1967, pp. 21-25.

911
The Migrant Workers. Publication #328. Washington, League of Women Voters, December 1967, 4p.

912
Morris, Austin P.
"Still Forgotten men." *America* 118, March 30, 1968, pp. 412-413.

913
Roysher, Martin, & Ford, D.
"California's Grape Pickers Will Soon be Obsolete." *New Republic,* April 13, 1968, pp. 11-12.

914
Loyd, C.
"Remembering Forgotten Americans: Leoti, Kansas." *NEA Journal* 56, June 1968, pp. 58-59.

915
"The Migratory Farm Worker." *Monthly Labor Review* 91, June 1968, pp. 10-12.

916
"The Rural Worker in America; Symposium." *Monthly Labor Review* 91, June 1968, pp. 1-32.

917
Tobin, Richard L.
"The Revolution is not Coming, it is Here." *Saturday Review* 51, August 17, 1968, pp. 12-15.

918
Compton, Neville
"The Green Valley Isn't so Jolly; Migrant Labor Camp Conditions, Yakima." *New Republic* 159, September 7, 1968, pp. 19-20.

919

Miller, Paul B., & Glasgow, John M.
"Job Crisis Along the Rio Grande." *Monthly Labor Review* 91, December 1968, pp. 18-23.

920

Sandage, Shirley M.
Child of Hope. Words by Shirley M. Sandage. Photos by Jo Moore Stewart. South Brunswick, N.J., A. S. Barnes, 1969, 135p.

921

Trupp, Philip
"The Migrant Worker." *Vista Volunteer* (5: 4), April 1969, pp. 12-17.

922

"For Amber Waves of Grain." *Vista Volunteer* (5: 5), May 1969, pp. 14-19.

923

"Wrath of Grapes." *Time,* May 16, 1969, p. 24.

924

Coyne, John R., Jr.
"Grapes of Wrath." *National Review* 21, July 1, 1969, p. 639.

925

Coles, Robert, & Hugh, Harry
"Peonage in Florida." *New Republic* 161, July 26, 1969, pp. 17-21.

926

Ramirez, Raúl
"Slim Pickings: Migrant Farm Hands Strain for $1 an Hour Harvesting Cucumbers." *Wall Street Journal* 174, September 16, 1969, p. 1- .

927

Greene, Sheldon L.
"Operation Sisyphus; Wetbacks, Growers and Poverty." *The Nation* 209, October 20, 1969, pp. 403-406.

928

"Ending the Misery of Migratory Farm Labor: an Agriculture Committee." *Looking Ahead* 17, January 1970, pp. 1-4.

929

National Planning Association. Agriculture Committee "Ending the Misery of Migratory Labor." *Looking Ahead* (17: 10), January 1970, pp. 1-4.

930
Reuel, Myrtle R.
"Communicating with the Migrant." *Child Welfare* 49, March 1970,
pp. 137-145.

931
Postelle, Y.
"Migrant Youngsters: our Forgotten Children." *Parents' Magazine &
Better Family Living* 45, May 1970, pp. 60-63.

932
Taylor, Paul S.
"Migrant Mother: 1936." *American West* 7, May 1970, pp. 41-45.

933
Sanchez, Arman J.
"Affluence Amid Poverty." *El Grito* (3: 4), Summer 1970, pp. 64-84.

934
"Senate Unit Airs Migrant Dispute." *Broadcasting* 79, August 3, 1970,
pp. 42-43.

935
"Candor That Refreshes: Coca-Cola to Improve Living Conditions of
Workers in Florida Citrus Groves." *Time* 96, August 10, 1970, p. 59.

936
Goodpaster, G. S.
"Peonage: the American System of Migratory Farm Labor." *Clearing-
house Review* (4: 6), October 1970, p. 237-   .

937
Gilmore, Tom
"The Migrant Worker: Needed, Exploited, Discarded." *Focus/Mid-
west* 53, 1971, pp. 14-16.

938
McBrearty, James C.
"Harvest of Plenty in Fields of Shame: the Migrant Worker Today."
Arizona Review 20, February 1971, pp. 1-8.

939
Marshall, Patricia
"From Migrant Stream to Mainstream: Ten-State Project Tests new
Routes to Better Life for Itinerant Workers." *Manpower* II, July 1971, pp.
11-17.

940
Wooley, A. E.
"Sending a boy to do a job you Wouldn't Even Wish on a Man." *To-
day's Health* 49, July 1971, pp. 44-49.

941

"Place in the sun for the Migrant: Coca-Cola's Housing Project." *Nation's Business* 59, September 1971, pp. 70-73.

942

Nelkin, Dorothy

"Invisible Migrant Workers." *Society* (9: 6), April 1972, pp. 36-41.

943

Hintz, Joy, & Mecartney, John

Who are Ohio's Migrants? Elizabeth S. Magee Education & Research Foundation (940 Engineers Bldg., Cleveland, Ohio 44114), 1974, 8p.

944

McQuarrie, Jack

Wildcrafting: Harvesting the Wilds for a Living, Brush-Picking, Fruit-Tramping, Worm-Grunting, and Other Nomadic Livelihoods. Santa Barbara, CA, Capra Press, 1975, 96p.

945

"Migrant Workers Based in La Grulla, Texas, Featured." *Los Angeles Times,* April 14, 1975, sec. I, p. 1, c. 1.

946

"Changes for Migrant Workers." *U.S. News & World Report* (78: 17), April 28, 1975, p. 54.

947

"Things are Better for Migrant Workers: Better pay and Healthier Living Conditions are Among the Sweeping Changes; yet Most Itinerant Farm Laborers Face an Uncertain Future." *U.S. News & World Report* 78, April 28, 1975, pp. 54-56.

948

Stewart, Don, & Perry, Phillip

"Harvesters." *New Times* (52: 2), July 25, 1975, p. 40.

949

"Working With Migrants." *New Republic* (175: 3223), October 16, 1975, p. 14.

950

"Lifestyle of the Migrant Worker Discussed." *Los Angeles Times,* October 31, 1975, sec. I-A, p. 4, c. 1.

951

Miller, J.

"Wisconsin Migrant Workers Rally for Bill." *Workers' World* (19: 3), January 21, 1977, p. 12- .

952
McMahon, B.
"Slavery in a Migrant Labor Camp." *Guardian* (29: 17), February 2, 1977, p. 5- .

953
"The Rio Grande Divides 2 Worlds." *The Economist* 262, February 5, 1977, p. 53.

954
McWilliams, Carey
"Earnings Gap." *The Nation* (224: 12), March 26, 1977, p. 356.

955
Daly, M.
"Migrants Stranded in Colorado." *Big Mama* 5, May 1977, p. 11- .

956
Dunn, Lucia, & Ullman, Jackie
"These Proud Americans." *Saturday Evening Post* (249: 6), September 1977, p. 42.

957
Tortorici, J.
"Slavery Today." *Militant* (41: 34), September 16, 1977, p. 12- .

958
Davidson, John
"Long Road North." *Texas Monthly* (5: 10), October 1977, p. 124.

959
National Catholic Conference of Bishops, U.S. Catholic Conference. Secretariat for Hispanic Affairs
The Farmworker Family: a People on the Move; Program Booklet in Celebration of Farm Worker Week, May 1-7, 1978. Washington, 1978, 22 & 22pp.

960
Coles, Robert, & Coles, J. H.
"Living on the Road; Excerpt from *Women of Crisis.*" *New York Times Magazine,* March 26, 1978, pp. 18-19.

961
Breiter, Toni
"They Sought Work and Found Terror." *Agenda* (8: 3), May/June 1978, pp. 22-26.

962
Malone, B.
"Tales of Migrant Horrors end in Victory." *Rochester Patriot* (6: 9), May 18, 1978, p. 1- .

963
Schwartz, Loretta
"The Plight of America's Five Million Migrants." *Ms.* 6, June 1978,
pp. 65-68.

964
Shenin, T.
"The Peasants are Coming." *Race and Class* (19: 3), Winter 1978, p.
277-   .

965
Adler, Stephen
"America 'Rediscovers' Migrant Workers." *New Society* (45: 831),
September 7, 1978, pp. 506-507.

966
Flowers, M.
"Ohio Migrants Press Union Recognition." *Guardian* (30: 47),
September 13, 1978, p. 3-   .

967
Karen, D.
"Migrant Workers . . . Still and Moving." *Socialist Review* 45, May
1979, p. 145-   .

968
Buyer, Bob
"Up-State Migrants: how do They Fare?" *Empire State Report* 5, Oc-
tober/November 1979, pp. 30-33.

969
Revenaugh, M.
"You Wake up in Potato Field." *Rochester Patriot* (7: 18), October 12,
1979, p. 1-   .

970
Castles, S.
"The Social Time Bomb." *Race and Class* (21: 4), Spring 1980, p.
369-   .

971
"Carpinteria Migrant Laborer's son Heads for Harvard University." *Los
Angeles Times,* June 28, 1980, sec. V, p. 1, c. 2.

972
"Economic Exiles." *Industrial Worker* (77: 8), July 16, 1980, p. 1-   .

973
"Migration and North America's Future." *The Futurist* 14, August 1980,
p. 23.

974
Levinger, Larry
"Nomads of the Prairie." *Readers Digest* 117, September 1980, pp. 95-100.

975
Forouzin, J.
"Conditions Scored Migrant Workers." *Workers' World* (22: 37), September 19, 1980, p. 12- .

976
North, David S.
"Non-Immigrant Workers: Visiting Labor Force Participation." *Monthly Labor Review* 103, October 1980, pp. 26-30.

977
"Migrant Farmworker Resources." *Southern Exposure* (9: 4), Winter 1981, p. 82- .

978
Portier, C.
"Raising Cane." *Southern Exposure* (9: 4), Winter 1981, p. 77- .

979
"Growers Lobby vs. Migrant Rights." *Dollars & Sense* 63, January 1981, p. 7.

980
"Plight and Future of Migrant Laborers Highlighted." *Los Angeles Times,* September 30, 1981, sec. IA, p. 4, c. 1.

981
"Migrant Education Program in Port Townsend, Washington," *Los Angeles Times,* October 24, 1981, sec. IA, p. 7, c. 1.

982
"Todd Darling's Documentary, 'Año Nuevo', on Migrant Labor." *Los Angeles Times,* November 4, 1981, sec. VI, p. 3, c. 1.

983
Martin, Philip L., & Mamer, J.
"Hired Workers on California Farms." *California Agriculture* 36, 1982, pp. 9-10.

984
Jacobs, Barry
"Slavery, American Style." *The Progressive* 46, January 1982, p. 18.

985
McMahon, B.
"Migrant Slaves . . . Harvest of Shame." *Guardian* (34: 20), February 17, 1982, p. 8- .

986

Koeppel, B.

"Migrants Stoop . . . Growers Conquer." *Progressive* (46: 3), March 1982, p. 42- .

987

"Travel Rights Under Attack." *Guardian* (34: 39), June 30, 1982, p. 19- .

988

Yale, A.

"The Travelers." *Southern Exposure* (10: 4), July 1982, p. 67- .

989

Chaze, W. L.

"Migrant Farm Workers Still Face a Harsh Life." *U.S. News & World Report* 93, August 9, 1982, pp. 36-37.

990

"A Look at Farm Worker Housing in California." *Los Angeles Times,* September 12, 1982, sec. II, p. 1, c. 2-P.

991

Foster, D.

"Desperate Migrants of Devil's Canyon." *Progressive* (46: 11), November 1982, p. 44- .

992

Sutton, Susan (Buck), & Brunner, Tracy

"Life on the Road: Midwestern Migrant Farmworker Survival Skills." *Migration Today* (11: 1), 1983, pp. 24-31.

993

"A Look at the Biggest Concentrations of Migrant Workers." *Los Angeles Times,* March 13, 1983, section I-B, p. 8, c. 1.

994

Foster, D.

"Land to the Landless." *Mother Jones* (8: 3), April 1983, p. 60- .

995

Camacho-de Schmidt, Aurora, & O'Loughlin, Frank

"H-2 Enemy: Institutionalized Injustice in our Fields." *Perspectives* 15, Summer 1983, pp. 6-9.

996

Thompson, Roger

"Migrants: Enduring Farm Problem." *Editorial Research Reports,* June 3, 1983, pp. 415-432.

997
"Series on Southern California Latinos—Migrant Pickers." *Los Angeles Times,* August 10, 1983, section I, p. 1, c. 1.

998
Buckley, William F., Jr.
"Doing the Impossible." *National Review* 35, September 2, 1983, p. 1097.

999
"Editorial on Funding for day Care Centers for California Migrant Workers." *Los Angeles Times,* September 7, 1983, section II, p. 4, c. 1-E.

1000
"Migrant Worker Tells House Committee About Slavery in Florida Fields." *Los Angeles Times,* September 23, 1983, section I, p. 15, c. 1.

1001
Martin, Philip L.
"Labor-Intensive Agriculture." *Scientific American* 249, October 1983, pp. 54-59.

1002
Meister, Dick
"Stoop Labor and who Will do it." *Christian Science Monitor,* February 8, 1984, p. 20.

E. AGRICULTURAL LABOR UNIONS

1003
Agricultural Workers Health and Medical Association *Report of Field Activities, California and Arizona.* [n.p.]

1004
"Farm Laborers' Union." *Outlook* 68, August 3, 1901, p. 755.

1005
Muls, Ernest E.
"The Labor Movement in New Mexico." *New Mexico Business Review* 4, 1935, pp. 137-140.

1006
"Unions of Agricultural Workers." *American Federationist* 43, June 1936, pp. 632-633.

1007
Stokes, Frank
"Let the Mexicans Organize." *The Nation* 143, December 19, 1936, pp. 731-732.

1008
"Farm Hands' Union; California Labor Federation Starts to Organize Workers in Fields and Canneries." *Business Week,* March 20, 1937, p. 53.

1009
"Coast Farmers map war on Unions." *Business Week,* December 2, 1939, p. 29.

1010
"Agricultural Labor-Contractor System in California." *Monthly Labor Review* 52, February 1941, pp. 345-348.

1011
Agricultural Workers Health and Medical Association *Monthly Statistical Report.* San Francisco, February 1941- .

1012
Mitchell, H. L.
"Farm Workers see the Light." *American Federationist,* January 1947, pp. 18-20.

1013
Wallace, Henry A.
"Report From California." *New Republic* 116, June 9, 1947, pp. 11-13.

1014
"To Stoop or lie." *Commonweal* 47, March 5, 1948, p. 509.

1015
Galarza, Ernesto
"Farm Struggle Continues." *American Federationist,* June 1949, pp. 23-25.

1016
Mitchell, H. L.
"Farm Toilers Make Progress." *American Federationist,* September 1950, p. 24.

1017
Mitchell, H. L.
"Workers in Agricultural and the big Corporations." *American Federationist,* August 1956, pp. 26-29.

1018
Burnham, P.
"Last Union." *Commonweal* 70, August 14, 1959, p. 421.

1019
"Valley of Decision: California's Central Valley." *Time* 76, July 4, 1960, pp. 76-77.

1020
"Pickets and Purpose." *Newsweek* 56, July 11, 1960, p. 76.

1021
Cooney, Robert B.
"New Hope Stirs Tattered Army of 50-Year Struggle." *American Federationist* 67, August 1960, pp. 6-9.

1022
Ball, C. D., & Fowler, B.
"AFL-CIO Goest After Farm Workers." *Farm Journal* 84, October 1960, p. 33- .

1023
"Fight to Organize Farm Help." *Farm Journal* 85, April 1961, pp. 32-33.

1024
"What the Farm Labor Battle is About . . ." *Californian* 2, November 1961, pp. 10-18.

1025
Bylin, James E.
"Farming Teamsters: Hoffa's Union Seems on Verge of Organizing Breakthrough." *Wall Street Journal* 168, August 23, 1966, p. 16.

1026
"Newcomer Wins on the Farm: Recently Chartered AFL-CIO Affiliate Defeats Teamsters as Bargaining Agent for Workers at 2 California Farms." *Business Week,* September 10, 1966, p. 158.

1027
"Farm Workers Choose a Union, and now the Southwest." *America* 115, September 17, 1966, p. 270.

1028
"Unionizing the Farm." *Business Week,* April 22, 1967, p. 164.

1029
Selvin, D. F.
"Rise of a Farm Workers Union." *American Federationist* 74, May 1967, pp. 1-5.

1030
"Collective Bargaining on the Farm." *Monthly Labor Review* 90, June 1967, pp. iii-iv.

1031
"Actos: Teatro Campesino, a Theatrical Part of the United Farmworkers Organizing Committee." *New Yorker* 43, August 19, 1967, pp. 23-25.

1032
Bylin, James E.
"Wine and Roses: AFL/CIO Doing Well With California Farm Labor, for now." *Wall Street Journal* 170, August 29, 1967, p. 12.

1033
Mills, Nicolaus C.
"Workers on the Farms: Agreement With the Western Conference of Teamsters." *New Republic* 157, September 23, 1967, p. 9.

1034
Chavez, Cesar
"The Organizer's Tale" (In Hale, Dennis, & Eisen, Jonathan, eds. *The California Dream*. New York, Macmillan, 1968, pp. 106-115).

1035
Morris, Austin P.
"Of Many Things: the Rights of Agricultural Labor to Organize and Bargain Collectively." *America* 118, January 13, 1968, inside front cover.

1036
Roysher, Martin, & Ford, Douglas
"California's Grape Pickers Will Soon be Obsolete." *New Republic* 158, April 13, 1968, pp. 11-12.

1037
Bailey, F., Jr.
"Bargaining Power—Elusive—Sought After—but is it Desirable?" *Banking* 60, May 1968, p. 82.

1038
Cohen, I. J.
"La Huelga! Delano and After." *Monthly Labor Review* 91, June 1968, pp. 13-16.

1039
Erenburg, Mark
"Obreros Unidos in Wisconsin." *Monthly Labor Review* (91: 6), June 1968, pp. 17-23.

1040
Glass, Judith (Chanin)
"Organizations in Salinas." *Monthly Labor Review* (91: 6), June 1968, pp. 24-27.

1041
"Will new Monopoly Force up Prices?" *Nation's Business* 56, June 1968, pp. 40-42.

1042
"Future of Collective Bargaining in U.S. Agriculture." Ottawa, *Labour Gazette* 68, December 1968, pp. 703-704.

1043
Logsdon, G.
"Wrath of Grapes; Unions Want to Organize all Hired Farm Labor." *Farm Journal* 93, February 1969, p. 33.

1044
"Rights for Farm Workers." *America* 120, April 26, 1969, pp. 492-493.

1045
Taylor, Ronald B.
"Labor in the Vineyard: the Boycott and the NLRA." *The Nation* 208, May 12, 1969, pp. 591-593.

1046
Matthiessen, Peter
"Cesar Chavez." *New Yorker* 45, June 21, 1969, pp. 43-44.

1047
Matthiessen, Peter
"Profiles: Organizer I and II." *New Yorker*, June 21, 1969, pp. 42-85; June 28, 1969, pp. 43-71.

1048
"Grapes Tabled." *The Economist* 231, June 28, 1969, pp. 49-50.

1049
Cabbell, Paul
A Free Press Interview with Cesar Chavez. [Los Angeles, UAW Wester Region Six, 1969], 4p. (Reprinted from the August 22, 1969 *Los Angeles Free Press*).

1050
Chavez, Cesar
"We Want Nothing More, we Want our Union." *American Federationist* 76, November 1969, p. 16.

1051
"For a Vote in the Vineyards." *America* 121, November 22, 1969, p. 482.

1052
United Farm Workers Organizing Committee
United Farm Workers Calendar 1970. Delano, CA, 1970? 26p.

1053
Hallett, D.L.
"Bitter Fruit in the Vineyards." *Nation's Business* 58, February 1970, pp. 80-83.

1054
Fitch, B., ed.
"Tilling With the System." *Christian Century,* 87, February 18, 1970, pp. 204-207.

1055
Weinstein, Harvey E.
"New Hows to Hoe: with the Grape Pacts Signed, Cesar Chavez Looks to Other Crops." *Wall Street Journal,* July 31, 1970, p. 1.

1056
Berman, J. J., & Hightower, J.
"Chavez and the Teamsters." *The Nation* 211, November 2, 1970, pp. 427-431.

1057
Mills, Nicolaus C.
"Eagle Over the Lettuce Fields." *Commonweal* 93, November 6, 1970, pp. 140-141.

1058
Politzer, J.
"Cesar's Salad." *Christianity Today* 15, January 1, 1971, p. 38.

1059
Gersmehl, Glen
"The Vision of Cesar Chavez; an Interview With Jim Drake." *Christianity and Crisis: a Journal of Christian Opinion* 30, January 11, 1971, pp. 296-300.

1060
"Cesar Chavez: 'La Causa' and the Man." *American Labor* 4, February 1971, pp. 20-30.

1061
"A Continuing Conversation With Cesar Chavez." *The Journal of Social Issues* (9: 3), November-December 1970, pp. 3-9; (9: 5), Spring 1971, pp. 30-31.

1062
Taylor, Ronald B.
"Why Chavez Spurns the Labor Act." *The Nation* 212, April 12, 1971, pp. 254-256.

1063
Dunne, John G.
"To Die Standing: Cesar Chavez and the Chicanos." *Atlantic* (227: 6), June 1971, pp. 39-45.

1064
Buckley, William F., Jr.
"Chavez Machine." *National Review* 23, August 10, 1971, pp. 888-889.

1065
"The Legal and Legislative Struggle of the Farmworkers, 1965-1972," *El Grito* (VI; 2), Winter 1972-73, entire issue.

1066
Bank, J.
"Farm Labor Laws: Breaking UFWOC's Back." *Christianity and Crisis: a Christian Journal of Opinion* 32, March 6, 1972, pp. 39-44.

1067
"Chavez Blight Spreads East." *Nation's Business* 60, May 1972, pp. 32-35.

1068
"Sociedad Protección Mutua de Trabajadores Unidos." *La Luz I,* October 1972, p. 6.

1069
Melloan, George
"Outside Cesar Chavez' Hiring Hall." *Wall Street Journal* 180, December 19, 1972, p. 14.

1070
Simonson, Mary E.
"New Chavez Strategy: Arizona Faces a Recall." *The Nation* (216: 16), April 16, 1973, p. 499.

1071
Wong, William
"Struggle in the Fields: Chavez Union Fights for Survival as the Teamsters Mount a Strong Drive to Represent Farm Laborers." *Wall Street Journal* 181, June 29, 1973, p. 32.

1072
Bernstein, Harry
"Duel in the sun: Union Busting Teamster Style." *Progressive* 37, July 1973, pp. 17-20.

1073
"Cesar Chavez's Decisive Battle." *Business Week,* August 4, 1973, p. 53.

1074
"Tug-of-war Over Farm Hands: is Chavez Losing his Fight?" *U.S. News & World Report* 75, September 17, 1973, pp. 96-98.

1075
White, Harold C.
"The Labor Unions in the Fields: the Arizona Farm Labor Law." *Arizona Business* 20, October 1973, pp. 17-26.

1076
Bank, J.
"Cesar Chavez and the Grape Boycott in Canada." Ottawa, *Labour Gazette* 74, February 1974, pp. 114-120.

1077
Friedland, William H., & Thomas, Robert J.
"Paradoxes of Agricultural Unionism in California." *Society* (11: 4), May 1974, p. 54.

1078
Bank, J.
"Farmworker Response to the Teamster Challenge." Ottawa, *Labour Gazette* 74, September 1974, pp. 629-633.

1079
D'Aiello, Charon
"Newsnote of the United Farmworkers Union." *La Raza* (2: 4), January 1975, pp. 3-4.

1080
"Chavez Escalates his Attack on Gallo." *Business Week,* January 27, 1975, p. 53.

1081
Coles, Robert
"Our Hands Belong to the Valley." *Atlantic* (235: 3), March 1975, p. 72.

1082
"A Law to Settle Farm Labor Strife; Secret Ballot and Elections Will Determine Which Union Will Represent the Workers." *Business Week,* June 2, 1975, p. 57.

1083
"Chavez Says California Gov. Brown to Address UFW Convention." *Los Angeles Times,* June 23, 1975, sec. I, p. 3, c. 6.

1084
Chavez, Cesar
"Interview, Cesar Chavez: The Undefeated Leader of the Migrant Farm Workers." *Penthouse,* July 1975, pp. 64-66, 99, 108, 110.

1085
"California Farm Board Votes to Allow Unions Access to Grower Lands." *Los Angeles Times,* August 30, 1975, sec. II, p. 1, c. 1.

1086
Kistler, Alan
"New Hope for the Farm Workers." *American Federationist* 82, September 1975, pp. 1-5.

1087
"U.S. Court Maintains Curb on Union Access to Farm Workers." *Los Angeles Times,* September 5, 1975, sec. I, p. 3, c. 5.

1088
Wong, William
"Harvesting Votes: Union Fight Over California Farmhands Goes to Polls . . . *Wall Street Journal* 186, September 9, 1975, p. 48.

1089
"California Lettuce Workers Cast Ballots in First Major Showdown." *Los Angeles Times,* September 10, 1975, sec. I, p. 26, c. 1.

1090
"Chavez vs. the Teamsters . . ." *U.S. News & World Report* 79, September 22, 1975, pp. 82-83.

1091
"Editorial on Administration of California's new Farm Labor Law." *Los Angeles Times,* October 3, 1975, sec. II, p. 6, c. 1.

1092
"Judge Orders Grower to Allow Union Organizers into Orchard." *Los Angeles Times,* October 11, 1975, sec. II, p. 1, c. 1.

1093
"UFW Workers Sign Contract With Minute Maid in Florida." *Los Angeles Times,* November 6, 1975, sec. I, p. 2, c. 6.

1094
Pawlicki, Joseph F.
"Big Fish and Small Fry in the Valley." *America* (133: 18), December 6, 1975, p. 399.

1095
Biffle, Christopher
"Bugs in a Frying pan: Chopping California's Cotton." *The Nation* (221: 20), December 13, 1975, p. 622.

1096
"California Assesses UFW $1 Million for Deficiencies in Jobless Fund." *Los Angeles Times,* December 18, 1975, sec. I, p. 3, c. 5.

1097
"Editorial on California Agricultural Labor Relations Board." *Los Angeles Times,* January 18, 1976, sec. IV, p. 2, c. 1.

1098
"UFW Union Signs First Contracts Under new California Labor law." *Los Angeles Times,* February 2, 1976, sec. I, p. 2, c. 5.

1099
"Violence Erupts Again Between UFW and Teamsters." *Los Angeles Times,* February 14, 1976, sec. II, p. 1, c. 1.

1100
"California ALRB Issues First Decision on Unfair Labor Practice." *Los Angeles Times,* February 27, 1976, sec. I, p. 3, c. 2.

1101
"California Grower-Backed Farm Labor Bill Gains Momentum." *Los Angeles Times,* March 4, 1976, sec. I, p. 26, c. 1.

1102
"UFW Signs Contract With Coachella Valley Cooperative." *Los Angeles Times,* March 22, 1976, sec. I, p. 2, c. 6.

1103
"UFW Signs 3-Year Contract With Admiral Packing Co." *Los Angeles Times,* March 28, 1976, sec. I, p. 2, c. 6.

1104
"California Governor Brown Strikes out at Opponents of Farm Labor law." *Los Angeles Times,* April 7, 1976, sec. I, p. 3, c. 5.

1105
"Teamsters and UFW Hold Secret Talks to Settle Labor Dispute." *Los Angeles Times,* June 11, 1976, sec. I, p. 1, c. 5.

1106
"Farm Workers Merge With East Coast Union." *Monthly Labor Review* 99, August 1976, pp. 48-49.

1107
"UFW Seeks Halt to Printing of Pamphlet on California Farm Initiative." *Los Angeles Times,* August 3, 1976, sec. I, p. 2, c. 5.

1108
"California Farmers say Union Organizers Harrass Their Farm Workers." *Los Angeles Times,* September 17, 1976, sec. I, p. 3, c. 5.

1109
"Hollywood Celebrities Attend Fund-Raiser for UFW Prop. 14." *Los Angeles Times,* October 11, 1976, sec. I, p. 24, c. 1.

1110
Brody, M.
"Hail to Cesar? Californians Have Another hot Issue to Weigh." *Barron's* 56, October 18, 1976, p. 3.

1111
"A Crucial Vote on Farm Unions: California's Proposition 14 Would Strengthen Farm Workers' Rights to Organize." *Business Week,* November 1, 1976, p. 60.

1112
Segur, Winthrop H., Jr., & Fuller, Varden
"California's Farm Labor Elections: an Analysis of the Initial Results." *Monthly Labor Review* 99, December 1976, pp. 25-30.

1113
"UFW Files Damage Suit vs. California Farm Labor Board Counsel." *Los Angeles Times,* March 8, 1977, sec. I, p. 23, c. 1.

1114
"AFL-CIO and United Farm Workers Peace Treaty due." *Los Angeles Times,* March 10, 1977, sec. I, p. 11, c. 1.

1115
"Editorial on Future Methods of the United Farm Workers Union." *Los Angeles Times,* March 11, 1977, sec. II, p. 6, c. 1.

1116
"Teamsters Union to Withdraw From Farm Union Activities in West." *Los Angeles Times,* March 11, 1977, sec. I, p. 1, c. 1.

1117
Koziara, Karen S.
"Agricultural Labor Relations Laws in Four States: a Comparison." *Monthly Labor Review,* May 1977, pp. 14-18.

1118
"UFW Wins 33 of 48 Farm Union Elections." *Los Angeles Times,* July 9, 1977, sec. I, p. 23, c. 1.

1119
"Cesar Chavez Seeks Nationwide Farm Union." *Los Angeles Times,* August 27, 1977, sec. II, p. 11, c. 1.

1120
Brody, M.
"Chavez Country; Fresh Fields lie Open to the United Farm Workers." *Barron's* 57, September 5, 1977, p. 9.

1121
"Race to the Orchards." *NACLA's Report on the Americas* (11: 8), November 1977, p. 29- .

1122
Rose, Cynthia
"Farmworker Organizations Hold Issue Forum." *Agenda* (8: 1), January/February 1978, pp. 22-24.

1123
"Last Threat to Chavez; Mechanization." *Business Week,* January 30, 1978, pp. 69-70.

1124
"Growers Prefer Machines to UFW". *Dollars and Sense* 35, March 1978, p. 14- .

1125
Chavez, Cesar
"Square Tomatoes and Idle Workers; the Farm Workers' Next Battle; University of California Mechanization Research." *The Nation* 226, March 25, 1978, pp. 330-332.

1126
Ring, H.
"Where is UFW Headed?" *Militant* (42: 15), April 21, 1978, p. 24- .

1127
"Cesar Chavez Column on Scene of Growers in Arizona and California." *Los Angeles Times,* June 25, 1978, sec. VI, p. 3, c. 1-C.

1128
Senia, A.
"From Vineyard to Onion Patch." *Sevendays* (2: 11), July 1978, p. 7- .

1129
"A Bill of Rights Written by Farm Workers, for Farm Workers." *Agenda* (8: 4), July/August 1978, p. 22.

1130
Martinez, Douglas R.
"Farm Workers Unions: Growth and Change." *Agenda* (8: 4), July/August 1978, pp. 14-17.

1131
"Latest Threat to Chavez: Mechanization." *Business Week,* July 31, 1978, pp. 77-78.

1132
Foster, D.
"UFW Moves Increase Political Clout." *In These Times* (2: 42), September 13, 1978, p. 5- .

1133
Gmeiner, K.
"Farmworkers Organize." *Guild Notes* (7: 4), October 1978, p. 7- .

1134
"My Life . . . Jesse Lopez de la Cruz." *Radical America* (12: 6), November 1978, p. 27- .

1135
Bedell, B.
"Farm Organizing . . . Union Busting." *Guardian* (31: 15), January 17, 1979, p. 2- .

1136
"Imperial County Officials Charge UFW With Unfair Labor Practices." *Los Angeles Times,* February 23, 1979, sec. I, p. 3, c. 3.

1137
Cloak, D.
"Farm Worker Organizers Face Trial." *Guardian* (31: 25), March 28, 1979, p. 6- .

1138
"Workers Denounce Planned U.S. Senate Farm Labor Law Hearing." *Los Angeles Times,* April 19, 1979, sec. I, p. 24, c. 5.

1139
"Split Creates new Farm Workers Union." *Just Economics* (7: 3), Summer 1979, p. 3- .

1140
Bernstein, Harry
"Cesar Chavez Fights a 2-Front Battle." *Christianity and Crisis: a Christian Journal of Opinion* 39, August 20, 1979, pp. 197-200.

1141
"Governor Brown Vetoes Bill Which Would Curtail Powers of the UFW." *Los Angeles Times,* September 8, 1979, sec. II, p. 1, c. 1.

1142
"UFW Negotiates new 3-Year Contracts with California Vegetable Growers." *Los Angeles Times,* September 14, 1979, sec. I, p. 3, c. 1.

1143
"UFW Wins in California/FLOC Fights in Ohio." *Industrial Worker* (76: 10), October 1979, p. 8- .

1144
Williams, C.
"UFW Under Attack." *Guild Notes* (8: 5), October 1979, p. 5- .

1145
Blake, P.
"FLOC Attorney Beaten." *Win Magazine* (15: 34), October 18, 1979, p. 17- .

1146
Avery, D.
"FLOC on the Move." *Guild Notes* (8: 6), November 1979, p. 16- .

1147
Kent, D.
"UFW Wins Lettuce Contract." *The Organizer* (5: 11), November 1979, p. 6- .

1148 \
"California ALRB Orders Payment of Back pay to Delano Nursery Workers." *Los Angeles Times,* December 8, 1979, sec. I, p. 33, c. 4.

1149
Barry, T.
"Farmworker Union Farms." *Guardian* (32: 10), December 12, 1979, p. 4- .

1150
Mann, W.
"Arizona Farmworkers Union." *Worker's World* (22: 1), January 4, 1980, p. 16- .

1151
"UFW President Chavez Announces Boycott of Lucky Stores Chain." *Los Angeles Times,* January 20, 1980, sec. I, p. 23, c. 1.

1152
"Farm Labor Leader Chavez Assails NBC and Farm Organizations." *Los Angeles Times,* January 25, 1980, sec. I. p. 3, c. 1.

1153
"California Assembly Approves Measure to Curb the United Farm Workers." *Los Angeles Times,* February 26, 1980, sec. I, p. 3, c. 5.

1154
Bruno, C. C.
"I Refuse to bow to the UFW Union." *Humanist* 39, November/December 1979, pp. 29-31; Discussion, *Humanist* 40, March/April 1980, pp. 46-49.

1155
"Sue Miner Honored for her 25 Years With Migrant Ministry." *Los Angeles Times,* May 5, 1980, sec. V, p. 1, c. 2.

1156
"UFW Fights IRS Claim of Owing $400,000 in Taxes." *Los Angeles Times,* July 19, 1980, sec. II, p. 1, c. 1.

1157
"California Senate Okays Bill to bar UFW Political Fund Payments." *Los Angeles Times,* August 26, 1980, sec. I, p. 3, c. 1.

1158
"FLOC Update." *Guild Notes* (9: 6), November 1980, p. 12- .

1159
Lacefield, P.
"Bread and Roses too." *Win Magazine* (16: 19), November 15, 1980, p. 30- .

1160
"California Appeal Court Backs ALRB on Farm Workers' Rights." *Los Angeles Times,* December 28, 1980, sec. I, p. 22, c. 1.

1161
Vandermeer, J.
"Agricultural Research and Social Conflict." *Science for the People* 13, January 1981, p. 5.

1162
"United Farm Workers Loses 5-Year-Old Gallo Vote to Teamsters." *Los Angeles Times,* January 3, 1981, sec. I, p. 23, c. 1.

1163
Fitzsimmons, M.
"FLOC Unionization vs. Mechanization." *Lucha* 5, February 1981, p. 7.

1164
Roth, A.
"Ohio Farmworkers Stop Sheriff's Case." *Workers' World* 23, February 27, 1981, p. 4.

1165
"Conference Presents Platform, Rural America." *Mountain Life & Work* 57, March 1981, p. 31.

1166
"Coalition Denounces Mexican Guest Worker Proposal." *Los Angeles Times,* June 10, 1981, sec. I, p. 10, c. 1.

1167
Bedell, B.
"Don't Mourn, Organize." *Guardian* (33: 43), July 29, 1981, p. 2- .

1168
"Dissidents Oppose Leadership of UFW President Cesar Chavez." *Los Angeles Times,* September 6, 1981, sec. I, p. 3, c. 6-P.

1169
"Cesar Chavez Warns Growers That UFW Will Resist Attack." *Los Angeles Times,* September 7, 1981, sec. I, p. 3, c. 1.

1170
"Feature on Problems Limiting Growth of United Farm Workers Union." *Los Angeles Times,* October 25, 1981, sec I, p. 1, c. 1-P.

1171
"United Farm Workers Union Seeks More Efficient Operation." *Los Angeles Times,* October 25, 1981, sec. I, p. 20, c. 1.

1172
"Two Former Anti-Poverty Aides Say Chavez Pressure led to Dismissal." *Los Angeles Times,* November 13, 1981, sec. I, p. 3, c. 5.

1173
"Reagan Administration Seeks Return of Federal Grant From 2 UFW Agencies." *Los Angeles Times,* December 10, 1981, sec. I, p. 3, c. 1.

1174
Keerdoja, E., & Lubenow, G. C.
"What Happened to Chavez's Union?" *Newsweek* 98, December 14, 1981, p. 22.

1175
"California ALRB Awards Millions to Farm Workers in 1979 Strike." *Los Angeles Times,* December 17, 1981, sec. II, p. 1, c. 4.

1176
"Farmers Ordered to Rehire 53 Workers Involved in 1979 Strike." *Los Angeles Times,* December 25, 1981, sec. I, p. 26, c. 1.

1177
"Gentlemen Farmers . . . Genteel Poverty." *Industrial Worker* (79: 1), January 1982, p. 1- .

1178
Bedell, B.
"Dissent Racks Farmworkers Union." *Guardian* (34: 14), January 6, 1982, p. 6- .

1179
"Teamsters Vote to Renew Peace Treaty With United Farm Workers."
Los Angeles Times, February 26, 1982, sec. I, p. 3, c. 5.

1180
"UFW Launches Texas Drive." *Southern Exposure* (10: 2), March 1982,
p. 7- .

1181
Thomas, R.
"3-Way Collective Bargaining . . . Goal." *Labor Notes* 40, May 1,
1982, p. 14- .

1182
Larson, Erik
"Internal Strains Split United Farm Workers as Movement Changes In-
to a Trade Union." *Wall Street Journal* 199, May 17, 1982, p. 29.

1183
Donohue, John W.
"Between Two Worlds." *America* 146, May 22, 1982, pp. 403-404.

1184
"California Supreme Court Supports Order Allowing Unionists on Farm
Land." *Los Angeles Times,* May 28, 1982, sec. I, p. 21, c. 1.

1185
Early, S.
"How to Organize Immigrant Labor." *Nation* (34: 22), June 5, 1982,
p. 680.

1186
"United Farmworkers and Political Power." *Southern Exposure* (10: 4),
July 1982, p. 14- .

1187
"Farmworkers win Arkansas Contract." *Southern Exposure* (10: 5), September 1982, p. 4- .

1188
"Deukmejian Hints of Deal Between Bradley and United Farm Workers." *Los Angeles Times,* September 2, 1982, sec. I, p. 3, c. 3.

1189
"Bradley Addresses National Agri-Marketing Association on Cesar Chavez." *Los Angeles Times,* September 25, 1982, sec. II, p. 1, c. 6.

1190
"UFW Dissidents use Some of Cesar Chavez's Tactics." *Los Angeles
Times,* December 6, 1982, sec. IV, p. 1, c. 2.

1191
"United Farm Workers Dissidents and Protest Aimed at Chavez." *Los Angeles Times,* December 8, 1982, sec. I, p. 17, c. 1.

1192
Tjerandsen, C.
"Your Organization is Your gun." *The Organizer* (9: 4), Winter 1983, p. 3- .

1193
"Not so United." *The Economist* 286, January 15-21, 1983, p. 30.

1194
Delgado, Gary
"Organizing Undocumented Workers." *Social Policy* 13, Spring 1983, pp. 26-29.

1195
"United Farm Workers Leader Chavez Says California ALRB General Counsel is Aiding Growers." *Los Angeles Times,* March 23, 1983, section I, p. 17, c. 1.

1196
"Workers at Sakioka Farms Issued Illegal Hoes." *Los Angeles Times,* April 9, 1983, Section I, p. 30, c. 1.

1197
"Editorial on use of Outlawed Short-Handled Hoe on California Farm." *Los Angeles Times,* April 13, 1983, section II, p. 6, c. 1-E.

1198
Terry, Jim
"Campbell Soup in hot Water With Organized Labor: Farmworkers Seek to Boycott America's Favorite Soups." *Business & Society Review,* Summer 1983, pp. 37-41.

1199
"California Farm Labor Board may Overturn Major Ruling on Bargaining." *Los Angeles Times,* June 20, 1983, section IV, p. 1, c. 1.

1200
"California ALRB Reverses Stand on Grower's Decisions and Bargaining." *Los Angeles Times,* June 21, 1983, section I, p. 3, c. 4.

1201
"Chavez's Son, Fernando, Elected President of Latino Political Association." *Los Angeles Times,* July 26, 1983, section I, p. 12, c. 4.

1202
"A Harvest of Troubles in California." *The Economist* 288, August 27, 1983, pp. 15-16.

1203
Newman, Patty
"Harvest of Power; in 1975 Cesar Chavez and his United Farm Workers Pushed Through an Unprecedented Labor Law in California; now They are Reaping the Rewards in Oppressive Control Over Farming and Farm Workers." *Reason: Free Minds and Free Markets* 15: September 1983, pp. 19-26.

1204
"Waldie Column on Agricultural Labor Board's Tilt to Agribusiness." *Los Angeles Times,* September 4, 1983, section IV, p. 5, c. 3.

1205
Yañez, A.
"Farm Workers Weigh Grower . . . Government Attack." *Militant* (47: 35), September 30, 1983, p. 10- .

1206
"United Farm Workers Political Arm Fined $25,000 by FPPC Over Funds Reporting." *Los Angeles Times,* November 9, 1983, section I, p. 18, c. 1.

1207
"Endicott Article in Power of United Farm Workers Leader Chavez in California." *Los Angeles Times,* January 29, 1984, section IV, p. 3, c. 1.

1208
Barger, W. K.
"Midwestern Farmworkers and the Farm Labor Movement." *La Red/The Net* 78, March 1984, pp. 2-7.

1209
"Farm Workers' Suit Attacks California Agricultural Research." *Chronicle of Higher Education,* March 21, 1984, p. 3.

F. FARM LABOR STRIKES

1210
Teller, Charlotte
"Labor Crisis in Colorado: Cripple Creek." *Harper's Weekly* 48, January 25, 1904, pp. 978-980.

1211
Teller, Charlotte
"Labor War in Colorado." *Harper's Weekly* 48, January 9, 1904, pp. 54-56; April 23, 1904, pp. 641-643; August 13, 1904, pp. 1253, 1259.

1212
Fitch, John H.
"Arizona's Embargo on Strike Breakers." *Survey Graphic* 37, 1916-1917, pp. 143-146.

1213
Seiler, C.
"Cantaloupes and Communists." *The Nation* 131, September 3, 1930, pp. 243-244.

1214
Rodriguez, T., & Fennell, W. G.
"Agrarian Revolt in California." *The Nation* 137, September 6, 1933, p. 272.

1215
Hunter, Stanley A.
"Churchmen Investigate Strikes in California." *Christian Century* 50, November 8, 1933, p. 1416.

1216
De Ford, Miriam A.
"Blood-Stained Cotton in California." *The Nation* 137, December 20, 1933, pp. 705-706.

1217
Winter, Ella
"California's Little Hitlers." *The New Republic,* December 27, 1933, pp. 188-190.

1218
Creel, George
"Blood-Stained Cotton in California; Reply." *The Nation* 138, February 21, 1934, p. 222.

1219
Shoaf, George H.
"California's Reign of Terror." *Christian Century* 51, February 28, 1934, pp. 282-284.

1220
Winter, Ella
"Fascism on the West Coast." *The Nation* 138, February 28, 1934, pp. 241-242.

1221
Williams, C. S.
"Imperial Valley Prepares for war." *World Tomorrow* 17, April 26, 1934, pp. 199-201.

1222
"Imperial Valley Labor Troubles." *Information Service* (Federal Council of the Churches of Christ in America), May 5, 1934, pp. 2-4.

1223
Levenson, Lew
"California Casualty List." *The Nation* 139, August 29, 1934, pp. 243-245.

1224
Mac Namara, John
"Berry Picker." *The Nation* 139, September 12, 1934, pp. 302-304.

1225
Taylor, Paul S., & Kerr, Clark
"Uprisings on the Farms." *Survey Graphic* 24, January 1935, pp. 19-22.

1226
Mini, Norman
"That California Dictatorship." *The Nation* 140, February 20, 1935, pp. 224-226.

1227
Kelly, F. C.
"Unrest in the Valley: California's Imperial Valley Watches Nervously as Labor Problems Grow and Vigilantes Keep an eye on all 'Agitators'." *Today*, May 11, 1935, pp. 14-15.

1228
Adamic, Louis
"Cherries are red in San Joaquin." *The Nation* 142, June 27, 1936, pp. 840-841.

1229
Steinbeck, John
"Dubious Battle in California." *The Nation* 143, September 12, 1936, pp. 302-304.

1230
"Poison gas in America's Salad Bowl; Vigilantes Hunt Reds in the Lettuce Fields of California." *Literary Digest* 122, October 10, 1936, pp. 5-6.

1231
"Riot-Spiced Salads; a California Sheriff Calms Lettuce Fields With gas Threats." *Literary Digest* 122, October 31, 1936, pp. 8-9.

1232
"Farmers Break Strike, California Fruit Growers . . ." *Business Week*, July 17, 1937, p. 26.

1233
"La Pasionaria de Texas; Pecan Pickers' Strike." *Time* 31, February 28, 1938, p. 17.

1234
McWilliams, Carey
"The Joads on Strike." *The Nation* 149, November 4, 1939, pp. 488-489.

1235
"Cotton Strike; California Pickers' Holdout ends After Disorder Flares." *Newsweek* 14, November 6, 1939, p. 51.

1236
Ficachi, Concepcion G.
"Habla Trujillo Gurria: Huelgas y Braceros." Mexico, *Hoy,* March 31, 1945, pp. 14-15.

1237
"Farmers Divided: One Group Helps Strikers, Another Forms Vigilante Committee." *Business Week,* March 2, 1946, p. 94.

1238
Nordyke, L.
"Texas Cleans up a Mess." *Saturday Evening Post* 219, July 27, 1946, pp. 26-27.

1239
Mitchell, H. L.
"Agricultural Workers Strike." *Commonweal* 47, November 14, 1947, p. 117.

1240
Flanagan, Daniel V.
"Farm Workers Strike: Conditions at the DiGiorgio Farm at Arvin, near Bakersfield." *American Federationist* 54, December 1947, pp. 12-13.

1241
McWilliams, Carey
"The Strike at DiGiorgio's." *The Nation* 166, February 28, 1948, pp. 234-235.

1242
Galarza, Ernesto
"Big Farm Strike at the DiGiorgio's." *Commonweal* 48, June 4, 1948, pp. 178-182.

1243
"Cane Mutiny." *Time* 62, November 2, 1953, p. 26.

1244

Carpenter, William

"Ferment in the Lettuce Fields, Imperial Valley." *The Nation* 180, April 9, 1955, inside cover.

1245

"Valley of Decision: California's Central Valley." *Time* 76, July 4, 1960, pp. 76-77.

1246

"AFL-CIO Organizers go After Farm Labor." *Business Week,* September 24, 1960, pp. 50-52.

1247

King, L. T.

"Pickets in the Valley." *Commonweal* 73, October 14, 1960, pp. 64-67.

1248

"Farmers Strike, Consumer Pays." *Business Week,* September 15, 1962, p. 36.

1249

"NFO Holding Action." *Farm Journal* 86, October 1962, p. 114.

1250

"What Farmers Think of NFO Holding." *Farm Journal* 86, October 1962, p. 10.

1251

"Asparagus Aspersions; Dispute over Employment of Domestic or Foreign Workers." *Newsweek* 65, April 5, 1965, p. 34.

1252

"New Alliance Shapes up in Dixie: AFL-CIO's Interest in Strike on Cotton Plantation." *Business Week,* July 10, 1965, p. 124.

1253

Ogle, A.

"Revolution in the Vineyards." *America* 113, December 11, 1965, pp. 747-748.

1254

Novak, Michael

"Grape Strike." *Commonweal* 83, December 24, 1965, pp. 366-369.

1255

"Grapes of Wrath: Delano District Strike." *Newsweek* 66, December 27, 1965, pp. 57-58.

1256

"Grapes of Wrath in California." *America* 114, January 8, 1966, p. 33.

1257
"Dispute in Delano." *Commonweal* 83, January 28, 1966, p. 49.

1258
Kopkind, Andrew
"Grape Pickers' Strike: war in California." *New Republic* 154, January 29, 1966, pp. 12-15.

1259
Degnan, James P.
"Monopoly in the Vineyards: Grapes of Wrath Strike." *The Nation* 202, February 7, 1966, pp. 151-154.

1260
"From Delano to Sacramento," *America* 114, April 2, 1966, p. 430.

1261
"Victory in the Vineyards; Support Given to Farm Workers in California." *Time* 87, April 15, 1966, p. 59.

1262
"Farm Unions Reap First California Victory." *Business Week,* April 16, 1966, p. 158.

1263
"Harvest in the Vineyards." *The Economist* 219, April 16, 1966, p. 248.

1264
"Viva la Huelga! Schenley Corp. Recognizes NFWA as Sole Bargaining Agent." *Newsweek* 67, April 18, 1966, p. 42.

1265
Davis, Thurston N.
"Viva la Huelga!" *America* 114: April 23, 1966, pp. 589-590.

1266
"Labor Comes to Life in the Grape Fields." *New Republic* 154, April 23, 1966, pp. 6-7.

1267
"Schenley Surrenders; Migrant Workers vs. California Grape Growers." *Christian Century* 83, April 27, 1966, pp. 515-516.

1268
"March of Migrants." *Life* 60, April 29, 1966, pp. 93-94.

1269
Wolfe, Jerome
"Church and Delano." *Commonweal* 84, April 29, 1966, pp. 168-169.

1270
Vizzard, James L.
"Grape Strike." *Commonweal* 84, May 27, 1966, pp. 295-296.

1271
Allen, Gary
"The Grapes: Communist Wrath in Delano." *American Opinion* 9, June 1966, pp. 1-14.

1272
Valdez, Luis, et al.
"Tales of the Delano Revolution." *Ramparts* 5, July 1966, pp. 37-50.

1273
Salandini, Victor
"Decision at Di Giorgio." *America* 115, October 8, 1966, p. 415.

1274
"Unionizing the Farm: Di Giorgio Signs an AFL-CIO Contract." *Business Week,* April 22, 1967, p. 164.

1275
Dunne, John G.
"Strike! California's Grape Pickers." *Saturday Evening Post* 240, May 6, 1967, pp. 32-36.

1276
"Trouble in the Melon Patch; Texas Rangers Break up Picket Lines in Picker's Strike." *Newsweek* 69, June 19, 1967, p. 38.

1277
Adair, Doug
"Cesar Chavez's Biggest Battle." *The Nation* 205, December 11, 1967, pp. 627-628.

1278
"Cesar's war; Grape Pickers' 35-Month-old Strike." *Time* 91, March 22, 1968, p. 23.

1279
Cohen, Irving J.
"La Huelga! Delano and After." *Monthly Labor Review* 91, June 1968, pp. 13-16.

1280
Watson, M. L.
"Boycott Seeks to aid Grape Workers." *Christian Century* 85, June 5, 1968, pp. 769-770.

1281
"Seething Vineyards: Struggle now Concentrated vs. Growers of Table Grapes." *Newsweek* 72, July 8, 1968, p. 62.

1282
Salandini, Victor
"More Grapes of Wrath." *America* 119, August 17, 1968, pp. 104-105.

1283
"Can They Pull off a Nationwide Boycott?" *Nation's Business* 56, October 1968, pp. 46-48.

1284
Meister, Dick
"La Huelga Becomes la Causa: California Grape Pickers Strike." *New York Times Magazine,* November 17, 1968, pp. 52-53.

1285
Krebs, A.V., Jr.
"Bishops Stay out of the Vineyard." *Commonweal* 89, December 20, 1968, pp. 393-394.

1286
"Churchmen and Table Grapes." *America* 120, January 4, 1969, p. 4.

1287
Logsdon, G.
"Wrath of Grapes." *Farm Journal* 93, February 1969, p. 33.

1288
Chavez, Cesar
"Non-Violence Still Works: UFWOC During California Grape Pickers' Strike: Interview." *Look,* April 1, 1969, p. 52.

1289
Chavez, Cesar
"Letter From Delano." *Christian Century* 86, April 23, 1969, pp. 539-540.

1290
Taylor, Ronald B.
"Labor in the Vineyard: the Boycott and the NLRA." *The Nation* 208, May 12, 1969, pp. 591-593.

1291
"Sundering of the Grape Growers." *America* 121: June 5, 1969, p. 2.

1292
Sanderson, R. K., & Barr, E. L.
"Why Grape Growers do not Render Unto Cesar." *Christian Century* 86, June 11, 1969, pp. 810-811.

1293
Bernstein, Harry
"Federal Mediators Enter Grape Strike." *Los Angeles Times,* June 19, 1969, p. 1.

1294
"Breakthrough for la Huelga: Breakthrough in Negotiations." *Time* 93, June 27, 1969, p. 18.

1295
"The Little Strike That Grew to La Causa." *Time* 94, July 4, 1969, pp. 16-21.

1296
"Four-Year Strike, Two-Year Boycott: Showdown." *U.S. News & World Report* 67, July 14, 1969, pp. 83-84.

1297
Buckley, William F., Jr.
"Don't Eat Grapes Along With me." *National Review* 21, July 15, 1969, p. 715.

1298
Day, Mark
"Clergy and the Grape Strike: Delano Verdict." *America* 121, August 30, 1969, pp. 114-117.

1299
Fusco, Paul
La Causa, the California Grape Strike. Photos by Paul Fusco. Written by George D. Horwitz. New York, Collier Books, 1970, 158p.

1300
Coyne, J. R., Jr.
"Doctored Grapes?" *National Review* 22, January 27, 1970, p. 88.

1301
Hudson, Wilson M.
"Huelga . . . a Strike for Decent Living." *Nursing Outlook* 18, February 1970, p. 40.

1302
"Black Eagle Wins." *Time* 96, August 10, 1970, pp. 10-11.

1303
Varela, Delfino
"The Farm Workers' Victory, too bog for Words." *Regeneración* (I: 5), August 28, 1970, pp. 9-10.

1304
Palmer, L. M.
"Grape Fight Spreads to Other Crops." *Farm Journal* 94, September 1970, p. 22.

1305
Henninger, D.
"And now Lettuce." *New Republic* 163, October 10, 1970, pp. 9-11.

1306
"Cesar Chavez: 'La Causa' and the Man." *American Labor* 4, February 1971, pp. 20-30.

1307
O'Connell, T. J.
"Lettuce Boycott Reaches New York: First of Lawsuits Against the Pentagon." *America* 124, February 13, 1971, pp. 143-149.

1308
Drake, J., & Gersmehl, G.
"Salad Days at the Pentagon." *Commonweal* 93, February 19, 1971, pp. 485-486.

1309
Arias, Pedro
"Coachella." *La Raza* (1: 12), 1973, pp. 22-23.

1310
Bernstein, Marcelle
"Battle of the Foodbowl." London, *New Statesman* 86, September 28, 1973, pp. 412-413.

1311
Levering, Bob
"The Gallo Wine-Cesar Chavez Confrontation . . ." *Business & Society Review,* Winter 1975-76, pp. 11-16.

1312
" 'Fighting for our Lives', Story of UFW Strike, Reviewed." *Los Angeles Times,* April 16, 1975, sec. IV, p. 13, c. 1.

1313
"Chavez Seeks Aid for Boycott on California College Campuses." *Los Angeles Times,* May 6, 1975, sec. II, p. 1, c. 6.

1314
"Catholic Leaders Reaffirm Support for UFW Boycotts." *Los Angeles Times,* August 28, 1975, sec. I, p. 26, c. 1.

1315
"Chavez and UFW Plan Boycott of Sunmaid and Sunsweet Growers."
Los Angeles Times, February 12, 1976, sec. I, p. 3, c. 5.

1316
"Opponent of California Farm Labor Board Sells Grapes to Gallo." *Los Angeles Times,* February 15, 1976, sec. I, p. 3, c. 5.

1317
Chavez, Cesar
"California Farm Workers' Struggle." *Black Scholar* 7, June 1976, pp. 16-19.

1318
"Gallo Fights a Boycott." *Industry Week* 189, June 28, 1976, p. 32.

1319
Lopez, David E.
"Cowboy Strikes and Unions." *Labor History* (18: 3), Summer 1977, pp. 325-340.

1320
Broyles, William
"Behind the Lines." *Texas Monthly* (5: 8), August 1977, p. 5.

1321
"Texas Farm Workers . . . Hunger Strike." *Common Sense* (5: 1), October 1977, p. 16- .

1322
Barry, T.
"Arizona Citrus Strikers." *Guardian* (30: 4), November 2, 1977, p. 5- .

1323
Barry, T.
"Arizona Farm Worker Wins Victory." *Militant* (41: 42), November 11, 1977, p. 23- .

1324
García, E.
"Arizona Farm Workers win Strike." *Militant* (41: 44), November 25, 1977, p. 2- .

1325
"Boycott Pet Products." *Workers' Power* 34, December 5, 1977, p. 5- .

1326
Barry, T.
"UFW Joins Arizona Onion Strikers." *Guardian* (30: 12), December 28, 1977, p. 5- .

1327

Barry, T.

"Undocumented Farmworkers win Second Citrus Strike." *Guardian* (30: 16), January 25, 1978, p. 3- .

1328

Bornstein, Leon

"Farm Workers end Longstanding Boycott." *Monthly Labor Review* 101, March 1978, p. 53.

1329

"UFW and Delano Area Grape Workers Reach Contract Agreement." *Los Angeles Times,* May 9, 1978, sec. II, p. 1, c. 1.

1330

"UFW Strikes Onion Growers." *Industrial Worker* (75: 7), July 1978, p. 3- .

1331

"Striking Tomato Workers in Ohio vow to Defy Eviction Notice." *Los Angeles Times,* September 4, 1978, sec. I, p. 4, c. 1.

1332

"Growers Threaten . . . Farm Workers." *Militant* (42: 34), September 15, 1978, p. 28- .

1333

Flowers, M.

"Ohio Farmworkers let Tomatoes rot." *Guardian* (30: 48), September 20, 1978, p. 5- .

1334

Lewis, K.

"Potato Growers Denounce Farmworkers." *Rochester Patriot* (6: 17), September 28, 1978, p. 1- .

1335

Rosenzweig, E.

"Farm Workers dig in on 2 Fronts." *Guardian* (31: 3), October 25, 1978, p. 4- .

1336

Downs, P.

"Ohio Farmworkers Strike." *Science for the People* (10: 6), November 1978, p. 6- .

1337

Margolis, Richard J.

"Trouble in Crystal City; Zavala County Economic Development Corporation." *New Leader* 61, November 20, 1978, pp. 12-13.

1338
Greenwood, R.
"Florida Farmworkers win Strike." *Guardian* (31: 13), January 3, 1979, p. 4- .

1339
"Strike by California Lettuce Pickers Reduces Nation's Lettuce Harvest." *Los Angeles Times,* January 23, 1979, sec. I, p. 3, c. 5.

1340
"Violent Farm Labor Confrontation in Imperial Valley Injures 24." *Los Angeles Times,* January 30, 1979, sec. I, p. 16, c. 1.

1341
"Strike vs. Lettuce Growers in the Southland Spreads." *Los Angeles Times,* February 1, 1979, sec. I, p. 18, c. 1.

1342
"California Farm Bureau Federation Reacts to Lettuce Boycott Threat." *Los Angeles Times,* February 3, 1979, sec. II, p. 12, c. 1.

1343
Rosenzweig, E.
"Lettuce Pickers Thwart Growers." *Guardian* (31: 18), February 7, 1979, p. 4- .

1344
"Nearly all Vegetable Farming in the Imperial Valley Halted." *Los Angeles Times,* February 13, 1979, sec. I, p. 3, c. 3.

1345
"Imperial County Supervisors Reject Protection Request by Lettuce Strikers." *Los Angeles Times,* February 14, 1979, sec. I, p. 29, c. 3.

1346
Remer, L.
"Farm Workers Strike for pay Hike." *In These Times* (3: 13), February 14, 1979, p. 7- .

1347
Malone, B.
"Tomato Struggle to be Told Here." *Rochester Patriot* (7: 3), February 15, 1979, p. 4- .

1348
Lee, J.
"Farmworker Killed . . . California Lettuce Strike." *Workers' World* (21: 7), February 16, 1979, p. 5- .

1349
"New Violence Reported in Imperial Valley Lettuce Strike." *Los Angeles Times,* February 22, 1979, sec I, p. 3, c. 4.

1350
Santos, J.
"UFW Lettuce Strike Spreads." *Militant* (43: 7), February 23, 1979, p. 32- .

1351
"Lettuce Strike Test of UFW." *Industrial Worker* (76: 3), March 1979, p. 8- .

1352
"California Lettuce Strikers Fight." *Militant* (43: 8), March 2, 1979, p. 8- .

1353
Loy, T.
"California Lettuce Strike Spreads." *Worker's World* 9, March 2, 1979, p. 2- .

1354
Sheils, M., & Maguire, S.
"Cesar's Lettuce Strike." *Newsweek* 93, March 5, 1979, pp. 81-82.

1355
"Why Chavez Needs a big win: California Lettuce Workers Strike." *Business Week,* March 5, 1979, pp. 23-24.

1356
"UFW Strikers Shun Slap in Face." *Guardian* (31: 22), March 7, 1979, p. 6- .

1357
"United Farm Workers Boycott Chiquita in new Labor Tactic." *Los Angeles Times,* March 7, 1979, sec. I, p. 3, c. 3.

1358
McCall, C.
"Lettuce Rots and a man Dies as Cesar Chavez's Dream Strike Turns Nightmare." *People* 11, March 12, 1979, pp. 24-27.

1359
Hackwell, B.
"Lettuce Strike Moves." *Workers' World* (21: 12), March 23, 1979, p. 12- .

1360
"Boycott Libby's . . . Campbell's." *The Workbook* (4: 2), April 1979, p. 64- .

1361
"FLOC Targets Boycott." *Guild Notes* (8: 2), April 1979, p. 5- .

1362
"UFW President Chavez Says U.S. INS Prolonging Lettuce Strike." *Los Angeles Times*, April 18, 1979, sec. I, p. 26, c. 4.

1363
Wright, M.
"Companies try to Break UFW Strike." *Guardian* (31: 30), May 2, 1979, p. 7- .

1364
Wright, M.
"UFW Condemns INS Scabbing." *Guardian* (31: 31), May 9, 1979, p. 9- .

1365
Kent, D.
"Farmworker Strike Intensifies." *The Organizer* (5: 6), June 1979, p. 8- .

1366
"UFW Wins Victory . . . Strike Lettuce." *The Black Panther* (19: 9), June 18, 1979, p. 6- .

1367
Rosenzweig, E.
"UFW Threatens . . . Expand Strike." *Guardian* (31: 37), June 20, 1979, p. 6- .

1368
Rosenzweig, E.
"UFW Flexes its Muscles in Strike." *Guardian* (31: 38), June 27, 1979, p. 4- .

1369
Kramer, S.
"UFW Negotiations Break." *Militant* (43: 25), June 29, 1979, p. 20- .

1370
"UFW in Fight for Survival." *Labor Notes* 6, July 21, 1979, p. 4- .

1371
Rosenzweig, E.
"UFW Rally Bolsters Strike." *Guardian* (31: 44), August 22, 1979, p. 4- .

1372
Sole, D.
"Ohio Tomato Farmers March for Justice." *Workers' World* (21: 35),
August 31, 1979, p. 4- .

1373
"UFW Boycotts Chiquita Banana." *Keep Strong* (4: 5), September 1979,
p. 65- .

1374
"Mann Packing Co. Reaches Agreement With United Farm Workers."
Los Angeles Times, September 11, 1979, sec. I, p. 3, c. 4.

1375
Bedell, B.
"FLOC/Growers Backs Against Wall." *Guardian* (31: 47), September
12, 1979, p. 3- .

1376
"UFW Winning Raises." *Labor Notes* 8, September 22, 1979, p. 3- .

1377
Bedell, B.
"Union Busting . . . Iowa Grain Workers." *Guardian* (31: 49),
September 26, 1979, p. 2- .

1378
"Red Coach Lettuce . . . Targeted . . . UFW." *Industrial Worker* (76:
10), October 1979, p. 8- .

1379
"UFW Wins Victory in California Strikes." *The Black Panther* (19: 10),
October 1, 1979, p. 10- .

1380
Crawford, G.
"FLOC Wins Court Victory." *Workers' World* (21: 39), October 5,
1979, p. 2- .

1381
Bedell, B.
"FLOC Tomato Strike Success." *Guardian* (32: 1), October 10, 1979,
p. 6- .

1382
"UFW Victorious." *Win Magazine* (15: 35), October 25, 1979, p. 17- .

1383
"Arizona Farmworkers on Strike." *Workers' World* (21: 42), October 26,
1979, p. 11- .

1384
Avery, D.
"FLOC on the Move." *Guild Notes* (8: 6), November 1979, p. 16-   .

1385
Rosenzweig, E.
"UFW Victories Evidence of Durability." *Guardian* (32: 8), November 28, 1979, p. 6-   .

1386
"Arizona Farmworkers Lose out." *Win Magazine* (15: 42), December 13, 1979, p. 28-   .

1387
Starr, A.
"UFW to Boycott Wegman's." *Rochester Patriot* (7: 23), December 20, 1979, p. 1-   .

1388
Street, Richard S.
"Lettuce Strike Story." *The Nation* 230, January 19, 1980, pp. 45-49.

1389
Mulligan, John E.
"Liturgy and la Lucha." *America* 142, February 23, 1980, pp. 144-147.

1390
Kushner, S.
"Lettuce Strike Continues." *In These Times* (4: 17), March 26, 1980, p. 6-   .

1391
Chacker, N.
"Fight for Justice hits Tomato Field." *Changes Socialist Monthly* (2: 6), July 1980, p. 8-   .

1392
Kelly, J.
"Strike at Sanderson Farms." *Big Mama* (8: 6), July 1980, p. 15-   .

1393
"What's Happening . . . Farm Labor." *Food Monitor* 17, July 1980, p. 20-   .

1394
Krass, Alfred C.
"Strikers and Ohio Churches: in the Soup." *Christian Century* 97, August 13-20, 1980, pp. 796-798.

1395
"Ohio Farmworkers . . . Strike Support." *Workers' World* (22: 34), August 22, 1980, p. 4- .

1396
"FLOC Pushes Canners to Bargain." *Just Economics* (8: 3), September 1980, p. 2- .

1397
Johnson, L.
"They Treat us Worse Than Chickens." *Win Magazine* (16: 14), September 1, 1980, p. 18- .

1398
Calderon, C.
"Farmworkers Onion Strike Part win." *Guardian* (32: 46), September 3, 1980, p. 7- .

1399
"Tomato Pickers ask 'Please Boycott'." *Industrial Worker* (77: 10), September 16, 1980, p. 1- .

1400
"Bud Antle, Inc., Nation's Largest Lettuce Grower, hit by Walkout." *Los Angeles Times,* September 20, 1980, sec. I, p. 25, c. 1.

1401
"Tomato Crop Below Normal in Ohio." *Labor Notes* 20, September 25, 1980, p. 7- .

1402
Rosenzweig, E.
"California Farmworkers Strike Lettuce Grower." *Guardian* (32: 50), October 1, 1980, p. 8- .

1403
Hackwell, B.
"Undocumented Worker on Strike in Ohio." *Workers' World* (22: 41), October 17, 1980, p. 6- .

1404
García, E.
"Undocumented Citrus Workers on Strike." *Militant* (44: 40), October 31, 1980, p. 18- .

1405
Zeiters, E.
"Arizona Farmworkers on Strike." *Workers' World* (22: 43), October 31, 1980, p. 5- .

1406
García, E.
"Arizona Farmworkers win Recognition." *Militant* (44: 44), November 28, 1980, p. 21- .

1407
Cutter, A.
"Farm Workers Fight Slave Conditions." *Guardian* (33: 10), December 10, 1980, p. 6- .

1408
Calderon, C.
"Texas Farm Workers Boycott RC Cola." *Guardian* (33: 26), April 1, 1981, p. 10- .

1409
McFerran, M.
"In the Tomato Fields." *Labor Today* (20: 5), May 1981, p. 5- .

1410
"California Supreme Court to Decide Farm Access by Strikers." *Los Angeles Times,* August 13, 1981, sec. I, p. 3, c. 3.

1411
Wilayto, P.
"Ohio Farmworkers in Fourth Year Strike." *Workers World* (23: 36), September 4, 1981, p. 16- .

1412
"Frontlines/Farmworkers on Strike." *Rochester Patriot* (9: 17), September 25, 1981, p. 4- .

1413
"Campbell's Boycott Continues." *Win Magazine* (17: 20), November 15, 1981, p. 26- .

1414
"UC Study Shows 1979 UFW Strike Aided Lettuce Growers' Profits." *Los Angeles Times,* January 15, 1982, sec. I, p. 1, c. 1.

1415
"UFW Strike Halts Lemon Harvesting at Ventura County Ranches." *Los Angeles Times,* March 12, 1982, sec. II, p. 5, c. 1.

1416
"UFW and Limoneria Company Reach Tentative Agreement on new Contract." *Los Angeles Times,* May 11, 1982, sec. I, p. 3, c. 6.

1417
"United Farm Workers to Intensify Boycott Against Lettuce Growers." *Los Angeles Times,* May 18, 1982, sec. I, p. 3, c. 1.

1418
Blake, B.
"Farmworkers Boycott Red Coach Lettuce." *Socialist Worker* 64, August 1982, p. 14- .

1419
Nichols, C.
"Fast Dramatizes Farmworkers' Strike." *Mountain Life* (58: 10), November 1982, p. 22- .

1420
Pepper, R.
"Pulpwood Cutters win Strike." *Southern Exposure* (11: 1), January 1983, p. 6- .

1421
Terry, R.
"Farmworkers Strike vs. Campbell." *Multinational Monitor* (4: 2), February 1983, p. 9- .

1422
"Campbell Boycott Continues." *Rural America* (8: 2), March 1983, p. 4- .

1423
"United Farm Workers End Strike vs. Ventura Mushroom Farm; Dole Boycott Ends." *Los Angeles Times,* March 17, 1983, section I, p. 21, c. 1.

1424
Bouton, D.
"A Long Road to Justice." *Rural America* (8: 2), July 1983, p. 5- .

1425
Sanders, B.
"It's Back to Boycott for Farmworkers." *Guardian* (35: 39), July 13, 1983, p. 8- .

1426
"United Farm Workers Loses Pay Fight but Wins key Issue on Strikebreaking." *Los Angeles Times,* July 16, 1983, section II, p. 1, c. 1.

1427
Sanders, B.
"Strikers Trek 540 Miles to Campbell." *Guardian* (35: 42), August 24, 1983, p. 6- .

1428
"California Farmworkers: Back to the Barricades?" *Business Week,* September 26, 1983, p. 86.

1429
Berman, N.
"Latino Strikers and White Scabs." *Guardian* (35: 46), September 28, 1983, p. 6- .

1430
"Labor Column on Battles Between Farm Workers and Growers in California." *Los Angeles Times,* October 24, 1983, section IV, p. 1, c. 1.

1431
"Abatti Produce, Inc. to Halt Farming Operations Over Labor Woes." *Los Angeles Times,* December 16, 1983, section II, p. 5, c. 1.

1432
"Lucky Stores to Stop Buying Lettuce From Boycotted Grower." *Los Angeles Times,* January 4, 1984, section I, p. 21, c. 1.

Scholarly and Specialized Materials

A. AGRICULTURAL LABOR, GENERAL

1. Bibliographies

1433
U.S. Library of Congress
List of References on Farm Labor in the United States (With Special Reference to Conditions of Life and Labor of Farm Workers). Washington, February 2, 1921, 10p.

1434
Colvin, Esther M., & Folsom, J. C.
Agricultural Labor in the United States, 1915-1935. Washington, U.S. Dept. of Agriculture, Bureau of Agricultural Economics (Agricultural Economics Bibliography #64), 1935, 493p.

1435
Benedict, Murray R.
Agricultural Labor in the Pacific Coast States: a Bibliography and Suggestions for Research. Berkeley, CA, Pacific Coast Regional Committee, Social Science Research Council, 1938, 64p.

1436
Colvin, Esther M., & Folsom, J. C.
Agricultural Labor in the United States, 1936-1937: a Selected List of References. Washington, U. S. Dept. of Agriculture, Bureau of Agricultural Economics (Agricultural Economics Bibliograph #72), 1938, 205p.

1437
Turner, Howard B.
Imperial County, California: a Selected List of References. Washington, U.S. Dept. of Agriculture, Bureau of Agricultural Economics, Library (Economist List #25), 1941, 77p.

1438
McNeill, John, & Folsom, J. C.
Agricultural Labor in the United States, 1938-June 1941: a Selected List of References. Washington, U.S. Dept. of Agriculture, Bureau of Agricultural Economics (Agricultural Economics Bibliograph #95), 1942, 268p.

1439
Moats, Ruby W., & McNeill, John
Agricultural Labor in the United States, July 1941-February 1943: a List of References. Washington, U.S. Dept. of Agriculture, Library (Library List #4), 1943, 59p.

1440
"Farm Labor in the United States: References to Materials Published Since 1943" (In California. Governor's Commission to Survey the Agricultural Labor Resources of the San Joaquin Valley. *Agricultural Labor in the San Joaquin Valley.* Sacramento, March 15, 1951, pp. 301-317).

1441
Folsom, J. C.
Agricultural Labor in the United States, 1943-1952: a Selected List of Annotated References. Washington, U.S. Dept. of Agriculture, Library (Library List #61), 1954, 170p.

1442
Slobodek, Mitchell
A Selective Bibliography of California Labor History. Los Angeles, UCLA, Institute of Industrial Relations, 1964, 265p.

1443
Nordin, Dennis S.
"Graduate Studies in American Agricultural History." *Agricultural History* 41, July 1967, pp. 275-312.

1444
Schideler, James H., & Lee, Lawrence B.
A Preliminary List of References for the History of Agriculture in California. Davis, University of California, Davis, Agricultural History Center, 1967, 62p.

1445
Hall, Carl W.
Bibliography on Mechanization and Labor in Agriculture. East Lansing, Rural Manpower Center, Michigan State University, 1968, 18p. (Special Paper #6)

1446
Taylor, Paul S.
"California Farm Labor: a Review." *Agricultural History* 42, January 1968, pp. 49-54.

1447
Fujimoto, Isao, & Schieffer, Jo Clare
Guide to Sources on Agricultural Labor, June 1969. Davis, California,

Dept. of Applied Behavioral Sciences, College of Agricultural and Environmental Sciences, University of California, Davis, 1969, 39p.

1448
Institute for Rural America
Poverty, Rural Poverty, and Minority Groups in Rural Poverty: an Annotated Bibliography. Lexington, KY, Spindletop Research, 1969, 159p.

1449
Ruesink, David C., & Baton, T. B.
Bibliography Relating to Agricultural Labor. College Station, TX, Texas A & M University, 1969, 93p.

1450
Schlebecker, John T.
Bibliography of Books and Pamphlets on the History of Agriculture in the United States, 1607-1967. Santa Barbara, CA, ABC-Clio Press, 1969, 183p.

2. Circulating Materials

1451
Colorado. Division of Employment and Training
Annual Rural Manpower Report. Denver, State of Colorado (annual).

1452
Connecticut. Employment Security Division
Annual Agricultural and Food Processing Report. Hartford [n.d.]

1453
Delaware. Dept. of Labor
Rural Employment and Services Report. Dover, State of Delaware, Dept. of Labor [n.d.] (annual).

1454
Farm Labor Report. Employment by County. Sacramento, Employment Development Dept., Employment Data & Research Division (semi-monthly). (At head of title: Farm Labor Information, Report 881-A).

1455
Montana. State Employment Service
Montana Annual Rural Manpower Report. Helena, Montana, State Employment Service, Employment Security Div., Dept. of Labor & Industry [n.d.] annual.

1456
New Jersey. Bureau of Rural Manpower Services. *Rural Manpower Report.* Trenton (annual).

1457
Oregon. Employment Division
Annual Rural Services Report. Salem, State of Oregon, Employment Division, Dept. of Human Resources (annual).

1458
Pennsylvania. Rural Manpower Services
Annual Report. Harrisburg [n.d.]

1459
Tennessee. Dept. of Employment Security
Tennessee Rural Manpower Services Report. Nashville [n.d.] annual.

1460
Washington (State). Employment Security Dept.
Rural Employment Report. Olympia, Washington State Employment Security Dept. (annual).

1461
"Half a Century of Farm Wages in the United States." (In *U.S. Industrial Commission Report.* Washington, volume 11, part 1, 1901, pp. 116-144).

1462
Barker, Eugene C.
"Land Speculation as the Cause of the Texas Revolution." *Texas State Historical Association Quarterly* 10, 1906, pp. 76-95.

1463
Eaves, Lucile
A History of California Labor Legislation, With an Introductory Sketch of the San Francisco Labor Movement. Berkeley, CA, University (of California) Press, 1910, 461p.

1464
Coulter, Ernest K.
"Agricultural Laborers in the United States." *Annals of the American Academy of Political and Social Science* 40, March 1912, pp. 40-44.

1465
Baker, C. C.
"Mexican Land Grants in California." *Southern California Quarterly* 9, 1914, pp. 236-243.

1466
Guinn, J. M.
"The Passing of the Rancho." *Historical Society of Southern California, Annual Publications X,* 1915-1916- p. 48.

1467
Love, Clara M.
"The History of the Cattle Industry of the Southwest." *Southwestern Historical Quarterly* (19: 4), April 1916, pp. 370-399; (20: 1), July 1916, pp. 1-18.

1468
Adams, R. L., & Kelly, T. R.
California—Study of Farm Labor. Berkeley, University of California, College of Agriculture, Experiment Station Circular #193, March 18, 1918, 75p.

1469
"Farm Labor" (In *Transactions of the Commonwealth Club of California*, volume 13, #3. San Francisco, May 1918, pp. 73-122).

1470
Adams, R. L.
"The Farm Labor Problem." *The University of California Chronicle* 22, April 1920, pp. 200-216.

1471
U.S. Dept. of Labor
Standards of Labor in the Hill Farms of Louisiana, by M. B. Oates and L. A. Reynoldson. Bulletin #961. Washington, August 13, 1921, 27p.

1472
"Ranch Labor" (In Texas. Agricultural and Mechanical College. Agricultural Experiment Station. Division of Farm and Ranch Economics. *Economic Study of a Typical Ranching Area on the Edwards Plateau of Texas*. College Station, Texas, July 1922, pp. 301-315).

1473
Morrow, William W.
Spanish and Mexican Private Land Grants. San Francisco, Bancroft Whitney Co., 1923, 27p.

1474
Renehan, Alois
The Pueblo Indians and Their Land Grants . . . Albuquerque, T. Hughes Printer, 1923, 78p.

1475
California. Bureau of Labor Statistics, San Francisco
Labor Laws of the State of California, 1925. Sacramento, 1925, 298p.

1476
U.S. Dept. of Agriculture
Truck Farm Labor in New Jersey, 1922, by J. C. Folsom. Dept. Bulletin #1825. Washington, April 1925, 38p.

1477
U.S. Dept. of Labor. Employment Service
Harvesting in the "big Wheat Belt." Washington, May 1, 1927, 8p.

1478
Hill, Joseph A.
Women in Gainful Occupations, 1870-1920 . . . (U.S. Bureau of the Census, Census Monographs IX). Washington, GPO, 1929, 416p.

1479
"The History of Wages in the United States From Colonial Times to 1928." *U.S. Bureau of Labor Statistics Bulletins* 499, 1929, pp. 124-128, 225-231.

1480
U.S. Senate. Committee on Agriculture and Forestry
Agricultural Labor Supply; Hearings, April 3-8, 1930, on S.J. Res. 86, a Joint Resolution Creating a Commission to Make a Study With Respect to the Adequacy of the Supply of Unskilled Agricultural Labor. 71st Congress, Second Session. Washington, GPO, 1930, 119p.

1481
Allen, Ruth A.
The Labor of Women in the Production of Cotton. Austin, University of Texas, Bureau of Business Research, Study #39), 1931.

1482
Folsom, J. C.
"Farm Labor Research in the United States." Geneva, *International Labour Review* 25, May 1932, pp. 646-665.

1483
Foscue, Edwin J.
"Agricultural History of the Lower Rio Grande Valley Region." *Agricultural History* (8: 3), 1934, pp. 124-137.

1484
Veblen, Thorstein B.
"Farm Labor and the I.W.W." (In his, *Essays in our Changing Order.* New York, Viking Press, 1934, pp. 319-336).

1485
Veblen, Thorstein B.
"Farm Labor for the Period of the War" (In his, *Essays in our Changing Order.* New York, Viking Press, 1934, pp. 279-318).

1486
Perlman, Selig, & Taft, Philip
History of Labor in the United States, 1896-1932. New York, Macmillan, 1935, v. 4, pp. 189-207.

1487
"California's Farm Labor Problems" (In *Transactions of the California Commonwealth Club, 30*. San Francisco, April 7, 1936, pp. 153-196).

1488
Taylor, Paul S., & Vasey, Tom
California Farm Labor. Washington, 1937, 13p. (Reprinted from *Rural Sociology*).

1489
Taylor, Paul S., & Vasey, Tom
"Contemporary Background of California Farm Labor." *Rural Sociology* 1, December 1936, pp. 401-419.

1490
Taylor, Paul S., & Vasey, Tom
"Historical Background of California Farm Labor." *Rural Sociology* 1, September 1936, pp. 281-295.

1491
U.S. Dept. of Agriculture. Farm Security Administration
Placer County, California. Survey of Agricultural Conditions in Placer County, California; by Tom Vasey and Josiah C. Folsom. (Prepared in Cooperation with Agricultural Economics Bureau). Washington, GPO, October 1937, 14p. (A61.11:C12)

1492
U.S. Dept. of Agriculture. Farm Security Administration & Bureau of Agricultural Economics
Survey of Agricultural Labor Conditions in Placer County, California, by Tom Vasey and J. C. Folsom. Washington, U.S. Farm Security Administration, October 1937, 14p.

1493
U.S. Dept. of Agriculture. Farm Security Administration
Archuleta County, Colorado. Survey of Agricultural Labor Conditions in Archuleta County, Colorado; by Tom Vasey and Josiah C. Folsom. (Prepared in Cooperation with Agricultural Economics Bureau). Washington, GPO, November 1937, 8p. (A61.11:C11)

1494
U.S. Dept. of Agriculture. Farm Security Administration
Karnes County, Texas. Survey of Agricultural Labor Conditions in Karnes County, Texas; by Tom Vasey and Josiah C. Folsom. (Prepared in Cooperation with Agricultural Economics Bureau). Washington, GPO, November 1937, 15p. (A61.11:T31)

1495
Texas. State Employment Service
Survey of Farm Placement in Texas, 1936 and 1937. Austin? 1938, 91p.

1496
Taylor, Carl C., et al.
Disadvantaged Classes in American Agriculture. (U.S. Dept. of Agriculture, Farm Security Administration, Social Research Report, VIII). Washington, GPO, April 1938, 124p.

1497
U.S. Dept. of Agriculture. Bureau of Agricultural Economics
The Farm Labor Situation in Texas, by W. C. Holley. Washington, 1940, 14p.

1498
U.S. Dept. of Labor
Report on the Citrus Fruit Packing Industry Made Under the Fair Labor Standards Act. Washington, Research and Statistics Division, Wages and Hours Division, U.S. Dept. of Labor, 1940, 86p.

1499
U.S. Senate. Committee on Education and Labor
Labor and Laboring Classes. Violations of Free Speech and Rights of Labor; Hearings before Subcommittee, 76th Congress, 3rd Session, pursuant to S. Res. 266 (74th Congress), to Investigate Violations of Right of Free Speech and Assembly and Interference with Right of Labor to Organize and Bargain Collectively. *Part 58:* Open Shop Activities, Dairy Industries, Inc., Milk Products Industries, Inc., Knudsen Truck & Warehouse Co., Associated Farmers of Imperial County, Inc., Jan. 23-24, 1940, pp. 21321-21730. *Part 59:* California Agricultural Background, California's Migrant Problem, Work of Federal and State Agencies, Jan. 25, 1940, pp. 21731-21941. *Part 60:* Industrial Association of San Francisco, Salinas Lettuce Strike, 1936, California Packing Corp., Associated Farmers of California, Inc., Stanislaus County, Inc., Jan. 26-27, 1940, pp. 21943-22263. *Part 61:* Campaign for Proposition #1, Committee of 43. Grower-Shipper Vegetable Association of Central California. Jan. 29, 1940, pp. 22265-22486. *Part 62:* Supplementary Exhibits, California Agricultural Background, Structure of Agricultural Economy, Agricultural Labor Market, Social and Economic Conditions Among Migratory Workers. Washington, 1940. (Y4.Ed8/3: L11/6).

1500
Tetreau, Elzer D. J.
"Social Aspects of Arizona's Farm Labor Problem." *Sociology and Social Research* 24, July 1940, pp. 550-557.

1501
Zeichner, Oscar
"The Legal Status of the Agricultural Laborers in the South." *Political Science Quarterly* 55, September 1940, pp. 412-428.

1502
Hall, William C.
A Study of 281 Farm Labor Families of South Texas. Kingsville, TX, 1942. (Master's Thesis, Texas College of Arts and Industries).

1503
Simons, Savilla (Millis)
"Study of Child Labor in Industrialized Agriculture in Hidalgo County, Texas." *Social Service Review* 16, September 1942, pp. 414-435.

1504
U.S. House. Committee on Appropriations
Farm Labor Program, 1944. Hearings Before the Subcommittee of the Committee on Appropriations, House of Representatives, 78th Congress, First Session . . . Washington, GPO, 1943, 306p.

1505
U.S. Dept. of Agriculture. Bureau of Agricultural Economics
The Farm Working Force of 1943, by Louis J. Ducoff and M. J. Hagood. Washington, August 1944, 54p.

1506
Magee, Elizabeth S.
"The Impact of the war on Child Labor." *Annals of the American Academy of Political and Social Science* 236, November 1944, pp. 101-109.

1507
Ahearn, D. J., Jr.
The Wages of Farm and Factory Laborers, 1914-1944. New York, Columbia University Press, 1945, 245p.

1508
California. Senate. Joint Legislative Fact-Finding Committee on Agricultural and Industrial Labor *Final Report, 1945.* Sacramento, 1945, 80p.

1509
Chandler, Alfred N.
. . . *Land Title Origins, a Tale of Force and Fraud.* New York, Robert Schalkenbach Foundation, 1945, 550p.

1510
U.S. Dept. of Agriculture. Bureau of Agricultural Economics
Two Years of Farm Wage Stabilization in California, by W. H. Metzler. Washington, February 1946, 65p.

1511
Goldschmidt, Walter
As You Sow. New York, Harcourt, Brace, 1947, 288p.

1512
Osgood, Ernest S.
The Day of the Cattleman. Chicago, University of Chicago Press, 1947, 283p.

1513
U.S. Senate. Committee on Agriculture and Forestry
Farm Labor Supply Program: Hearings, March 7-12, 1947, on H.R. 2102 and S. 724 (80th Congress, First Session). Washington, GPO, 1947, 111p.

1514
Goldschmidt, Walter
"Employment Categories in American Agriculture." *Journal of Farm Economy* 29, May 1947, pp. 554-564.

1515
Johns, Bryan T.
Field Workers in California Cotton. Berkeley, CA, 1948. (Master's Thesis, University of California, Berkeley)

1516
Robinson, William W.
Land in California . . . Berkeley, CA, University of California Press, 1948, 291p.

1517
U.S. Farm Placement Service
Labor Recruitment for Agriculture. Washington, 1948-

1518
California. Joint Committee on Agriculture and Livestock Problems
Partial Report: Part 2: General Information on Farm Labor Supply Centers and Photos Illustrating Types of Housing. Sacramento, California State Senate, 1949, 79p.

1519
Ducoff, Louis J.
"Farm Laborers" (In Taylor, Carl C., et al., eds. *Rural Life in the United States.* New York, Knopf, 1949, pp. 281-294).

1520
Wilson, Frank E.
El Cerrito: a Changing Culture. Portales, New Mexico, 1949. (Master's Thesis, New Mexico Highlands University)

1521
Chambers, Clarke A.
A Comparative Study of Farmer Organizations in California During the Depression Years, 1929-1941. Berkeley, CA, 1950, 117p. (Ph.D. Dissertation, University of California, Berkeley)

1522

Governor's Committee to Survey the Agricultural Labor Resources of the
San Joaquin Valley
*Agricultural Labor in the San Joaquin Valley; Recommendations and
Preliminary Report, December 15, 1950.* Sacramento, CA, State Printer,
1950, 60p.

1523

U.S. Farm Placement Service
Handbook for Farm Placement Service. Washington, GPO, 1950, 77p.

1524

California. Legislature. Joint Committee on Agriculture and Livestock
Problems
*The Recruitment and Placement of Farm Laborers in California 1950,
with Special Consideration and Recommendations Concerning Proposals
for Extension of Unemployment Insurance; Special and Partial Report of
the Joint Legislative Committee on Agriculture and Livestock Problems.*
Sacramento, Senate, State of California, 1951, 376p.

1525

Maudslay, Robert
Texas Sheep Man. Austin, University of Texas Press, 1951.

1526

Pendleton, Edwin C.
History of Labor in Arizona Irrigated Agriculture. Berkeley, 1951,
150p. (Ph.D. Dissertation, University of California, Berkeley)

1527

Taylor, Paul S.
Building the CVP (Central Valley Project). [n.p.] 1951? 17p.

1528

U.S. House. Committee on Agriculture. Subcommittee on Farm Labor
Farm Labor Investigations; Hearings . . . 81st Congress, 2nd Session
(Serial BBB). Washington, GPO, 1951, 260p.

1529

California. Governor's Committee to Survey the Agricultural Labor Resources of the San Joaquin Valley
*Agricultural Labor in the San Joaquin Valley; Final Report and Recom-
mendations.* Sacramento, March 15, 1951, 405p.

1530

Perry, Pettis
"The Farm Question in California." *Political Affairs,* July 1951, pp.
50-64.

1531
Fisher, Lloyd H.
"Harvest Labor Market in California." *Quarterly Journal of Economics* 65, November 1951, pp. 463-491.

1532
Chambers, Clarke A.
California Farm Organizations; a Historical Study of the Grange, the Farm Bureau, and the Associated Farmers, 1929-1941. Berkeley, University of California Press, 1952, 277p.

1533
Shapiro, Harold A.
The Workers of San Antonio, 1900-1940. Austin, TX, 1952, 164p. (Ph.D. Dissertation, University of Texas at Austin)

1534
Dance, Maurice
"The Current Status of Agricultural Labor in the United States" (In Western Economic Association. *Proceedings, 1952.* Claremont, California, 1953, pp. 86-90).

1535
Fisher, Lloyd H.
The Harvest Labor Market in California. Cambridge, Harvard University Press, 1953, 183p.

1536
Greenfield, Margaret
Unemployment Insurance for Farm Workers. Berkeley, Bureau of Public Administration, University of California, 1953, 49p. (1953 Legislative Problem, #8).

1537
U.S. Dept. of Agriculture. Agricultural Research Service
Unemployment and Partial Employment of Hired Farm Workers: Selected Areas of Los Angeles, by E. M. Birch and J. R. Motheral. Washington, June 1954, 42p.

1538
Tennessee. Agricultural Experiment Station
Labor Used in Crop Production in Tennessee, 1953; Part 3: Small Grain, Soybeans and Miscellaneous Seed Crops, by W. P. Ranney. Farm Economy Circular #5). Knoxville, December 1954, 28p.

1539
California. University. University at Berkeley. Institute of Industrial Relations
Labor Relations in Agriculture, by Varden Fuller. Berkeley, 1955, 46p.

1540
Haystead, Ladd, & Fite, Gilbert C.
The Agricultural Regions of the United States. Norman, University of Oklahoma Press, 1955, 288p.

1541
Cowan, Robert G.
Ranchos of California; a List of Spanish Concessions 1775-1822, and Mexican Grants, 1822-1846. Fresno, CA, Academy Library Guild, 1956, 151p.

1542
Gates, P. W.
"Frontier Estate Builders and Farm Laborers" (In Wyman, Walker D., & Kroeber, Clifton B., eds. *The Frontier in Perspective.* Madison, WI, University of Wisconsin Press, 1957, pp. 143-163).

1543
Weatherford, Willis D.
Geographic Differentials of Agricultural Wages in the United States. Cambridge, Distributed for the Harvard Graduate School of Public Administration of Harvard University by the Harvard University Press, 1957, 99p.

1544
U.S. Dept. of Agriculture
Area Variations of Agricultural Labor in the United States, by Sheridan T. Maitland and Dorothy A. Fisher (Technical Bulletin #177). Washington, March 1958, 54p.

1545
U.S. Dept. of Labor
Farm Labor Fact Book. Washington, 1959, 240p. (L 1.2: F22).

1546
Wells, Robert
"The Agricultural Workers in California." *Political Affairs* 38, August 1959, pp. 1-11.

1547
U.S. Dept. of Labor
Problems Involved in Applying a Federal Minimum Wage to Agricultural Workers. Volume 2: Statistical Appendix. Washington, 1960, 253p.

1548
U.S. House. Committee on Agriculture
Farm Labor Program. Report From Committee on Agriculture to Accompany H.R. 12176, May 23, 1960. Washington, 86th Congress, first session, 1960, 26p. (Item 1008-A).

1549
Ornelas, Charles
"The Development of Agriculture in the El Paso Valley: the Spanish Period." *Password* 5, October 1960, pp. 139-145.

1550
U.S. Dept. of Labor. Bureau of Employment Security
Hired Farm Workers in the United States. Washington, 1961, 46p.

1551
U.S. Dept. of Agriculture. Economic Research Service. Economic and Statistical Analysis Division. Farm Population Branch
Education and Earnings of the Hired Farm Working Force of 1960, by James D. Cowhig. Agricultural Information Bulletin #262. Washington, May 1962, 29p.

1552
Jacobs, Paul
"A Matter of Spirit" (In his, *The State of the Unions,* New York, Atheneum, 1963, pp. 192-196).

1553
Knowlton, Clark
"Causes of Land Loss Among the Spanish Americans in Northern New Mexico." *Rocky Mountain Social Science Journal,* April 5, 1963, pp. 201-211.

1554
Foner, Philip
The History of the Labor Movement in the United States. New York, International Publishers, 1964, v. 3, pp. 276-277.

1555
MacGillivray, John H., & Stevens, Robert A.
Agricultural Labor and its Effective Use. Palo Alto, CA, National Press, 1964, 107p.

1556
Metzler, William H.
Technological Change and Farm Labor use, Kern County, California, 1961. Berkeley, University of California, Berkeley, Giannini Foundation Research Report #277, 1964- .

1557
Stevens, Paul
Changes in Land Tenure and Usage Among the Indians and Spanish Americans in Northern New Mexico. Lubbock, TX, 1964. (Master's Thesis, University of Texas at Austin)

1558
U.S. Dept. of Labor. Bureau of Labor Standards
Agricultural Workers and Workmen's Compensation, by Donald L. Ream, et al. Revised. Washington, 1964, 19p.

1559
Knowlton, Clark
"An Approach to the Economic and Social Problems of Northern New Mexico." *New Mexico Business Review* (17: 9), September 1964, pp. 15-22.

1560
Heady, Earl O.
Roots of the Farm Labor Problem; Changing Technology, Changing Capital use, Changing Labor Needs. Ames, Iowa, Iowa State University, Center for Agricultural Economic Development, 1965, 224p.

1561
Jones, Lamar B.
Mexican American Labor Problems in Texas. Austin, Texas, 1965, 244p. (Ph.D. Dissertation, University of Texas, Austin).

1562
Myers, Robin, comp.
Poverty on the Land; in a Land of Plenty. Report on the Public Hearings Held by the National Advisory Committee on Farm Labor, Washington, D.C., May 18-19, 1964. 1965, 65p. (ED 068 207).

1563
Padfield, Harland, & Martin, William E.
Farmers, Workers and Machines: Technological and Social Change in Farm Industries of Arizona. Tucson, University of Arizona Press, 1965, 325p.

1564
U.S. Dept. of Agriculture. Economic Research Service
Characteristics of the Population of Hired Farmworker Households, by Gladys K. Bowles and Calvin L. Beale. Washington, (Agricultural Economic Report #84). Washington, 1965, 21p.

1565
Arrington, Leonard J.
Beet Sugar in the West; a History of the Utah-Idaho Sugar Company, 1891-1966. Seattle, University of Washington Press, 1966, 234p.

1566
Lamar, Howard R.
The Far Southwest, 1846-1912: a Territorial History. New Haven, Yale University Press, 1966, 560p.

1567
Selvin, David F.
Sky Full of Storm; a Brief History of California Labor. Berkeley, CA, University of California, Berkeley, Center for Labor Research & Education, Institute of Industrial Relations, 1966, 86p.

1568
Schmidt, Fred H.
"Rationalizing the Farm Labor Market . . ." *Southwestern Social Science Quarterly* 47, June 1966, pp. 12-21.

1569
Primack, Martin L.
"Farm Capital Formation as a use of Farm Labor in the United States, 1850-1919." *Journal of Economic History* 26, September 1966, pp. 348-362.

1570
"The Agricultural Labor Problem." *Journal of Farm Economics* 48, December 1966, pp. 1121-1153.

1571
Adams, Leonard P., ct al.
Viable Farmer-Worker Relationships; a Study of Selected Cases in New York State in 1966. Ithaca, N.Y. (Agricultural Experiment Station, Bulletin #1019), 1967, 70p.

1572
Bishop, Charles E., ed.
Farm Labor in the United States. New York, Columbia University Press, 1967, 143p.

1573
Gallego, José J.
Justicia al Obrero del Campo. Chicago, Fabet Press Service, 1967, 40p.

1574
Knowlton, Clark
"Recommendations for the Solution of Land Tenure Problems Among the Spanish Americans" (In *Testimony Presented at the Cabinet Committee Hearings on Mexican Affairs.* Washington, U.S. Interagency Committee on Mexican-American Affairs, 1967, pp. 233-239).

1575
Maloney, Thomas J.
Cattle Ranching as a Cultural Ecology Problem in San Miguel County, New Mexico. St. Louis, 1967. (Ph.D. Dissertation, Washington University)

1576
U.S. House. Committee on Agriculture
The Application of Minimum Wages in Agriculture; Hearing, February 27, 1967, 90th Congress, First Session (Serial B). Washington, 1967, 48p.

1577
Fuller, Varden
"New era for Farm Labor?" *Industrial Relations* 6, May 1967, pp. 285-302.

1578
Knowlton, Clark
"Land Grant Problems Among the State's Spanish Americans." *New Mexico Business* (20: 6), June 1967, pp. 1-13.

1579
North Carolina. Agricultural Extension Service
Farm Labor and Minimum Wages, by Charles R.. Pugh. Circular #481. Raleigh, North Carolina State University at Raleigh, June 1967, 28p.

1580
Bauer, Larry L.
The Effect of Technology on the Farm Labor Market. Raleigh, N.C., 1968, 76p. (Ph.D. Dissertation, North Carolina State University at Raleigh)

1581
Ferman, Louis A., et al.
Poverty in America; Book of Readings. Rev. ed. Ann Arbor, University of Michigan Press, 1968, 669p.

1582
Given, Charles W., et al.
A Study of Interpersonal Relations Among Managers and Employees of Fruit and Vegetable Farms With Emphasis on Labor Management Practices Utilized. East Lansing, MI, Rural Manpower Center, Michigan State University. Available from National Technical Information Service (Springfield, VA 22151), 1968, 71p.

1583
Jacobs, Paul
"The Man With a hoe, 1964" (In Blaustein, Arthur I., & Woock, Roger R., eds. *Man Against Poverty: World War III; a Reader on the World's Most Crucial Issue.* New York, Random House, 1968, pp. 128-136).

1584
McWilliams, Carey
The California Revolution. New York, Grossman, 1968, 240p.

1585
Oregon. Dept. of Employment
1967 Agricultural Worker age Study. Prepared by Research and Statistics Division. Salem, 1968, 48p.

1586
Ranenofsky, Ann F.
The Rise of Guadalupe Yaqui Factions From Legal Claims to Plaza Land. Tempe, AZ, 1968. (Master's Thesis, Arizona State University)

1587
Taylor, Paul S.
"California Farm Labor: a Review." *Agricultural History* (42: 1), January 1968, pp. 49-54.

1588
Gallaway, Lowell E.
"Geographic Flows of Hired Agricultural Labor: 1957-1960." *American Journal of Agricultural Economics* (50: 2), May 1968, pp. 199-212.

1589
Colberg, Marshall R.
"Agriculture and the Minimum Wage." *Mississippi Valley Journal of Business & Economics,* Fall 1968, pp. 15-25.

1590
Rushing, William A.
"Objective and Subjective Aspects of Deprivation in a Rural Poverty Class." *Rural Sociology* (33: 3), September 1968, pp. 269-284.

1591
Bowden, J. J.
The Ponce de Leon Land Grant. El Paso, TX, Texas Western College Press, 1969, 56p.

1592
Lehmann, Valgene W.
Forgotten Legions: Sheep in the Rio Grande Plain of Texas. El Paso, Texas Western College Press, 1969, 226p.

1593
Salandini, Victor
The Short-run Effects of the Termination of Public Law 78 on the California Farm Labor Market for 1965-1967. Washington, 1969, 300p. (Ph.D. Dissertation, Catholic University of America).

1594
U.S. Dept. of Agriculture. Economic Research Service.
Farm Labor Inputs, 1964, by Walter E. Sellers, Jr., and Theodore R. Eichers. Statistical Bulletin #438. Washington, GPO, 1969, 45p.

1595
U.S. Dept. of Labor. Wage and Hour and Public Contracts Divisions
Hired Farmworkers: a Study of the Effects of the $1.15 Minimum Wage, under the Fair Labor Standards Act: submitted to the Congress, 1969. Washington, 1969, 56 & 70 pp.

1596
Hiestand, F. J.
"The Politics of Poverty Law" (In Wasserstein, Bruce, & Green, Mark J., eds. *With Justice for Some; an Indictment of the Law by Young Advocates.* Boston, Beacon Press, 1970, pp. 160-189).

1597
Holden, William C.
The Espuela Land and Cattle Company: the Study of a Foreign-Owned Ranch in Texas. Austin, Texas State Historical Association, 1970, 268p.

1598
Legal Problems of Agricultural Labor. Davis, CA, School of Law, University of California, Davis, 1970, 269p.

1599
Leonard, Olen E.
The Role of the Land Grant: the Social Processes of a Spanish American Village in New Mexico. Albuquerque, Calvin Horn, Inc., 1970, 108p.

1600
Dow, J. K.
Historical Perspective of the Florida Citrus Industry and the Impact of Mechanical Harvesting on the Demand for Labor. Gainesville, University of Florida, Dept. of Agricultural Economics, April 1970, 110p.

1601
U.S. Dept. of Agriculture. Economic Research Service
Labor Used on U.S. Farms, 1964 and 1966, by Walter E. Sellers, Jr. (Statistical Bulletin #456). Washington, June 1970, 24p.

1602
Smith, T. Lynn
"Farm Labour Trends in the United States, 1910-1969." Geneva, *International Labour Review* 102, August 1970, pp. 149-169.

1603
Berger, Samuel R.
Dollar Harvest; the Story of the Farm Bureau. Lexington, MA, Heath Lexington Books, 1971, 221p.

1604
Bowden, J. J.
Spanish and Mexican Land Grants in the Chihuahuan Acquisition. El Paso, TX, Texas Western Press, 1971, 231p.

1605
Colorado. Legislative Council. Committee on Farm Labor
Committee on Farm Labor. Report to the Colorado General Assembly
(Research Publication #181). Denver, 1971, 62p.

1606
Fearis, Donald F.
The California Farm Workers, 1930-1943. Davis, CA, 1971, 328p.
(Ph.D. Dissertation, University of California, Davis)

1607
Knorr, A. L., & Elterich, G. J.
Analysis of Delaware's Full-time Hired Farm Labor Situation. Newark,
DE, Agricultural Experiment Station (Bulletin #385), University of Delaware, 1971, 27p.

1608
Reynolds, Lloyd G.
*The Structure of Labor Markets; Wages and Labor Mobility in Theory
and Practice.* Westport, CT, Greenwood Press, 1971, 328p.

1609
U.S. Dept. of Agriculture. Economic Research Service
The Hired Farm Working Force of 1970: a Statistical Report, by Robert
C. McElroy. Agricultural Economic Report #201. Washington, GPO,
1971, 30p.

1610
U.S. Dept. of Agriculture. Economic Research Service
Variations in Length of the Farm Workweek, by Walter E. Sellers, Jr.
Statistical Bulletin #474. Washington, GPO, 1971, 20p.

1611
Miller, Paul B.
*The Role of Farm Labor Market Institutions in the Lower Rio Grande
Valley of Texas.* December 1971, 184p. (ED 072 888).

1612
Fritsch, Conrad F.
*Agricultural Employment and Economic Growth in the Lower Rio
Grande Region: Input-Output Analysis.* Austin, TX, Office of Information
Services, Office of the Governor, 1972, 90p.

1613
Minnesota. Dept. of Manpower Services
*Economic Security for Hired Farm Workers: Implications of Extending
Unemployment Insurance to Hired Agricultural Labor.* St. Paul, 1972,
93p.

1614
U.S. Dept. of Labor. Manpower Administration. Special Review Staff
Review of the Rural Manpower Service. Washington, 1972, 152p.

1615
U.S. Senate. Committee on Labor and Public Welfare
Farmworkers in Rural America, 1971-1972: Hearings: parts 4A-4B,
June 19 & 20, 1972, on the Role of Land-Grant Colleges. 92nd Congress,
first and second sessions. Washington, 1972, 2v.

1616
Newby, Howard
"Agricultural Workers in the Class Structure." *Sociological Review*
(20: 3), August 1972, pp. 413-439.

1617
Bradfute, Richard W.
*The Court of Private Land Claims and the Adjudication of Spanish and
Mexican Land Grant Titles, 1891-1904.* Boulder, CO, 1973, 261p. (Ph.D.
Dissertation, University of Colorado)

1618
South Carolina. Rural Manpower Service
Annual Rural Manpower Report. Columbia, South Carolina State
Employment Service, 1973-   (annual).

1619
Taylor, Ronald B.
Sweatshops in the Sun, Child Labor on the Farm. Boston, Beacon Press,
1973, 216p.

1620
Ohio. Agricultural Research & Development Center
*Hired Farm Workers, Agricultural Employers and Ohio Agriculture; Im-
plications for Unemployment Insurance,* by Bernard L. Erven. Research
Bulletin #1067. Wooster, Ohio, November 1973, 77p.

1621
Employment in Agricultural and Agribusiness Occupations/Economic Research Service, U.S. Dept. of Agriculture, in Cooperation with Bureau
of the Census, U.S. Dept. of Commerce, et al. Washington, U.S. Dept.
of Agriculture, 1974, 11v.

1622
Fritsch, Conrad F., et al.
*The Economic Impact From the Extension of Unemployment Insurance
to Texas Agriculture.* College Station, TX, Texas A & M University System, Texas Agricultural Experiment Station, 1974, 26p. (Bulletin 1146).

1623
Maryland Farm Manpower Activities. Compiled by Ray A. Murray. College Park, Dept. of Agricultural and Resource Economics, University of Maryland, 1974?-1980, volumes 1-5.

1624
Villareal, Roberto M.
Farm Workers and the Minimum Wage. Austin, Texas, National Migrant Information Clearinghouse, 1974, 16p.

1625
Villareal, Roberto M.
Workmen's Compensation: Guide for Farmworkers. Austin, National Migrant Information Clearinghouse, 1974, 21p.

1626
Scott, L. C., & Jones, L. B.
"U.S. Dept. of Agriculture and Wages in the Sugar Crop Industry." *Labor Law Journal* 25, January 1974, pp. 18-30.

1627
Schluter, Gerald E., & Heady, Earl O.
Projected 1980 Overall Agricultural Employment by Regions, Commodities, and Related Sectors. Ames, Iowa, Center for Agricultural and Rural Development, Iowa State University, 1975, 85p. (CARD Report; 59).

1628
Schob, David E.
Hired Hands and Plowboys; Farm Labor in the Midwest, 1815-60. Urbana, University of Illinois Press, 1975, 329p.

1629
Simons, Algie M.
The American Farmer. Reprint of the 1902 edition published by C. H. Kerr, Chicago. New York, Arno Pres, 1975, 208p.

1630
U.S. House. Committee on Education and Labor. Subcommittee on Agricultural Labor
Oversight Hearing on Labor Certification of the use of Offshore Labor; Hearing, March 20, 1975, 94th Congress, first session. Washington, 1975, 460p.

1631
U.S. House. Committee on Education and Labor. Subcommittee on Equal Opportunities
Poverty, Equal Opportunity and Full Employment: Hearings . . . 94th Congress, first session, on H.R. 50, H.R. 2276, H.R. 5937 . . . Held in Santa Fe, New Mexico, May 2 & 3, 1975. Washington, GPO, 1975, 474p.

1632
Friedland, William H., & Barton, Amy
Destalking the Wily Tomato: a Case Study in Social Consequences in California Agricultural Research. Research Monograph #15. Davis, University of California, Davis, Dept. of Applied Behavioral Sciences, June 1975, 79p.

1633
Swartz, Joel
"Poisoning Farmworkers: the new Chemicals." *Environment* 17, June 1975, pp. 26-33.

1634
Smith, Leslie (Whitener)
Socioeconomic Characteristics of the Spanish Origin Hired Farm Working Force, 1973. Paper Presented at the Annual Meeting of the Rural Sociological Society, San Francisco, California, August 22, 1975. 31p. (ED 111 547).

1635
McCurry, Dan C., comp.
Children in the Fields. New York, Arno Press, 1975, 294p.

1636
New Jersey. Legislature. Office of Fiscal Affairs. Division of Program Analysis
Analysis of New Jersey's Seasonal Farm Labor Protection Programs. Trenton, 1975, 47p.

1637
Pierce, James M.
The Condition of Farmworkers and Small Farmers in 1975: Report to the National Board. Charlotte, N.C., National Sharecroppers Fund 1975, 15p.

1638
Smith, Richard B., et al.
"Analysis of Employment Conditions for Full-Time Hired Farm Labor on Eastern Iowa hog Farms." Ames, Iowa, Agricultural and Home Economics Experiment Station, Iowa State University of Science and Technology, 1976, pp. 811-842 of *Research Bulletin,* Iowa Agricultural and Home Economics Experiment Station.

1639
Thedinger, Bob
Research into the Current Plight of Farmworkers in the United States. Prepared by the Social Action Dept., Catholic Diocese of Kansas City-St. Joseph, MO, April 11, 1976, 50p. (ED 121 513).

1640
U.S. House. Committee on Education & Labor. Subcommittee on Agriculture
Oversight Hearings in the Farm Labor Contractor Registration Act: Hearings, October 1 & 11, 1975. 94th Congress, first session. Washington, 1976, 337p.

1641
Galarza, Ernesto
Farm Workers and Agribusiness in California, 1947-1960. Notre Dame, IN, University of Notre Dame Press, 1977, 405p.

1642
"Farm Labor Markets." *American Journal of Agricultural Economics* 59, December 1977, pp. 1045-1051.

1643
Feise, Christopher F.
A Radical Analysis of the Transformation of American Agriculture and its Impact on Labor, 1910-1975. Pullman, WA, 1978, 210p. (Ph.D. Dissertation, Washington, State University)

1644
Texas. Legislature. House of Representatives. Committee on Labor
Report of the Committee on Labor, Texas House of Representatives, 65th Legislature, to the Speaker and Members of the Texas House of Representatives, 66th Legislature/Bill Blythe, Chairman. Austin, The Committee, 1978, 79p.

1645
Armstrong, Richard
"Tangled web: Federal Programs." *Commonweal* 105, May 26, 1978, pp. 334-336.

1646
Ryan, Vernon D., & Warland, Rex H.
"Race and the Effect of Family Status Among Male Agricultural Laborers." *Rural Sociology* 43, Fall 1978, pp. 335-347.

1647
Barton, Amy E.
Campesinas: Women Farmworkers in the California Agricultural Labor Force. Report of a Study Project by the California Commission on the Status of Women. Sacramento, California State Commission on the Status of Women, December 1978, 77p. (ED 167 322).

1648
Rowe, Gene A.
The Hired Farm Working Force of 1977. Washington, U.S. Dept. of

Agriculture, Economic, Statistics and Cooperative Services, 1979, 53p. (Agricultural Economic Report #437).

1649

Emerging Occupations in Agriculture: Impact Upon Curricula and People, Part I: Yolo County, 1979. Final Report. Davis, University of California, Davis, Dept. of Applied Behavioral Sciences, May 1979, 100p. (ED 170 563).

1650

U.S. House. Committee on Government Operations. Manpower and Housing Subcommittee *Administration of Laws Affecting Farmworkers.* Hearing Before the Manpower and Housing Subcommittee, House of Representatives, 96th Congress, First Session, November 13, 1979. Washington, GPO, 1980, 264p.

1651

Gisser, M., & Willett, K.
"Benefits of Resource Scarcity: a Case Study of the Farm Sector." *Land Economics* 56, May 1980, pp. 227-237.

1652

Janiewski, D.
"Women . . . Proletariat . . . Tobacco Belt." *Insurgent Sociologist* (10: 1), Summer 1980, p. 16- .

1653

Occupational Employment in Selected Non-Manufacturing Industries. San Francisco-Oakland SMSA. Sacramento, State of California, Employment Development Dept., Employment and Research Division, December 1980, 44p.

1654

Daniels, Cletus E.
Bitter Harvets, a History of California Farmworkers, 1870-1941. Ithaca, N.Y., Cornell University Press, 1981, 348p.

1655

Golomb, Susha
Changing Patterns of Employment in Agriculture in the United States, 1967-1977. Columbus, Ohio 1981, 194p. (Ph.D. Dissertation, Ohio State University)

1656

Liebman, Ellen
The Evolution of Large Agricultural Landholdings in California. Berkeley, CA, 1981, 386p. (Ph.D. Dissertation, University of California, Berkeley)

1657
Pollack, Susan J.
The Hired Farm Working Force of 1979. Washington, U.S. Dept. of Agriculture, Economic Research Service, 1981, 59p.

1658
Smith, Leslie (Whitener), & Smith, Robert C.
Hired Farmworkers, Background and Trends for the '80's. Washington, U.S. Dept. of Agriculture, Economic Research Service, 1981, 31p. (Rural Development Research Report #32). (Superintendent of Documents number A93.41:32).

1659
Wells, Miriam J.
"Social Conflict, Commodity Constraints and Labor Market Structure in Agriculture." *Comparative Studies in Society and History* (23: 4), 1981, pp. 679-704.

1660
Althoff, P.
"Basic Facts on Agricultural Workers." *Political Affairs* (60: 3), March 1981, p. 30.

1661
Wells, Miriam J.
"Alienation, Work Structure, and the Quality of Life: Can Cooperatives Make a Difference?" *Social Problems* 28, June 1981, pp. 548-562.

1662
Alston, Lee J.
"Tenure Choice in Southern Agriculture, 1930-1960." *Explorations in Economic History* 18, July 1981, pp. 211-232.

1663
Majka, Linda C., & Majka, Theo J.
Farm Workers; Agribusiness and the State. Philadelphia, Temple University Press, 1982, 346p.

1664
Martin, Philip L., & Mamer, John
"The Farm Labor Market." *Proceedings of the Academy of Political Science* (34: 3), 1982, pp. 223-234.

1665
Ross, Peggy (Johnston)
Farmwomen's Participation in United States Agricultural Production: Selected Assessments. Columbus, Ohio, 1982, 268p. (Ph.D. Dissertation, Ohio State University)

1666
Wells, Miriam J.
"Political Mediation and Agricultural Cooperation: Strawberry Farms in California." *Economic Development and Cultural Change* 30, January 1982, pp. 413-432.

1667
Lyson, T. A.
"Stabilizing Change in Farming Plans: Results From a Longitudinal Study of Young Adults." *Rural Sociology* 47, Fall 1982, pp. 544-556.

1668
Holt, J. S.
"Labor Market Policies and Institutions in an Industrializing Agriculture." *American Journal of Agricultural Economics* 64, December 1982, pp. 999-1006.

1669
Security Pacific Bank. Research Dept.
California Agriculture. Los Angeles, December 1982, 45p.

1670
Calavita, Kitty
"California's Employer Sanctions Legislation: now you see it, now you Don't." *Politics & Society* (12:2), 1983, pp. 205-230.

1671
Pollack, Susan J., & Jackson, William R., Jr.
The Hired Farm Working Force of 1981. Report Number AER-507. Washington, GPO, 1983, 70p.

1672
Martin, Philip L.
"Labor-Intensive Agriculture." *Scientific American* 249, October 1983, pp. 54-59.

B. IMMIGRATION OF MEXICAN AGRICULTURAL LABOR

1. Bibliographies

1673
U.S. Library of Congress
Mexican Labor in the United States: a Brief Bibliographical List. Washington, January 11, 1928, 5p.

1674
Bogardus, Emory S.
The Mexican Immigrant: an Annotated Bibliography. Los Angeles, Council on International Relations, 1929, 21p.

1675
Jones, Robert C.
Selected References on the Labor Importation Program Between Mexico and the United States. Washington, Pan American Union, 1948, 5p.

1676
The Immigrant Worker in America. (Labor-Management Relations, volume 4, #2). Urbana, IL, College of Education and Institute of Labor and Industrial Relations, University of Illinois, 1951, 7p.

1677
Massa Gil, Beatriz
Bibliografía Sobre Migración de Trabajadores Mexicanos a los Estados Unidos. México, Depto. de Estudios Económicos, Banco de México, 1959, 122p.

1678
Heslet, Mary R.
The Mexican Farm Labor Program: References, 1951-1965. Washington, Library of Congress, Legislative Reference Service, 1965, 14p.

1679
"Mexican Immigration History 1900-1970: Literature and Research." *Latin American Research Resources* (8: 2), 1973, pp. 3-24.

1680
Sharma, Prakash, C.
A Selected Research Bibliography on Mexican Immigration to the United States (Exchange Bibliography #672). Monticello, IL, Council of Planning Librarians, 1974, 18p.

2. Circulating Materials

1681
U.S. Community Services Administration
The Problem of the Undocumented Worker. Ed. by Robert S. Landmann. Washington [n.d.] 89p.

1682
Immigration Association of California
Annual Report. First- , San Francisco, 1881/82-

1683

U.S. Dept. of Labor

Annual Reports of the Commission General of Immigration, 1895-1932. Washington, GPO, 1896-   (annual).

1684

Cox, Isaac J.

"The Early Settlers of San Fernando." *Texas State Historical Association Quarterly* 5, October 1901, pp. 142-160.

1685

"Agricultural Distribution of Immigrants" (In *U.S. Industrial Commission Report.* Washington, volume 15, 1902, pp. 492-646).

1686

Ward, Robert D.

"Agricultural Distribution of Immigrants." *Popular Science Monthly* 66, December 1904, pp. 166-175.

1687

Hening, H. B.

Deprived Children. Albuquerque, Bureau of Immigration of the Territory of New Mexico, 1908.

1688

Clark, Victor S.

"Mexican Labor in the United States." *Bureau of Labor Bulletin* #78 (U.S. Bureau of Labor Statistics), September 1908, pp. 417-644.

1689

Guinn, James M.

"The Sonoran Migration." *Historical Society of Southern California Annual Publications* 8, 1909-1911, pp. 50-60.

1690

Coulter, John L.

"Influence of Immigration on Agricultural Development." *Annals of the American Academy of Political and Social Science* 33, March 1909, pp. 373-379.

1691

U.S. Commission on Immigration

Abstract of Report on Recent Immigrants in Agriculture, by Alexander E. Cance. Washington, GPO, 1911, 267p. (Y3.Im6:Ag8)

1692

U.S. Commission on Immigration

Abstract of Statistical Review of Immigration to United States, 1820-1910, by Fred Croxton, Assisted by Ralph D. Fleming. Washington, GPO, 1911, 54p. (Y3.Im6:St2)

1693
U.S. Commission on Immigration
Peonage and Treatment and Conditions of Work of Immigrants. Washington, GPO, 1911, 13p. (Y3.Im6:P39).

1694
U.S. Committee on Mexican Labor in California
Annual Reports, 1918-1934. Washington, GPO, 1918-1935.

1695
"Amended and Revised Rules for the Admission of Agricultural and Other Laborers." *U.S. Immigration and Naturalization Service Bulletin* 1, June 1, 1918, pp. 1-4.

1696
"Terms of Labor Department's Order Allowing Mexican Workmen to Come into United States During the War." *Official Bulletin* 2, June 20, 1918, p. 3.

1697
Veblen, Thorstein B.
"Farm Labor for the Period of the War." *Public* 21, July 13-August 3, 1918, pp. 882-885, 918-922.

1698
Alvarado, Ernestine M.
"Mexican Immigration to the United States." (In National Conference of Social Work. *Proceedings, 1920.* Chicago, 1920, pp. 479-480).

1699
Alvarado, Ernestine M.
"The Uniting of Native and Foreign-Born in America: Mexican Immigration to the United States" (In *Proceedings of the National Conference of Social Work.* Chicago, University of Chicago Press, 1920).

1700
Sturgess, Vera L.
"The Progress of Adjustment in Mexican and U.S. Life." (In National Conference of Social Work. *Proceedings, 1920.* Chicago, 1920, pp. 481-486).

1701
U.S. House. Committee on Immigration and Naturalization
Farm Labor. Admission of Mexican Agricultural Laborers. Hearing Pursuant to S. J. Res. 66, Suspending Temporarily Operation of Certain Provisions of Immigration Act Relating to Alien Contract Laborers and Illiterate Aliens. Washington, GPO, 1920, 28p. (Y4.Im6/2 : M57).

1702
U.S. House. Committee on Migration and Naturalization
Farm Labor. Temporary Admission of Illiterate Mexican Laborers,
Hearings on H.J. Res. 271, January 26-February 2, 1920. Washington,
GPO, 1920, 375p. (Y4. Im6/1: N21/5).

1703
Stowell, Jay S.
The Near Side of the Mexican Question. New York, Home Missions
Council, 1921, 123p.

1704
"The Mexican Immigrant." *Annals of the American Academy of Political
and Social Science* 93, January 1921, pp. 131-133.

1705
Slayden, James L.
"Some Observations on Mexican Immigration." *Annals of the American Academy of Political and Social Science* 93, January 1921, pp. 121-
126.

1706
Wallis, Wilson D.
"The Mexican Immigrant of California." *Pacific Review* 2, December
1921, pp. 444-454.

1707
"Mexican Immigration" (In *Transactions of the Commonwealth Club of
California.* San Francisco, March 1923, pp. 1-34).

1708
McLean, Robert N., & Thomson, Charles A.
Spanish and Mexican in Colorado . . . New York, Board of National
Missions of the Presbyterian Church in the USA, 1924, 61p.

1709
Sullenger, T. E.
"The Mexican Population of Omaha." *Journal of Applied Sociology* (8:
5), May-June 1924, pp. 288-293.

1710
Bamford, E. F.
"The Mexican Casual Problem in the Southwest." *Journal of Applied
Sociology* 8, July 1924, pp. 363-371.

1711
McCombs, Vernon M.
From Over the Border, a Study of the Mexicans in the United States.
New York, Council of Women for Home Missions and Missionary Educa-
tion Movement, 1925, 192p.

1712
Martin, Mabelle (Eppard)
"California Emigrant Roads Through Texas." *Southwestern Historical Quarterly* 28, April 1925, pp. 287-301.

1713
Bloch, Louis
"Report on the Mexican Labor Situation in Imperial Valley" (In *22nd Biennial Report, California State Bureau of Labor Statistics.* Sacramento, 1926, 277p.

1714
Cramp, Kathryn
A Study of the Mexican Population of Imperial Valley, California. Berkeley, CA, 1926. (University of California, Berkeley, Bancroft Library).

1715
Gwin, J. B.
"Some Problems of our Mexican Population"; "The Immigrant in Texas", by Max S. Handman (In National Conference of Social Work. *Proceedings, 1926.* Columbus, Ohio, 1926, pp. 327-339).

1716
Handman, Max S.
"The Mexican Immigrant in Texas" (In National Conference of Social Work. *Proceedings, 1926.* Chicago, 1926, pp. 332-339).

1717
Hanson, Stella (Endicott)
Mexican Laborers in the Southwest. Clarement, CA, 1926. (Master's Thesis, Pomona College)

1718
U.S. House. Committee on Immigration and Naturalization
Seasonal Agricultural Laborers From Mexico; Hearing on H.R. 6741, H.R. 7559, H.R. 9036, January 28-29, February 2, 9, 11 and 23, 1926 (69th Congress, First Session). Washington, U.S. House of Representatives, 1926, 345p.

1719
Holmes, Samuel J.
"An Argument Against Mexican Immigration" (In Commonwealth Club of California. *Transactions,* volume 21, #1. San Francisco, March 23, 1926, pp. 21-27).

1720
Panunzio, Constantine
Immigration Crossroads. New York, Macmillan, 1927, 307p.

1721
Dobie, J. Frank
The Mexican Vaquero of the Texas Border. Austin, TX, 1927? 12p.
(Reprinted from Southwestern Political & Social Science Quarterly,
volume VIII, #1, June 1927).

1722
Thomson, Charles A.
"Restriction of Mexican Immigration." *Journal of Applied Sociology,*
August 1927, pp. 274-278.

1723
Allwell, Patrick J.
Mexican Immigration Into the United States. Columbia, MO, 1928.
(Master's thesis, University of Missouri)

1724
Batten, James H.
"The Mexican Immigration Problem." *Pan-Pacific Progress* 8, 1928,
pp. 39-52.

1725
Garis, Roy L.
Immigration Restriction: a Study of the Opposition to and Regulation of
Immigration into the United States. New York, Macmillan, 1928, 376p.

1726
Perron, Marius
Employment Agencies on the Mexican Border. Austin, TX, 1928, 50p.
(Master's Thesis, University of Texas at Austin)

1727
Taylor, Paul S.
Mexican Labor in the United States. Berkeley, University of California
(Publications in Economics), 1928-34, 3v.

1728
U.S. Senate. Committee on Immigration
Restriction of Western Hemisphere Immigration, Hearing, 70th Con-
gress, First Session, on S. 1437, to Subject Certain Immigrants Born in
Countries of Western Hemisphere to Quota Under Immigration Laws, Feb-
ruary 1, 1928. (This Hearing Relates to Mexicans Only). Washington,
GPO, 1928, 11p. (Y4.Im6/2:W52).

1729
U.S. House. Committee on Immigration and Naturalization
Mexicans. Immigration from Countries of Western Hemisphere. Hearings, 70th Congress, First Session, on H.R. 6465, H.R. 7358, H.R.
10955, H.R. 11687, February 21-April 5, 1928. (Hearing #70.1.5). (The

Principal Subject Discussed in These Hearings is the Mexican Immigration Problem). Washington, GPO, 1928, 801p. (Y4.Im6/1:W52).

1730
Walker, Helen W.
"Mexican Immigrants as Laborers." *Sociology and Social Research* 13, 1928-29, pp. 55-62.

1731
Municipal League of Los Angeles
"The League's Investigations and Arizona's Demands Concerning Mexican Immigration." *Municipal League of Los Angeles Bulletin* 5, April 1928, pp. 1-3.

1732
Stowell, Jay S.
"The Danger of Unrestricted Mexican Immigration." *Current History* 28, August 1928, pp. 763-768.

1733
Bresette, L. E.
Mexicans in the United States; a Report of a Brief Survey. Washington, National Catholic Welfare Conference, 1929, 45p.

1734
Dobie, J. Frank
A Vaquero of the Brush Country. Dallas, TX, Southwest Press, 1929, 314p.

1735
Fabila, Alfonso
El Problema de la Emigración de Obreros y Campesinos Mexicanos. México, Talleres Gráficos de la Nación, 1929, 37p. (at head of title: Publicaciones de la Secretaría de Gobernación).

1736
Gamio, Manuel
Number, Origin and Geographic Distribution of the Mexican Immigrants in the United States. Honolulu? Institute of Pacific Relations, 1929, 14p.

1737
Hufford, Charles H.
The Social and Economic Effects of the Mexican Migration Into Texas. Boulder, CO, 1929, 70p. (Master's Thesis, University of Colorado).

1738
McLean, Robert N.
"Mexican Workers in the United States" (In National Conference of Social Work. *Proceedings, 1929.* Chicago, 1929, pp. 531-538).

1739

Morrison, Ethel M.

A History of Recent Legislative Proposals Concerning Mexican Immigration. Los Angeles, 1929, 85p. (Master's Thesis, University of Southern California)

1740

Thomson, Charles A.

"Mexicans: an Interpretation" (In *Proceedings of the National Conference on Social Work, 1929.* Chicago, University of Chicago Press, 1929, pp. 499-503).

1741

Whitaker, Arthur P.

"The Spanish Contribution to American Agriculture." *Agricultural History* 3, January 1929, pp. 1-14.

1742

Bloch, Louis

"Facts About Mexican Immigration Before and Since the Quota Restriction Laws." *Journal of the American Statistical Association* 24, March 1929, pp. 50-60.

1743

Holmes, Samuel J.

"Perils of the Mexican Invasion." *North American Review* 227, May 1929, pp. 615-623.

1744

"Mexican Immigration." *Conference Board Bulletin* #32, August 1929, pp. 253-256.

1745

Hoover, Glen E.

"Our Mexican Immigrants." *Foreign Affairs* 8, October 1929, pp. 99-107.

1746

Redfield, Robert

"Antecedents of Mexican Immigration to the United States." *American Journal of Sociology* 35, November 1929, pp. 433-438.

1747

California. Dept. of Industrial Relations. Dept. of Agriculture, and Dept. of Social Welfare

Mexicans in California: Report of Governor C. C. Young's Mexican Fact-Finding Committee. San Francisco, 1930, 214p.

1748
Santibañez, Enrique
Ensayo Acerca de la Inmigración Mexicana en los Estados Unidos. San Antonio, Clegg Co., 1930, 165p.

1749
Taylor, Paul S.
Mexican Labor in the United States Dimmit County, Winter Garden District, South Texas . . . Berkeley, University of California Press, 1930 (Publications in Economics, volume 6, #5), pp. 293-464.

1750
Taylor, Paul S.
"Note on Streams of Mexican Migration." *American Journal of Sociology* 36, 1930/31, pp. 287-288.

1751
U.S. Bureau of Immigration
Annual Report of Commissioner General of Immigration to Secretary of Labor, Fiscal Year 1930. Washington, GPO, 1930, 267p. (L3.1:930)

1752
U.S. House. Committee on Immigration and Naturalization
Mexico. Restriction of Immigration From Republic of Mexico, Report (and Minority Reports) to Accompany S.51 [to Amend Subdivision (c) of Section 4 of Immigration Act of 1924, as Amended]. 3 parts. House Report 1594, 71st Congress, Second Session. (Part 1: Report Submitted by Mr. Johnson of Washington, May 23 1930, 8p. Part 2: Minority Report, Submitted by Mr. Dickstein, May 28, 1930, 11p. Part 3: Minority Report, Submitted by Mr. Cooke, June 9, 1930, 1p.). Washington, 1930, 3 pts.

1753
Handman, Max S.
"Economic Reasons for the Coming of the Mexican Immigrant." *American Journal of Sociology* 35, January 1930, pp. 601-611.

1754
Crawford, Remsen
"The Menace of Mexican Immigration." *Current History* 31, February 1930, pp. 902-907.

1755
Hull, Harry E.
"Protective Immigration." *American Labor Legislation Review* 20, March 1930, pp. 97-98.

1756
Bogardus, Emory S.
"The Mexican Immigrant and Segregation." *American Journal of Sociology* 36, July 1930, pp. 74-80.

1757
Albig, John W.
"Opinions Concerning Unskilled Mexican Immigrants." *Sociology & Sociological Research* 15, September 1930, pp. 62-72.

1758
Batten, James H.
"New Features of Mexican Immigration: The Case Against Further Restrictive Legislation." *Pacific Affairs* 3, October 1930, pp. 955-966.

1759
Taylor, Paul S.
"Some Aspects of Mexican Immigration." *Journal of Political Economy* 38, October 1930, pp. 609-615.

1760
Bogardus, Emory S.
"Attitudes and the Mexican Immigrant" (In Young, Kimball, ed. *Social Attitudes*, by L. L. Bernard, et al. New York, Holt, 1931, pp. 291-327).

1761
Gamio, Manuel
"The Influence of Migrations in Mexican Life. Mexico? 1931? 10p.

1762
Loyo, Gilberto
La Emigración de Mexicanos a los Estados Unidos. Rome, Instituto Poligrafico dello Stato, 1931.

1763
"Mexican Immigration" (In Howland, Charles P., ed. *Survey of American Foreign Relations.* New Haven, CT, Yale University Press, 1931, pp. 202-233).

1764
Ohno, Kakijiro
History and Economic Significance of Mexican Labor in California. Los Angeles, 1931, 61p. (Master's thesis, University of Southern California)

1765
Watson, A. C.
"Mexicans in Texas"; "Mexicans in California", by J. H. Batten (In Herring, Hubert C., & Terrill, Katharine, eds. *The Genius of Mexico*; Lectures Delivered Before the Fifth Seminar in Mexico, 1930. New York, The Committee on Cultural Relations With Latin America, 1931, pp. 235-243).

1766
O'Brien, Robert
"That Northern Mexican." *Pomona College Magazine*, October 1931, pp. 29-33.

1767
"Migration to and From Mexico in 1930." Geneva, *International Labour Review* 24, November 1931, pp. 604-606.

1768
"The Mexicans in California" (In White House Conference on Child Health and Protection. *Dependent and Neglected Children,* section 4. New York, Appleton-Century, 1933, pp. 312-350).

1769
U.S. Dept. of Labor
Annual Report of the Secretary of Labor, 1932-1933 to 1939-1940. (Condensed Reports of the U.S. Immigration and Naturalization Service.) Washington, GPO, 1933-1941, 8v.

1770
Murray, Katherine M.
"Mexican Community Service." *Sociology & Social Research* 17, July-August 1933, pp. 545-550.

1771
Bogardus, Emory S.
"Mexican Repatriates." *Sociology & Social Research* 18, November/December 1933, pp. 169-176.

1772
Gilbert, James C.
A Field Study in Mexico of the Mexican Repatriation Movement. Los Angeles, 1934. (Ph.D. Dissertation, University of Southern California)

1773
Hardy, Osgood
"Los Repatriados." *Pomona College Magazine* XXI, 1934, pp. 71-73.

1774
Martínez de Alva, Ernesto
Vida Rural; los Campesinos de México. México, Talleres Gráficos de la Nación, 1934, 344p.

1775
Wilmoth, G. C.
Mexican Border Procedure. Washington, U.S. Dept. of Labor, Immigration and Naturalization Service (Lecture #23), November 19, 1934, 10p.

1776
Foscue, Edwin J.
"Agricultural History of the Lower Rio Grande Valley Region." *Agricultural History* VIII, March 1934, pp. 124-138.

1777
"Immigration into the United States, 1820 to 1934." *U.S. Bureau of Labor Statistics Bulletins* 616, 1936, pp. 257-264.

1778
Rak, Mary (Kidder)
Border Patrol. Boston, Houghton, Mifflin, 1938, 242p.

1779
México. Departamento del Trabajo
Proposiciones del Departamento del Trabajo a la Primera Convención Nacional de Población. Mexico, D. A. P. P., 1939, 39p.

1780
Hidalgo, Ernesto
La Protección de Mexicanos en los Estados Unidos. Defensorías de Oficio, Anexas a los Consulados; un Proyecto. México, Talleres Gráficos de la Nación, 1940, 71p.

1781
Hinojosa, Federico A.
El México de Afuera, y su Reintegración a la Patria. San Antonio, TX, Artes Gráficas, 1940, 71p.

1782
Bogardus, Emory S.
"Current Problems of Mexican Immigrants." *Sociology & Social Research* 25, November-December 1940, pp. 166-174.

1783
Rak, Mary (Kidder)
They Guard the Gates; the Way of Life on the American Borders. Evanston, IL, Row, Peterson & Co., 1941, 64p.

1784
U.S. Works Progress Administration
Mexican Migratory Workers of South Texas, by Seldon C. Menefee. Washington, GPO, 1941.

1785
Waters, Lawrence L.
"Transient Mexican Agricultural Labor." *Southwestern Social Science Quarterly* 22, June 1941, pp. 49-66.

1786
Humphrey, Norman D.
"Mexican Repatriation From Michigan." *Social Service Review* 15, September 1941, pp. 497-513.

1787
Atwater, Ernesta E.
A Tabulation of Facts on Conditions Existent in Hicks' Mexican Camp.
El Monte, CA, 1942.

1788
"Defense Migration in the United States." Geneva, *International Labour Review* 45, March 1942, pp. 320-321.

1789
Irigoyen, Ulises
"El Problema Económico de las Ciudades Fronterizos." Chihuahua, *Boletín de la Sociedad Chihuahuense de Estudios Históricos* 4, July 20, 1942, pp. 64-68.

1790
"Bilateral Agreement Concerning the Temporary Migration of Mexican Farm Workers to the United States." Geneva, *International Labour Review* 46, October 1942, pp. 469-471.

1791
Mexico. Dept. of State for Foreign Affairs. Bureau of International News Service
The Good Neighbor Policy and Mexicans in Texas, by C. R. Stevenson and Ezequiel Padilla. Mexico, 1943, 22p.

1792
Rasmussen, Wayne D.
The U.S. Dept. of Agriculture and Inter-American Relations During the First Year of the War. Washington, U.S. Bureau of Agricultural Economics (War Records Project, Report #1), 1943, 9p.

1793
U.S. Treaties, etc., 1933- (Franklin D. Roosevelt)
. . . *Temporary Migration of Mexican Agricultural Workers.* Agreement Between the United States of America and Mexico, Effected by Exchange of Notes, Signed August 1942. Washington (U.S. Dept. of State, Publication #1872), GPO, 1943, 13p.

1794
Warburton, Amber (Arthun), et al.
The Work and Welfare of Children of Agricultural Laborers in Hidalgo County, Texas. Washington, U.S. Children's Bureau (Publication #298); GPO, 1943, 74p.

1795
"El Exodo de Nuestros Braceros Mexicanos." México, *Revista Económica* (6: 2), February 28, 1943, pp. 24-26.

1796
Broadbent, Elizabeth
The Distribution of Mexican Populations in the United States. Chicago, 1944. (Master's Thesis, University of Chicago)

1797
U.S. Treaties, etc., 1933-   (Franklin D. Roosevelt)
. . . *Temporary Migration of Mexican Agricultural Workers.* Agreement Between the United States of America and Mexico, Revising the Agreement of August 4, 1942 Effected by Exchange of Notes Signed at Mexico City, April 26, 1943. Washington (U.S. Dept. of State, Publication #2066), GPO, 1944, 13p.

1798
Prieto Yeme, Guillermo
"La Emigración de Braceros. Aspectos Interesantes." México, *Población,* July-August 1944, pp. 37, 54-55.

1799
Haggerty, John J.
"Mexico and the United States Discuss Mutual Farm Problems." *Agriculture in the Americas,* September 1944, pp. 168-171, 176, 178.

1800
International Labour Office
"Migration. Temporary Migration of Mexican Workers to the United States." Montreal, *International Labour Review,* October 1944, pp. 519-521.

1801
Jones, Robert C.
Mexican War Workers in the United States: the Mexico-United States Manpower Recruiting Program and its Operation. Washington, Pan American Union, Division of Labor and Social Life, 1945, 46p.

1802
Mexico. Dept. of Foreign Affairs
With the Mexican Laborers in the United States, by Ezequiel Padilla. (International Policy Series, #5). Mexico, 1945, 9p.

1803
Mexican-American Commission for Economic Cooperation
"Report of Activities From September 1943 to January 1945." *Pan American Union Bulletin* 79, April 1945, pp. 211-216.

1804
Pinal, Jorge del
"Los Trabajadores Mexicanos en los Estados Unidos." Mexico. *Trimestre Economico,* April-June 1945, pp. 1-45.

1805
Henderson, Julia
"Foreign Labour in the United States During the War." Montreal, *International Labour Review,* December 1945, pp. 609-631.

1806
McWilliams, Carey
Southern California Country; an Island on the Land. New York, Duell, Sloan & Pearce, 1946, 387p.

1807
México. Dirección de Previsión Social
Los Braceros. México, Talleres Gráficos de la Cía. Editora y Librería ARS, S.A., for the Secretaría del Trabajo y Prevision Social, 1946, 120p.

1808
Texas A & M College. Extension Service
Farm Labor Program in Texas, 1943-1947. College Station, Texas, 1947, 31p.

1809
"Puntos de Vista Sobre la Salida del Trabajador Mexicano a los Estados Unidos de Norteamérica." Mexico, *Boletín Mensual de la Dirección de Economía Rural* 257, October 1947, pp. 878-882.

1810
Bruno, Frank J.
"Migration, Immigration and Transiency" (In his, *Trends in Social Work, as Reflected in the Proceedings of the National Conference of Social Work, 1874-1946.* New York, Columbia University Press, 1948, pp. 120-129).

1811
Bruno, Frank J.
"Transients, Immigrants and Refugees" (In his, *Trends in Social Work, as Reflected in the Proceedings of the National Conference of Social Work, 1874-1946.* New York, Columbia University Press, 1948, pp. 322-330).

1812
Perales, Alonso S., comp.
Are we Good Neighbors? San Antonio, Perales Book Store, 1948, 298p.

1813
Jones, Robert C.
"Los Braceros Mexicanos en los Estados Unidos Durante el Período Bélico." Mexico, *Acción Social,* January-February 1946, pp. 17-28, 47.

1814

Dearman, Cecil J.

A Socio-Economic Study of Latin American Farm Migrants in Texas.
College Station, TX, Texas A & M College, 1947. (Master's Thesis,
Texas A & M College).

1815

Weston, George M.

The History of Treatment of Foreign and Minority Groups in California.
Stanford, CA 1948. (Ph.D. Dissertation, Stanford University)

1816

Martínez D., Guillermo

"Los Braceros, Experiencias que Deben Aprovecharse." México,
Revista Mexicana de Sociología (10: 2), May-August 1948, pp. 177-195.

1817

"Admission of Agricultural Workers into the United States: new Mexico-
United States Agreement." Geneva, *International Labour Review* 58,
August 1948, pp. 236-248.

1818

Minnesota. Governor's Inter-Racial Committee

*The Mexican in Minnesota: a Report to Governor Luther W. Youngdahl
of Minnesota.* St. Paul, August 15, 1948, 64p.

1819

Humphrey, Norman D.

"The Cultural Background of the Mexican Immigrant." *Rural Economy*
(13: 3), September 1948, pp. 239-255.

1820

Sanchez, George I., & Saunders, Lyle

*Wetbacks; a Preliminary Report to the Advisory Committee, Study of
Spanish-Speaking People.* Austin, University of Texas, 1949, 39p.

1821

U.S. House. Committee on Agriculture

Importation of Foreign Farm Labor; Hearings Before Subcommittee #2,
July 14, 1949, on H.R. 5557, 81st Congress, First Session (Serial CC).
Washington, GPO, 1949, 32p.

1822

Carter, H., ed.

"Reappraising our Immigration Policy." Annals of the American
Academy of Political and Social Science 262, March 1949, pp. 1-192.

1823

Davis, Kingsley, & Senior, Clarence

"Immigration From the Western Hemisphere." *Annals of the American
Academy of Political and Social Science* 262, March 1949, pp. 76-77.

1824
Miller, Watson B.
"Administering our Immigration Laws." *Annals of the American Academy of Political & Social Science* 262, March 1949, pp. 178-184.

1825
Moore, Wilbert E.
"America's Migration Treaties During World War II." *Annals of the American Academy of Political and Social Science* 262, March 1949, pp. 31-38.

1826
"American States Members of the ILO Fourth Conference, Montevideo, April-May 1949." Geneva, *International Labour Review* 60, September 1949, pp. 217-237.

1827
Merla, Pedro
"El Bracero Mexicano en la Economía Nacional." México, *Revista del Trabajo* (3: 143), December 1949, pp. 5-10.

1828
Casey, Robert J.
"The Texas Border and Some Borderliners: a Chronicle and a Guide. Indianapolis, Bobb-Merrill, 1950, 440p.

1829
Flores, Edmundo
"Los Braceros Mexicanos en Wisconsin." México, *El Trimestre Económico* (17: 1), January-March 1950, pp. 23-80.

1830
Gamio, Manuel
"Anglosajones y Latinoamericanos en la Frontera de Estados Unidos con México." México, *América Indígena* (10: 3), July 1950, pp. 191-194.

1831
Radtke, Theodore J.
The Wetback Situation in the Rio Grande Valley. Report of the Bishop's Committee for the Spanish-Speaking. Corpus Christi, Texas, August 1950.

1832
Saunders, Lyle, & Leonard, Olen E.
The Wetback in the Lower Rio Grande Valley of Texas. (Inter-American Education, Occasional Papers, #7). Austin, University of Texas Press, 1951, 92p.

1833

U.S. Dept. of Agriculture
A History of the Emergency Farm Labor Supply Program, 1943-1947.
(Agriculture Monograph #13). Washington, 1951, 208p.

1834

Flores, Edmundo
"Un Millón de Braceros Ilegales." México, *Revista de Economía* (14: 3), March 1951, pp. 42-43.

1835

Green, Alfred M.
"Ripple of 'Wetbacks' Becomes a Tidal Wave." *Machinists Monthly Journal* (63: 12), December 1951, pp. 364-366.

1836

Calderón, Miguel G.
"El Problema Económico Social de los Braceros" (In *México, Realización y Esperanza.* México, Editorial Superación, 1952, 782p.).

1837

Coalson, George O.
"Mexican Contract Labor in American Agriculture." *Southwestern Social Science Quarterly* 33, 1952-53, pp. 228-238.

1838

Tubbs, Lowell L.
A Survey of the Problems of the Migratory Mexicans. Austin, TX, 1952, 117p. (Unpublished Master's Thesis, University of Texas at Austin)

1839

U.S. Farm Placement Service
Information Concerning Entry of Mexican Agricultural Workers into the United States. Public Law 78, 82nd Congress. Agreement Between Government of United States and Mexico Concerning Migrant Labor, Approved August 1951 and Amended June 1952. Standard Work Contract, as Amended, Washington, GPO, 1952, 14p.

1840

U.S. Treaties, etc., 1945-   (Truman)
Mexican Agricultural Workers. Agreement Between the United States of America and Mexico Effected by Exchange of Notes Signed at Mexico, August 1, 1949, Entered into Force August 1, 1949, and Amendments and Interpretations Effected by Exchange of Notes. (U.S. Dept. of State Publication #4284). Washington, GPO, 1952, 107p.

1841
Leroy, George P.
"Contribution to the Study of the 'Wetback' Problem: Illegal Mexican Immigration to the United States." *Population* 7, April-June 1952, pp. 334-337.

1842
U.S. Dept. of Labor
"Migrant Labor Agreement with Mexico." Washington, *The Labor Market & Employment Security,* July 1952, pp. 1-2.

1843
Luengo Muñoz, Manuel
"El Problema Migratorio en la Frontera Mejicano-Estadounidense." Seville, Spain, *Estudios Americanos* (4: 15), September 1952, pp. 619-635.

1844
American GI Forum of Texas
What Price Wetbacks? Austin, American GI Forum of Texas, and Texas State Federation of Labor, 1953? 59p.

1845
Kibbe, Pauline (Rochester)
"The Economic Plight of Mexicans" (In McDonagh, Edward C., & Richards, E. S., eds. *Ethnic Relations in the United States.* New York, Appleton, 1953, pp. 174-200).

1846
" 'Wetbacks' and Mexican National Agreements" (In *Transactions of the Commonwealth Club of California, 47.* San Francisco, April 20, 1953, pp. 153-172).

1847
Puente, Armando
"La Situación de los Braceros Mexicanos en los Estados Unidos." Buenos Aires, *Dinámica Social* (3: 33/34), May-June 1953, pp. 51-52.

1848
Busey, James L.
The Political Geography of Mexican Migration." *Colorado Quarterly* 2, Autumn 1953, pp. 181-190.

1849
Lopez Malo, Ernesto
"The Emigration of Mexican Laborers." México, *Ciencias Sociales* 5, 1954, pp. 220-227.

1850

U.S. Dept. of State

Mexican Agricultural Workers; Agreement Between the U.S. and Mexico, Renewing and Amending the Agreement of August 11, 1951, as Amended, and Establishing Joint Migratory Labor Commission, Effected by Exchange of Notes Signed Mexico, March 10, 1954. Publication 5457. Washington, 1954, 36p.

1851

U.S. House. Committee on Agriculture

Mexican Farm Labor; Hearings, 83rd Congress, Second Session, on H.J. Res. 355, February 3-11, 1954. Washington, 1954, 239p. (Y4.Ag8/1: M57).

1852

U.S. Senate. Committee on the Judiciary

To Control Illegal Immigration. Hearings before the Subcommittee on Immigration and Naturalization . . . 83rd Congress, Second Session, on S. 3660, to Make the Employment, and Related Practices, of any Alien Known by an Employer to have Entered the U.S. Illegally Within 3 Years Thereof Unlawful . . . and S. 3661, to Provide for the Seizure and Forfeiture of any Vessel or Vehicle Used in the Transportation of any Alien Known by the Owner . . . to Have Entered the U.S. Illegally . . . July 12, 13, & 14, 1954. Washington, GPO, 1954, 108p.

1853

Lopez Malo, Ernesto

"Emigrantes. El Problema de los Trabajadores Mexicanos." México, *Universidad de México* (8: 6), February 1954, pp. 1-2, 17-18.

1854

"Wetbacks: can the States act to Curb Illegal Entry?" *Stanford Law Review* 6, March 1954, pp. 287-323.

1855

Salinas Ramos, Alberto

"El Problema de los Braceros." México, *Tierra* (9: 4), April 1954, pp. 309-311.

1856

U.S.-Mexican Migratory Labor Commission Membership." *U.S. Dept. of State Bulletin* 30, April 12, 1954, p. 565.

1857

U.S. House. Committee on Agriculture

Mexican Farm Labor Programs. Hearings Before the Subcommittee on Equipment Supplies and Manpower on H.R. 3822. (84th Congress, Serial H). Washington, GPO, 1955, 328p. (Y4. Ag 8/1: M57/955).

1858
U.S. Treaties, etc., 1953-   (Eisenhower)
Mexican Agricultural Workers. Agreement Between the United States of America and Mexico, Amending Agreement of August 11, 1951, as Amended, Effected by Exchange of Notes, Signed at Mexico, August 6, 1954, Entered into Force August 6, 1954. (U.S. Dept. of State Publication #5670). Washington, GPO, 1955, 23p.

1859
Daniel, James M.
The Advance of the Spanish Frontier and the Despoblado. Austin, TX, 1955, 318p. (Ph.D. Dissertation, University of Texas at Austin)

1860
García Tellez, Ignacio
La Migración de Braceros a los Estados Unidos de Norteamérica. México, 1955, 55p.

1861
Higham, John
Strangers in the Land; Patterns of American Nativism, 1860-1925. New Brunswick, N.J., Rutgers University Press, 1955, 431p.

1862
Lázaro Salinas, José
La Emigración de los Braceros: Visión Objetiva de un Problema Mexicano. Léon, México, Imprenta Cuauhtemoc, 1955, 204p.

1863
Nichols, Garrett C.
Agricultural Influences on the Mexican Residents of the Coachella Valley as Particularly Related to Education. Claremont, CA, 1955. (Master's Thesis, Claremont Graduate School)

1864
Texas State Federation of Labor
Down in the Valley; a Supplementary Report on Developments in the Wetback and Bracero Situation of the Lower Rio Grande Valley of Texas Since Publication of "What Price Wetbacks?" Austin, 1955, 11p.

1865
Hayes, E. F., et al.
" 'Operation Wetback': Impact on the Border States." *Employment Security Review,* March 1955, pp. 16-21.

1866
"U.S. Dept. of State Agreement on Migratory Workers." *U.S. Dept. of State Bulletin* 32, April 25, 1955, p. 701.

1867
Starr, M.
"Labor and Immigration." *Current History* 29, November 1955, pp. 300-304.

1868
Casarrubías Ocampo, Daniel
El Problema del Exodo de Braceros en México y sus Consecuencias. (Instituto Nacional de la Juventud Mexicana, Publicación v. 15). México, Editorial Injumex, 1956, 74p.

1869
Galarza, Ernesto
Strangers in our Fields. Based on a Report Regarding Compliance with the Contractual, Legal and Civil Rights of Mexican Agricultural Contract Labor in the United States, Made Possible Through a Grant-in-aid From the Fund for the Republic. Washington, 1956, 80p.

1870
U.S. Treaties, etc., 1953-   (Eisenhower)
Mexican Agricultural Workers; Recommendations by Joint Migratory Labor Commission. Agreement Between the U.S.A. and Mexico, Effected by Exchange of Notes dated at Mexico, D.F., April 14, 1955. (U.S. Dept. of State Publication #6020). Washington, GPO, 1956, 14p.

1871
California. Agricultural Experiment Station
Domestic and Imported Workers in the Harvest Labor Market, Santa Clara County, California, 1954, by Varden Fuller, et al. (Mimeo Report #184). Berkeley, University of California, Berkeley, Division of Agricultural Sciences, January 1956, 52p.

1872
Lee, John F.
"Statutory Provision for Admission of Mexican Agricultural Workers; an Exception to the Immigration and Nationality Act of 1952." *George Washington Law Review* 24, March 1956, pp. 464-477.

1873
Hadley, Eleanor M.
"Critical Analysis of the Wetback Problem." *Law and Contemporary Problems* 21, Spring 1956, pp. 334-357.

1874
Norman, Arthur
"Migration to Southwest Texas: Peoples and Words." *Southwestern Social Science Quarterly* 37, September 1, 1956, pp. 149-158.

1875
Thompson, Albert N.
"The Mexican Immigrant Worker in Southwestern Agriculture."
American Journal of Economics & Sociology (16: 1), October 1956, pp.
73-82.

1876
Vasconcelos, José
"A National Exodus." *Central America & Mexico* (IV: 2), October
1956, pp. 7-9.

1877
Carney, John P.
*Postwar Mexican Migration, 1945-1955, with Particular Reference to
the Policies and Practices of the United States Concerning its Control.* Los
Angeles, 1957. (Ph.D. Dissertation, University of Southern California)

1878
Michigan. State University of Agriculture & Applied Science, East Lansing. Dept. of Political Science. *Selected Readings on Mexico.* Prepared
for a Seminar on Foreign Affairs Sponsored by the Dept. of Political
Science . . . and the Great Decisions Program, Foreign Policy Association, Lansing, Michigan. East Lansing, 1957, Various pagings.

1879
Tomasek, Robert D.
*The Political and Economic Implications of Mexican Labor in the United
States Under the non-Quota System, Contract Labor Program and Wet-
back Movement.* Ann Arbor, 1957, 309p. (Dissertation, University of
Michigan).

1880
U.S. Treaties, etc., 1953-   (Eisenhower)
Mexican Agricultural Workers. Agreement Between the United States of
America and Mexico, Relating to Article 7 of Agreement of August 11,
1951, as Amended, Effected by Exchange of Notes Signed at Washington
June 17, 1957. (Treaties and Other International Acts Series, 3848).
Washington, GPO, 1957, 4p.

1881
Kelton, Elmer
These are Braceros. San Angelo, Texas, The San Angelo Standard,
Inc., 1958.

1882
McDonnell, Donald C.
"The Bracero Program in California" (In Ninth Regional Conference,
Catholic Council for the Spanish-Speaking, April 15-17, 1958. *Proceed-
ings.* San Antonio, Texas, Schneider Printing Company, 1958, pp.
11-17).

1883
U.S. House. Committee on Agriculture
Farm Labor. Hearings Before the Subcommittee on Equipment, Supplies and Manpower, on Problems in the Southwest . . . and Mexican Labor, on H.R. 7028 . . . House of Representatives, 85th Congress, Serial CCC). Washington, GPO, 1958, 633p.

1884
Galarza, Ernesto
"Trabajadores Mexicanos en Tierra Extraña." México, *Problemas Agrícolas e Industriales de México* (10: 1/2), January-June 1958, pp. 1-84.

1885
Meneffee, Selden C.
"Los Trabajadores Migratorios Mexicanos del sur de Texas!" México, *Problemas Agrícolas e Industriales de México* (10:1/2), January-June 1958, pp. 181-214.

1886
U.S. President's Commission on Migratory Labor
"Los Trabajadores Migratorios en la Agricultura Norteamericana." México, *Problemas Agrícolas e Industriales de México* (10: 1/2), January-June 1958, pp. 85-180.

1887
Form, William, et al.
"The Place of Returning Migrants in the Stratification System." *Rural Sociology* 23, September 1958, pp. 286-297.

1888
Hutchinson, E. P.
"Immigration Statistics of the United States." *American Statistical Association Journal* 53, December 1958, pp. 963-1025.

1889
Hancock, Richard H.
The Role of the Bracero in the Economic and Cultural Dynamics of Mexico: a Case Study of Chihuahua. Stanford, CA, 1959, 245p. (Ph.D. Dissertation, Stanford University)

1890
U.S. Dept. of Labor. Bureau of Employment Security
Report of Operations of Mexican Farm Labor Program, Made Pursuant to Conference Report 1449, House of Representatives, 84th Congress, First Session, January 1-June 30, 1959. Washington, 1959, 7p. (L7.2: M57/3).

1891
U.S. Secretary of Labor's Consultants on the Mexican Farm Labor Program
Mexican Farm Labor Program, Consultants Report, October 1959.
Washington, 1959, 17p. `

1892
Velasco Gil, Carlos M.
Nuestros Buenos Vecinos. 4th ed enl. México, Ed. Azteca, 1959, 331p.

1893
Form, William H., & Rivera, Julius
"Work Contacts and International Evaluations: the Case of a Mexican Border Village." *Social Forces* 37, May 1959, pp. 334-339.

1894
U.S. Dept. of Labor
Mexican Farm Labor Program; Consultants Report. Washington, October 1959, 17p.

1895
Beegle, J. A., et al.
"Demographic Characteristics of the United States-Mexican Border." *Rural Sociology* 25, 1960, pp. 107-162.

1896
Padilla de Alba, Felipe
La Protección del Trabajador Mexicano en el Extranjero, México, 1960, 93p.

1897
"Invitation to Peonage." *IUD Digest* 5, Fall 1960, pp. 38-46.

1898
Anderson, Henry
The Bracero Program in California . . . Berkeley, School of Public Health, University of California, Berkeley, 1961, 328p.

1899
Elac, John C.
The Employment of Mexican Workers in United States Agriculture, 1900-1960: a Binational Economic Analysis. Los Angeles, 1961, 45p. (Ph.D. Dissertation, UCLA)

1900
Moore, Woodrow
El Problema de la Emigración de los Braceros Mexicanos. Mexico, 1961, 109p.

1901

Park, Joseph F.
The History of Mexican Labor in Arizona During the Territorial Period.
Tucson, 1961. (Master's Thesis, University of Arizona)

1902

Ramirez Lewall, I.
El Tesoro del Bracero; Recuerdo. Woodland, CA, Fisher Bros.
Creative Printing & Stationery, 1961, 21p.

1903

U.S. Dept. of Labor. Bureau of Employment Security
Report of Operations of Mexican Farm Labor Program, Made Pursuant to Conference Report 1449, House of Representatives, 84th Congress, First Session, January 1-June 30, 1961. (Farm Labor Service); Washington, 1961, 10p.

1904

Gamio, León C.
"Braceros Bring Home new Ways." *Americas* 13, May 1961, pp. 28-30.

1905

Scruggs, Otey M.
"United States, Mexico, and the Wetbacks, 1942-1947." *Pacific Historical Review* 30, May 1961, pp. 149-164.

1906

Rooney, James F.
"Effects of Imported Mexican Farm Labor in a California City."
American Journal of Economics 20, October 1961, pp. 513-521.

1907

Spradlin, T. R.
"The Mexican Farm Labor Importation Program." *George Washington Law Review* 30, October 1961, pp. 84-122; December 1961, pp. 311-327.

1908

Jensen, Joan M.
The American Protective League, 1917-1919. Los Angeles, 1962.
(Ph.D. Dissertation, UCLA)

1909

Lipschultz, Robert J.
American Attitudes Toward Mexican Immigration, 1924-1952. Chicago, 1962, 97p. (Ph.D. Dissertation, University of Chicago)

1910
Silva, Luciano V.
"Characteristics of Mexican Immigration" (In Los Angeles Committee for the Protection of the Foreign Born. *12th Annual Conference Journal.* Los Angeles, 1962, pp. 14-16).

1911
U.S. Dept. of Labor. Bureau of Employment Security
Information Concerning the Entry of Mexican Agricultural Workers into the United States. Washington, GPO, 1962, 51p. (L7 35: M57 962).

1912
U.S. Dept. of Labor. Bureau of Employment Security
Mexican Green Carders: Preliminary Report, by Lloyd Gallardo. Washington, 1962.

1913
U.S. Dept. of State
Migratory Workers: Mexican Agricultural Workers: Agreement Between the United States of America and Mexico; Amending and Extending the Agreement of August 11, 1951, as Amended and Extended, and Including Joint Interpretations of 1961; Effected by Exchange of Notes, Signed at Mexico, D.F., December 29, 1961. Washington (Treaties and other International Acts, Series 5160), 1962, 43p.

1914
U.S. House. Committee on Appropriations
Mexican Farm Labor Program; Hearing Before Subcommittee on Equipment, Supplies and Manpower, 87th Congress, 2nd Session, Jan. 19, 1962. Washington (Serial), 1962, 46p. (Y4.Ag 8/1: M57/962).

1915
U.S. Treaties, etc. (Kennedy)
Migratory Workers: Mexican Agricultural Workers. Agreement Between the United States of America and Mexico, Amending and Extending the Agreement of August 11, 1951, as Amended and Extended; and Including Joint Interpretations of 1961 Effected by Exchange of Notes Signed at Mexico, December 29, 1961. (Treaties and Other International Acts Series, 5160). Washington, GPO, 1962, 43p.

1916
"Employment of Foreign Workers in 1961." *Farm Labor Market Developments,* February 1962, pp. 1-12.

1917
Scruggs, Otey M.
"The Bracero Program Under the Farm Security Administration, 1942-1943." *Labor History* 3, Spring 1962, pp. 149-168.

1918
Gilmore, N. R., & Gilmore Gladys W.
"Bracero in California." *Pacific Historical Review* 32, August 1962,
pp. 265-282.

1919
Scruggs, Otey M.
"Texas, Good Neighbor?" *Southwestern Social Science Quarterly* 43,
September 1962, pp. 118-125.

1920
Anderson, Henry
*Fields of Bondage; the Mexican Contract Labor System in Industrialized
Agriculture.* Martinez, CA? 1963, 104p.

1921
Copp, Nelson G.
*Wetbacks and Braceros: Mexican Migrant Laborers and American
Immigration Policy, 1930-1960.* Boston, 1963, 265p. (Ph.D. Dissertation,
Boston University)

1922
Guzmán Rodríguez, Rubén G.
*El Exodo de los Trabajadores Mexicanos y su Relación con la Reforma
Agraria.* México, 1963, 138p.

1923
Krassowski, Witold
*Naturalization and Assimilation-Proneness of California Immigrant
Populations: a Statistical Study.* Los Angeles, 1963, 183p. (Ph.D. Disser-
tation, UCLA)

1924
Leal Carrillo, Stella
*Importancia Económica y Social de la Población Mexicana en Estados
Unidos de Norteamérica.* México, 1963, 125p. (Licenciatura, Univer-
sidad Nacional Autónoma de México)

1925
McBride, John
Vanishing Bracero, Valley Revolution. San Antonio, Naylor Co., 1963,
83p.

1926
Silva, Luciano V.
"Recent Developments in Mexican Immigration" (In Los Angeles
Committee for the Protection of the Foreign Born. *13th Annual Con-
ference Journal.* Los Angeles, 1963, pp. 17-20).

1927
U.S. Dept. of Agriculture. Economic Research Service *Economic, Social, and Demographic Characteristics of Spanish-American Wage Workers on U.S. Farms,* by Reed E. Friend and Samuel Baum. (Agricultural Economic Report #27.) Washington, 1963, 21p.

1928
U.S. Dept. of State
Migratory Workers; Mexican Agricultural Workers; Agreement Between United States and Mexico, Amending Agreement of August 11, 1951, as Amended and Extended, Effected by Exchange of Notes Signed Mexico, January 10 and February 25, 1963. Washington, 1963, 4p.

1929
U.S. House. Committee on Agriculture
Mexican Farm Labor Program. Hearings Before Subcommittee on Equipment, Supplies and Manpower, 88th Congress, First Session, on H.R. 1836 and H.R. 2009, March 27-29, 1963. Washington, GPO, 1963, 349p. (Y4.Ag8/1: M57/963).

1930
Gilmore, N. R.
"The Bracero in California." *Pacific Historical Review* 32, August 1963, pp. 265-282.

1931
Scruggs, Otey M.
"Texas and the Bracero Program." *Pacific Historical Review* (32: 3), August 1963, pp. 251-264.

1932
Shannon, Lyle W., & Lettau, Kathryn
"Measuring the Adjustment of Immigrant Laborers." *Southwestern Social Science Quarterly* 44, September 1963, pp. 139-148.

1933
Galarza, Ernesto
Merchants of Labor: the Mexican Bracero Story; an Account of the Managed Migration of Mexican Farm Workers in California, 1942-1960. San Jose? 1964, 284p.

1934
Schmidt, Fred H.
After the Bracero: an Inquiry into the Problems of Farm Labor Recruitment. Los Angeles, Institute of Industrial Relations, University of California, 1964, 139 & 34pp.

1935
Vargas y Campos, Gloria R.
El Problema del Bracero Mexicano. México, 1964, 144p.

1936
The Bracero Program and its Aftermath: an Historical Summary. Sacramento, CA, Legislative Reference Service, Assembly, California Legislature, 1965.

1937
California. Legislature. Assembly. Legislature Reference Service
The Bracero Program and its Aftermath: an Historical Summary. Sacramento, 1965, 22p.

1938
Grebler, Leo, et al.
Mexican Immigration to the United States: the Record and its Implications. Los Angeles, University of California, Graduate School of Business, Division of Research (Advance Report #2), 1965, 106p.

1939
U.S. Dept. of Agriculture. Economic Research Service
Termination of the Bracero Program: Some Effects on Farm Labor and Migrant Housing Needs, by Robert C. McElroy and Earle E. Gavett. Agricultural Economic Report #77. Washington, GPO, 1965, 29p.

1940
Bogardus, Emory S.
"The Mexican Immigrant and the Quota." *Sociology and Social Research* 12, Autumn 1965, pp. 371-378.

1941
Cormack, Joseph M., & Barker, Frederick F.
"The Mexican Labor Law." *Southern California Law Review,* September 29, 1965, pp. 251-294.

1942
Creagan, James F.
"Public Law 78: a Tangle of Domestic and International Relations." *Journal of Inter-American Studies,* October 1965, pp. 541-556.

1943
Peón, Máximo
Como Viven los Mexicanos en los Estados Unidos. Mexico, Costa-Amic, 1966, 270p.

1944
Alvarez, José
"A Demographic Profile of the Mexican Immigrant to the United States, 1910-1950." *Journal of Inter-American Studies* 8, July 1966, pp. 471-496.

1945
Braceros, Mexico and Foreign Trade. July 1966, 6p. (ED 014 599).

1946
Hawley, Ellis W.
"The Politics of the Mexican Labor Issue, 1950-1965." *Agricultural History* 140, July 1966, pp. 157-176.

1947
Hernandez-Alvarez, José
"Demographic Profile of the Mexican Immigration to the United States, 1910-1950." *Journal of Inter-American Studies* 8, July 1966, pp. 471-496.

1948
Dellon, Howard N.
"Foreign Agricultural Workers and the Prevention of Adverse Effect." *Labor Law Journal* 17, December 1966, pp. 739-748.

1949
Friends, Society of. American Friends Service Committee
Final Report of the Farm Workers Opportunity Project. Pasadena, CA, 1967, 130p.

1950
U.S. Dept. of Agriculture. Economic Research Service
Effects of Changes in use of Seasonal Workers in U.S.-Mexican Agricultural Trade and Balance of Payments, by Hans G. Hirsch. Washington (ERS-Foreign 195), 1967, 51p.

1951
Fineberg, Richard A.
Green Card Labor and the Delano Grape Strike: a Study of Postbracero Mexican National Farm Workers in the San Joaquin Valley, 1968. San Francisco, Council for Christian Social Action, Board for Homeland Ministries, United Church of Christ, 1968, 34p.

1952
Nathan (Robert R.) Associates, Washington, D.C.
Industrial and Employment Potential of the United States-Mexican Border . . . Washington, U.S. Dept. of Commerce, Economic Development Administration, 1968, 286p.

1953
Report of Select Commission on Western Hemisphere Immigration, January 1968. Washington, GPO, 1968, 1979p. (Y3. W52: 1/968).

1954
U.S. Select Committee on Western Hemisphere Immigration
The Impact of Commuter Aliens Along the Mexican and Canadian Borders: Hearings, parts 1-2, January 26-February 10, 1968. Washington, GPO, 1968, 2v.

1955

Levenstein, Harvey A.

"The AFL and Mexican Immigration in the 1920's: an Experiment in Labor Diplomacy." *Hispanic American Historical Review* 48, May 1968, pp. 206-219.

1956

Rischin, Moses

"Beyond the Great Divide: Immigration and the Last Frontier." *Journal of American History,* June 1968, pp. 42-53.

1957

Gamio, Manuel

The Mexican Immigrant: his Life Story, with Autobiographical Documents. New York, Arno Press (reprint of 1931 edition), 1969, 288p.

1958

Gamio, Manuel

Mexican Immigration to the United States. New York, Arno Press (reprint of 1930 edition), 1969, 262p.

1959

Gamio, Manuel, ed.

El Inmigrante Mexicano: la Historia de su Vida. México, UNAM, 1969, 271p.

1960

Salandini, Victor

The Short-run Socioeconomic Effects of the Termination of Public Law 78 on the California Farm Labor Market for 1965-1967. Washington, 1969, 300p.

1961

U.S. House. Committee on Education and Labor

Employment of Green Card Aliens During Labor Disputes, Hearing Before Special Subcommittee on Labor, 91st Congress, First Session, on H.R. 12667, July 16-August 8, 1969. Washington, 1969, 250p. (Y4.Ed8/1 : Al 4).

1962

Worker Certification Program Under the Immigration and Nationality Act. Fiscal Year 1968. (U.S. Dept. of Labor, Manpower Administration). 1969, 43p. (ED 033 218).

1963

LaBrucherie, Roger A.

"Aliens in the Fields: the Green Card Commuter Under the Immigration and Naturalization Law." *Stanford Law Review* (XXI: 6), June 1969, pp. 1750-1776.

1964
Scruggs, Otey M.
"Evolution of the Mexican Farm Labor Agreement of 1942." *Agricultural History* 34, July 1969, pp. 140-149.

1965
Christopherson, Helge
Meksikanerne i USA. Oslo, Norsk Utenrikspolitisk Institutt, 1971, 28p. (Reprinted from *Tidens Ekko,* 1970-1971, v. 10).

1966
Fineberg, Richard A.
Green Card Workers in Farm Labor Disputes; a Study of Postbracero Mexican National Farm Workers in the San Joaquin Valley. Claremont, CA, 1970, 118p. (Ph.D. Dissertation, Claremont Graduate School and University Center).

1967
Fricke, Carl H.
Mexican Braceros in California Agriculture. Los Angeles, 1970. (Master's Thesis, UCLA)

1968
Gonzalez, N. L.
"Bracero Politics: a Special Report." (In Servin, Manuel P. *The Mexican Americans: an Awakening Minority.* Beverly Hills, Glencoe Press, 1970, pp. 179-199).

1969
Hoffman, Abraham
The Repatriation of Mexican Nationals From the United States During the Great Depression. Los Angeles, 1970, 281p. (Ph.D. Dissertation, UCLA)

1970
McCain, Johnny M.
Contract Labor as a Factor in United States-Mexican Relations, 1942-1947. Austin, TX, 1970, 399p. (Ph.D. Dissertation, University of Texas at Austin)

1971
North, David S.
The Border Crossers; People who Live in Mexico and Work in the United States. Washington, TransCentury Corp., 1970, 319p.

1972
Texas Migrant Labor. Annual Report, 1970. Austin, Good Neighbor Commission of Texas, 1970, 85p. (Ed 057 936).

1973
Jones, Lamar B.
"Labor and Management in California Agriculture, 1864-1974." *Labor History* 11, Winter 1970, pp. 23-40.

1974
Gonzalez Navarro, Moisés
"Los Efectos Sociales de la Crisis del '29'." México, *Historia Mexicana* (XX: 2), April/June 1970, pp. 536-558.

1975
Inter-Agency Task Force on Migrant Labor. Austin, Good Neighbor Commission of Texas, December 1970, 222p.

1976
Craig, Richard B.
The Bracero Program: Interest Groups and Foreign Policy. Austin, University of Texas Press, 1971, 233p.

1977
Fellows, Lloyd
Economic Aspects of the Mexican Rural Population in California, With Special Emphasis on the Need for Mexican Labor in Agriculture. San Francisco, R & E Research Associates, 1971, 95p. (Reprint of the 1929 edition).

1978
Hymer, Evangeline
A Study of the Social Attitudes of Adult Mexican Immigrants in Los Angeles and Vicinity. San Francisco, R & E Associates, 1971, 68p. (Reprint of Master's Thesis, University of Southern California)

1979
Martinez, John R.
Mexican Emigration to the U.S., 1910-1930. San Francisco, R & E Research Associates, 1971, 100p.

1980
Samora, Julian
Los Mojados: the Wetback Story. Notre Dame, Indiana, University of Notre Dame Press, 1971, 205p.

1981
Schlesinger, Andrew B.
"Las Gorras Blancas, 1889-1891." *Journal of Mexican-American History* (I: 2), Spring 1971, pp. 87-143.

1982
Bustamante, Jorge A.
"The Wetback as a Deviant: an Application of Labeling Theory." *American Journal of Sociology* 77, 1972, pp. 706-718.

1983
Galarza, Ernesto
"The Braceros" (In Valdez, Luis, and Steiner, Stan, eds. *Aztlan: an Anthology of Mexican American Literature*. New York, Knopf, 1972, pp. 77-80).

1984
Norquest, Caroll
Rio Grande Wetbacks: Migrant Mexican Workers. Albuquerque, University of New Mexico Press, 1972, 159p.

1985
Ortega, Joe C.
"The Plight of the Mexican Wetback." *ABA Journal* 58, March 1972, pp. 251-254.

1986
Rischin, Moses
"Immigration, Migration and Minorities in California: a Reassessment." *Pacific Historical Review* 4, February 1972, pp. 71-90.

1987
Corwin, Arthur F.
˙ "Historia de la Emigración Mexicana 1900-1970. Literatura e Investigación." México, *Historia Mexicana* (22: 2), October-December 1972, pp. 188-220.

1988
Meador, Bruce S.
"Wetback" Labor in the Lower Rio Grande Valley. San Francisco, R & E Research Associates, 1973, 80p.

1989
Newton, Horace E.
Mexican Illegal Immigration into California, Principally Since 1945: a Socioeconomic Study. San Francisco, R & E Research Associates, 1973, 69p.

1990
North, David S., & Weissert, William G.
Immigrants and the American Labor Market. Washington, TransCentury Corp., 1973, 208p.

1991
Bustamante, Jorge A.
"El Espalda Mojada: Informe de un Observador Participante." México, *Revista Mexicana de Ciencia Política* 71, January-March 1973, pp. 81-107.

1992
Cardoso, Lawrence A.
Mexican Emigration to the United States, 1900 to 1930: an Analysis of Socio-Economic Causes. Storrs, CT, 1974, 234p. (Ph.D. Dissertation, University of Connecticut)

1993
Hoffman, Abraham
Unwanted Mexican-Americans in the Great Depression; Repatriation Pressures, 1929-1939. Tucson, University of Arizona Press, 1974, 207p.

1994
Portes, Alejandro
"Return of the Wetback." *Society* (11: 3), March/April 1974, pp. 40-46.

1995
Roach, J. M.
"Weighing the Foreign Work Force." *Conference Board Record* 11, December 1974, pp. 6-10.

1996
Wise, Donald E.
"The Effect of the Bracero on Agricultural Production in California." *Economic Inquiry* 12, December 1974, pp. 547-558.

1997
Briggs, Vernon M., Jr.
Mexican Migration and the U.S. Labor Market: a Mounting Issue for the '70's. (Studies in Human Resources Development, #3). Austin, Bureau of Business Research, Center for the Study of Human Resources, University of Texas-Austin, 1975, 44p.

1998
Briggs, Vernon M., Jr.
The Migration of Mexican Nationals into the United States: a Mounting Issue for the '70's. Austin, Center for the Study of Human Resources and Bureau of Business (Studies in Human Resource Development, #3), University of Texas at Austin, 1975, 37p.

1999
Dagodag, W. T.
"Source Regions and Composition of Illegal Mexican Immigration to California." *International Migration Review* (9: 4), 1975, pp. 499-511.

2000
Romo, Ricardo
"Responses to Mexican Immigration, 1910-1930." *Aztlan* (6: 2), 1975, pp. 173-196.

2001
"Labor Migration Under Capitalism." *Science & Society* (43: 4), Winter 1975, p. 498- .

2002
Frisbie, Parker
"Illegal Migration From Mexico to the United States: a Longitudinal Analysis." *International Migration Review* (9: 1), Spring 1975, pp. 3-13.

2003
Briggs, Vernon M., Jr.
"Mexican Immigrants and the Labor Market." *Texas Business Review* (49: 4), April 1975, pp. 85-90.

2004
Briggs, Vernon M., Jr.
"Mexican Workers in the United State Labour Market: a Contemporary Dilemma." Geneva, *International Labour Review* 112, November 1975, pp. 351-368.

2005
Bataillon, Claude
"Le Départ des Migrant Méxicains: Commentaire à Propos de Trois Etudes au Méxique Central, 1971-1974." (In Monbeig, Pierre, ed. *Les Migrations au Méxique* . . . Paris, Institut des Hautes Études de l'Amérique Latine, 1976, pp. 69-80).

2006
Bustamante, Jorge A.
"Espaldas Mojadas: Migración-Mercancia." (In Monbeig, Pierre, ed. *Les Migrations au Méxique* . . . Paris, Institut des Hautes Études de l'Amérique Latine, 1976, pp. 275-314).

2007
Mexican Migration to the United States. New York, Arno Press, 1976, 92 & 92 & 59 pp.

2008
Meyer, Jean A.
"Les Migrations Méxicaines vers les États-Unis au XXᵉ Siècle." (In Monbeig, Pierre, ed. *Les Migrations au Méxique* . . . Paris, Institut des Hautes Études de l'Amérique Latine, 1976, pp. 255-273).

2009
Reisler, Mark
By the Sweat of Their Brow; Mexican Immigrant Labor in the United States, 1900-1940. Westport, CT, Greenwood Press, 1976, 298p.

2010
Revel-Mouroz, Jean
"Les Migrations vers la Frontière Méxique-Etats-Unis." (In Monbeig, Pierre, ed. *Les Migrations au Méxique* . . . Paris, Institut des Hautes Etudes de l'Amérique Latine, 1976? pp. 315-350).

2011
Stoddard, Elwyn R.
"A Conceptual Analysis of the 'Alien Invasion': Institutionalized Support of Illegal Aliens in the United States." *International Migration Review* 10, 1976, pp. 157-189.

2012
"On the Problem of Illegal Mexican Aliens: Excerpt From the Comptroller-General's Report to the Congress, titled: 'Immigration, Need to Reassess U.S. Policy.' " *Inter-American Economic Affairs* 30, Winter 1976, pp. 93-96.

2013
North, David S., & Houstoun, Marion F.
The Characteristics and Role of Illegal Aliens in the U.S. Labor Market; an Exploratory Study (PB-252-616). Washington, Linton (for the U.S. Dept. of Labor, Employment & Training Division), March 1976 (distributed by NTIS, Springfield, VA), various paged.

2014
Blejer, Mario I, et al.
"Un Análisis de los Determinantes Económicos de la Migración Mexicana Legal e Ilegal Hacia los Estados Unidos." México, *Demografía y Economía* (11: 3), 1977, pp. 326-340.

2015
Bustamante, Jorge A.
Espaldas Mojadas, Materia Prima para la Expansión del Capital Norteamericano. 2d ed. corr. Mexico, Central de Estudios Sociológicos, Colegio de México, 1977, 46p. (Cuadernos del CES, #9).

2016
Kerstein, Peter N.
Anglo Over Bracero: a History of the Mexican Worker in the United States From Roosevelt to Nixon. San Francisco, R & E Research Associates, 1977, 113p.

2017
Machiels, Pierre J. M. P.
"Flores y Dólares": the Mexican Migrant to Half-Moon Bay, California. San Francisco, 1977, 213 p. (Master of Arts Thesis, San Francisco State University)

2018
Levering, R.
"Is Business pro or con Illegal Immigration?" *Business & Society Review* 24, Winter 1977-78, pp. 55-59.

2019
Smith, Barton, & Newman, Robert
"Depressed Wages Along the U.S.-Mexican Border: an Empirical Analysis." *Economic Inquiry* 15, January 1977, pp. 51-66.

2020
Fogel, Walter A.
"At the Center: Major Changes to Control Immigrant Flows." *Center Magazine* (10: 2), March 1977, p. 46-B.

2021
Bustamante, Jorge A.
"Undocumented Immigration From Mexico: Research Report." *International Migration Review* (1: 2), Summer 1977, pp. 149-177.

2022
Jenkins, J. C.
"Push/pull in Recent Mexican Migration to the United States." *International Migration Review* (11: 12), Summer 1977, pp. 178-189.

2023
"Race, Class and the State." *Race and Class* (19: 1), Summer 1977, p. 69-   .

2024
Hardin, Garrett, & Sereseres, Caesar
"Mexico—the Special Case: Should the United States tie Strings to aid?" *Center Magazine* (10: 4), July 1977, p. 74.

2025
Briggs, Vernon M., Jr.
"Immigration." *Labor Law Journal* 28, August 1977, pp. 495-500.

2026
Corwin, Arthur F., ed.
Immigrants—and Immigrants; Perspectives on Mexican Labor Migration to the United States. Westport, CT, Greenwood Press, 1978, 378p.

2027
Halsell, Grace
The Illegals. New York, Stein & Day, 1978, 216p.

2028
Alba, Francisco
"Mexico's International Migration as a Manifestation of its Development Pattern." *International Migration Review* (12: 4), Winter 1978, pp. 502-513.

2029
Bach, Robert L.
"Mexican Immigration and the American State." *International Migration Review* (12: 4), Winter 1978, pp. 536-558.

2030
Castillo, Leonel J.
"Dealing With the Undocumented Alien: an Interim Approach." *International Migration Review* (12: 4), Winter 1978, pp. 570-577.

2031
Chapman, Murray
"On the Cross-Cultural Study of Circulation." *International Migration Review* (12: 4), Winter 1978, pp. 559-569.

2032
Dinerman, Ina R.
"Patterns of Adaptation Among Households of U.S.-Bound Migrants From Michoacán, Mexico." *International Migration Review* (12: 4), Winter 1978, pp. 485-501.

2033
"Illegal Mexican Immigrants to the United States." *International Migration Review,* Winter 1978, entire issue.

2034
Jenkins, J. C.
"The Demand for Immigrant Workers: Labor Scarcity or Social Control?" *International Migration Review* 12, Winter 1978, pp. 514-535.

2035
Bustamante, Jorge A.
"Emigración Indocumentada a los Estados Unidos." México, *Foro Internacional* 18, January-March 1978, pp. 430-463.

2036
Cornelius, Wayne A.
"La Migración Ilegal Mexicana a los Estados Unidos . . ." México, *Foro Internacional* 18, January-March 1978, pp. 399-429.

2037
Reubens, Edwin P.
"Aliens, Jobs and Immigration Policy." *Public Interest* 51, Spring 1978, pp. 113-134.

2038
Rochin, Refugio I.
"Illegal Aliens in Agriculture: Some Theoretical Considerations." *Labor Law Journal* 29, March 1978, pp. 149-167.

2039
Kelly, Philip L.
Illegal Mexican Aliens in Southern Colorado: a Sampling of Their Views on Living and Working in the U.S. and Mexico. Paper Presented at the Annual Meeting of the Rocky Mountain Council for Latin American Studies, El Paso, Texas, May 3-5, 1978. (ED 215 797).

2040
Mumme, Stephen P.
"Mexican Politics and the Prospects for Emigration Policy: a Policy Prospective." *Inter-American Economic Affairs* 32, Summer 1978, pp. 67-94.

2041
Hirschman, Charles
"Prior U.S. Residence Among Mexican Immigrants." *Social Forces* 56, June 1978, pp. 1179-1202.

2042
Cornelius, Wayne A.
Mexican Migration to the United States: Causes, Consequences and U.S. Responses. Cambridge, Massachusetts Institute of Technology, Center for International Studies, Migration & Development Study Group (Monograph 78/9), July 1978, 124p.

2043
Portes, Alejandro, et al.
"Immigrant Aspirations." *Sociology of Education* 51, October 1978, pp. 241-260.

2044
Illegal Aliens: Problems and Policies. Washington, American Enterprise Institute for Public Policy Research, October 18, 1978, 33p.

2045
Reubens, Edwin P.
"Illegal Immigration and the Mexican Economy." *Challenge* 21, November 1978, pp. 13-19.

2046
Baird, Peter, & McCaughan, Ed
Beyond the Border: Mexico and the U.S. Today . . . New York, North American Congress on Latin America, 1979, 205p.

2047
Bustamante, Jorge A.
"Immigrants From Mexico: the Silent Invasion" (In Bryce-Laporte, Roy S., ed. *Sourcebook on the New Immigration.* New Brunswick, N.J., Transaction Books, 1979, pp. 140-145).

2048
Cornelius, Wayne A.
"Mexican Immigration: Causes and Consequences for Mexico " (In Bryce-Laporte, Roy S., ed. *Sourcebook on New Immigration*. New Brunswick, N.J., Transaction Books, 1979, pp. 69-84).

2049
Ehrlich, Paul R., et al.
The Golden Door: International Migration, Mexico and the United States. New York, Ballantine Books, 1979, 402p.

2050
Heer, David M.
"What is the Annual Net Flow of Undocumented Mexican Immigrants to the United States?" *Demography* 16, 1979, pp. 417-423.

2051
Iowa. Governor's Spanish-Speaking Task Force
Conóceme en Iowa; the Official Report of the Governor's Spanish-Speaking Task Force. Des Moines, Iowa, The Task Force, 1979, 117p.

2052
Martin, Philip L., & Richards, Alan
"International Migration of Labor: Boon or Bane?" (In Lucas, Robert E.B., ed. *International Migration: Causes, Consequences, Evaluation and Policies*. (Working Paper #26). Boston, Boston University African Studies Center, 1979, pp. 4-9).

2053
Pierri, Ettore
Braceros: la Frontera Explosiva. 2d ed. México, Eds. Mexicanos Unidos, 1979, 194p.

2054
Rivera, Julius
"The Mexican Illegal Alien and the U.S. Border Community" (In Bryce-Laporte, Roy S., ed. *Sourcebook on the New Immigration*. New Brunswick, N.J., Transaction Books, 1979, pp. 239-244).

2055
Rivera, R.
"Apple Pickers, Many Called . . . few Chosen." *NACLA Report on the Americas* (13: 1), January 1979, p. 44- .

2056
Abrams, E.
"The Myth of the Illegal Alien Crisis." *Journal of the Institute of Socioeconomic Studies* (4: 1), Spring 1979, pp. 27-35.

2057
Evans, John S., & James, Dilmus D.
"Conditions of Employment and Income Distribution in Mexico as Incentives for Mexican Migration to the United States: Prospects to the end of the Century." *International Migration Review* (13: 1), Spring 1979, pp. 4-24.

2058
Hansen, Niles
"International Labor Migration: Europe's Guest Worker Policies and Mexican in the United States." *Growth and Change* 10, April 1979, pp. 2-8.

2059
Portes, Alejandro
"Illegal Immigration and the International System, Lessons From Recent Legal Mexican Immigrants to the United States." *Social Problems* 26, April 1979, pp. 425-438.

2060
Graham, Otis L., Jr.
"Illegal Immigration and the new Restrictionism." *Center Magazine* 12, May 1979, pp. 54-64.

2061
McWilliams, Carey
"Mexico's Needy Neighbor." London, *New Statesman* 97, May 11, 1979, pp. 679-681.

2062
Salcido, Ramón M.
"Undocumented Aliens: a Study of Mexican Families." *Social Work* 24, July 1979, pp. 306-311.

2063
Bustamante, Jorge A., & Martinez, Gerónimo G.
"Undocumented Immigration From Mexico: Beyond Borders but Within Systems." *Journal of International Affairs* 33, Fall/Winter 1979, pp. 265-284.

2064
"Migrant Machines." *NACLA Report on the Americas* (13: 6), November 1979, p. 34-   .

2065
Newton, John R., & Osborn, T. N.
"A Profile of Legal Mexican Migration to the United States" (In Poulson, Barry W., & Osborn, T.N., eds. *United States-Mexico Economic Relations*. Boulder, CO, Westview Press, 1979, pp. 261-272).

2066
Cardoso, Lawrence A.
Mexican Emigration to the United States, 1897-1931; Socioeconomic Patterns. Tucson, University of Arizona Press, 1980, 192p.

2067
Coronado, Richard J.
A Conceptual Model of the Harvest Labor Market, the Bracero Program, and Factors Involved in Organization Among Farm Workers in California, 1946-1970. Notre Dame, Indiana, 1980, 434p. (Ph.D. Dissertation, University of Notre Dame)

2068
Diez-Canedo Ruiz, Juan
A new View of Mexican Migration to the United States. Cambridge, MA 1980. (Ph.D. Dissertation, Massachusetts Institute of Technology)

2069
García, Juan R.
Operation Wetback: the Mass Deportation of Mexican Undocumented Workers in 1954. Westport, CT, Greenwood Press, 1980, 268p.

2070
García y Griego, Manuel
El Volumen de la Migración de Mexicanos no Documentados los Estados Unidos: Nuevas Hipótesis. México, Centro Nacional de Información y Estadísticas del Trabajo, 1980, 659p.

2071
Hinojosa, José R.
Discretionary Authority over Immigration: an Analysis of Immigration Policy and Administration Toward Mexico. Notre Dame, IN, 1980, 281p. (Ph.D. Dissertation, University of Notre Dame).

2072
México. Central Nacional de Información y Estadística del Trabajo
Encuesta Nacional de Emigración a la Frontera Norte del País y a los Estados Unidos. México, Secretaría del Trabajo y Previsión Social, 1980.

2073
Pedraza-Bailey, Silvia
Political and Economic Migrants in America: Cubans and Mexicans. Chicago, 1980. (Ph.D. Dissertation, University of Chicago)

2074
Reichert, Joshua S., & Massey, Douglas S.
Guestworker Programs: Evidence From Europe and the United States, and Some Implications for U.S. Policy. (Working Paper #1). Berkeley, University of California, Institute of International Studies, Program in Population Research, 1980? 30p.

2075
Roberts, Kenneth D.
Agrarian Structure and Labor Migration in Rural Mexico: the Case of Circular Migration of Undocumented Workers to the United States. Madison, WI, 1980, 301p. (Ph.D. Dissertation, University of Wisconsin-Madison)

2076
U.S. Commission on Civil Rights. Texas Advisory Committee
Sin Papeles: the Undocumented in Texas, a Report. Washington, January 1980, 68p. (S/N 005-000-00230-3).

2077
U.S. Library of Congress. Congressional Research Service
Temporary Worker Programs: Background and Issues: a Report, prepared by Joyce Vialet, and Barbara McClure. Senate Report 55-752, 96th Congress, 2d session; Committee Print. Washington, GPO, 1980, 144p. (Y4. J 89/2: W 89/3). (S/N 052-070-05222-8).

2078
Reichert, Joshua S., & Massey, Douglas S.
"History and Trends in U.S.-Bound Migration From a Mexican Town." *International Migration Review* (14: 4), Winter 1980, pp. 475-491.

2079
Dominguez, Miguel
"Los Indocumentados en los Estados Unidos: una Perspectiva Chicana." *Mexico, Problemas del Desarrollo* (11: 41), January-April 1980, pp. 205-211.

2080
Martin, Philip L., & Sehgal, Ellen B.
"Illegal Immigration: the Guestworker Option." *Public Policy* 28, Spring 1980, pp. 207-229.

2081
Parrilla Bonilla, Antulio
"El Trabajo de los Latinoamericanos en los Estados Unidos." Barranquilla, Colombia, *Desarrollo Indoamericano* (15: 61), August 1980, pp. 41-42.

2082
Pfeffer, M.
"Mexican Workers in California." *Insurgent Sociologist* (10: 2), Fall 1980, p. 25-   .

2083
Teitelbaum, Michael S.
"Right vs. Right: Immigration and Refugee Policy in the United States." *Foreign Affairs* (59: 1), Fall 1980, pp. 21-59.

2084
Perspectives on Undocumented Workers: Black and Hispanic Viewpoints.
Washington, National Council of La Raza, prepared in 1979, updated September 1980, 39p.

2085
Miller, Hubert J.
Mexican Migration to the United States, 1900-1920, With a Focus on the Texas Lower Rio Grande Valley. Paper Presented at the LASA Meeting, Bloomington, Indiana, October 17, 1980, 33p. (ED 220 223).

2086
Mines, Richard A.
"Las Animas, California": *a Case Study of International Network Village Migration.* Berkeley, CA, 1980, 205p. (Ph.D. Dissertation, University of California, Berkeley)

2087
Arias, Armando A., Jr.
Undocumented Mexicans: a Study in the Social Psychology of Clandestine Migration to the United States. San Diego, 1981, 380p. (Ph.D. Dissertation, University of California, San Diego)

2088
Belsasso, G.
"Undocumented Mexican Workers in the United States: a Mexican Perspective" (In McBride, R. H., ed. *Mexico and the United States.* Englewood Cliffs, N.J., Prentice-Hall, 1981, pp. 128-157).

2089
Cornelius, Wayne A.
The Future of Mexican Immigrants in California: a new Perspective for Public Policy. La Jolla, Center for U.S.-Mexican Studies, University of California, San Diego, 1981, 73p. (RR 6).

2090
Cornelius, Wayne A.
"Immigration, Mexican Development Policy, and the Future of U.S.-Mexican Relations" (In McBride, R. H., ed. *Mexico and the United States.* Englewood Cliffs, N.J., Prentice-Hall, 1981, pp. 104-127).

2091
Cornelius, Wayne A.
Legalizing the Flow of Temporary Migrant Workers From Mexico: a Policy Proposal. La Jolla, Center for U.S.-Mexican Studies, University of California, San Diego, 1981, 17p. (RR 7)

2092
Cornelius, Wayne A.
Mexican Migration to the United States: the Limits of Government Intervention. La Jolla, Center for U.S.-Mexican Studies, University of California, San Diego, 1981, 11p. (RR 5)

2093
Craig, Ann L.
Mexican Immigration: Changing Terms of the Debate in the United States and Mexico. La Jolla, Center for U.S.-Mexican Studies, University of California, San Diego, 1981, 29p. (RR 4)

2094
Garcia y Griego, Manuel
The Importation of Mexico Contract Laborers to the United States, 1942-1964: Antecedents, Operations and Legacy. La Jolla, Center for U.S.-Mexican Studies, University of California, San Diego, 1981, 59p. (RR 11)

2095
Gonzalez, Rosalinda (Mendez)
Capital Accumulation and Mexican Immigration to the United States: a Comparative Historical Study of the Political Economy of International Labor Migrations. Irvine, CA, 1981, 467p. (Ph.D. Dissertation, University of California, Irvine)

2096
Haas, Lisbeth
The Bracero in Orange County, California: a Work Force for Economic Transition. La Jolla, Center for U.S.-Mexican Studies, University of California, San Diego, 1981, 54p. (RR 29)

2097
Johnson, Kenneth F., & Williams, M. W.
Illegal Aliens in the Western Hemisphere; Political and Economic Factors. New York, Praeger, 1981, 207p.

2098
Kazemi-Aalam, Behnam
Management and Organizational Development: Mexican Labor Force in San Diego. San Diego, 1981. (Ph.D. Dissertation, U.S. International University)

2099
Kessner, T., & Caroli, B. B.
Today's Immigrants, Their Stories: a new Look at the Newest Americans. New York, Oxford University Press, 1981, 317p.

2100
Mines, Richard A.
Developing a Community Tradition of Migration: A Field Study in Rural Zacatecas, Mexico and California Settlement Areas. La Jolla, Center for U.S.-Mexican Studies, University of California, San Diego, 1981, 219p. (M 3).

2101
North, David S.
"The Migration in U.S.-Mexican Relations" (In Erb, Richard D., & Ross, Stanley R., eds. *United States Relations With Mexico; Context and Content.* Washington, American Enterprise Institute for Public Policy Research, 1981, pp. 121-134).

2102
North, David S., & Wagner, J. R.
"Illegal Migrants in North America." (In *International Population Conference: Solicited Papers/Congrès Internade la Population: Communications Solicitées, Manila, 1981.* Liège, Belgium, International Union for the Scientific Study of Population; v. 2. 1981, pp. 473-489).

2103
Sain, Gustavo E.
A Migration Model of Undocumented Mexican Workers. Davis, CA, 1981, 157p. (Ph.D. Dissertation, University of California, Davis)

2104
Sandos, J. A., & Cross, H. E.
National Development and International Labor Migration: Mexico, 1940-1965. (PDP Worker Paper Series, #18). Washington, Battelle Human Affairs Research Center, Population & Development Policy Program, 1981, 26p.

2105
Schaeffer, Peter V.
Temporary International Labor Migration. Los Angeles, 1981. (Ph.D. Dissertation, University of Southern California)

2106
Shafer, Robert J.
Neighbors—Mexico and the United States: Wetbacks and oil. Chicago, Nelson-Hall, 1981, 241p.

2107
Stuart, James, & Kearney, Michael
   Causes and Effects of Agricultural Labor Migration From the Mixteca of Oaxaca to California. La Jolla, Center for U.S.-Mexican Studies, University of California, San Diego, 1981, 39p. (RR28).

2108
Weintraub, Sidney, & Ross, Stanley R.
   "The Illegal Alien From Mexico" (In Erb, Richard D., & Ross, Stanley R., eds. *United States Relations With Mexico; Context and Content.* Washington, American Enterprise Institute for Public Policy Research, 1981, pp. 135-154).

2109
Baca, Reynaldo, & Bryan, Dexter
   "Mexican Undocumented Workers in the Binational Community: a Research Note." *International Migration Review* 15, Winter 1981, pp. 737-748.

2110
McPheters, Lee R., & Schlagenhauf, Don E.
   "Macroeconomic Determinants of the Flow of Undocumented Aliens in North America." *Growth and Change* (12: 1), January 1981, pp. 2-8.

2111
Sanderson, Steven E.
   "Florida Tomatoes, U.S.-Mexican Relations, and the International Division of Labor." *Inter-American Economic Affairs* (35: 3), Winter 1981, pp. 23-52.

2112
Reichert, Joshua S.
   "The Migrant Syndrome: Seasonal U.S. Wage Labor and Rural Development in Central Mexico." *Human Organization* (40: 1), Spring 1981, pp. 56-66.

2113
U.S. Select Commission on Immigration & Refugee Policy
   U.S. Immigration Policy and the National Interest. Washington, 11 volumes, 1981- .
(See Appendix B: Papers on International Migration. 1981; Appendix E: Papers on Undocumented/Illegal Migration to the United States, 1981; Appendix F: Papers on Temporary Workers. April 1981, 36p.; Appendix I: Summary of Commission Recommendations and Votes. April 1981, 139p.).

2114
Cuthbert, Richard W., & Stevens, Joe B.
"Net Economic Incentive for Illegal Mexican Migration: a Case Study." *International Migration Review* 15, Fall 1981, pp. 543-550.

2115
McCrea, Joan M.
"Illegal Labor Migration From Mexico to the United States." Geneva, *Labour & Society* 6, October/December 1981, pp. 355-373.

2116
Bustamente, Jorge A.
"One More Time/the Undocumented." *Radical America* (15: 6), November 1981, p. 7- .

2117
Omi, M.
"New Wave Dread/Immigration." *Socialist Review* 60, November 1981, p. 77- .

2118
Bustamante, Jorge A.
"Facts, Perceptions, and the Issue of Undocumented Immigration" (In Montgomery, Tommy S., ed. *Mexico Today.* Philadelphia, Institute for the Study of Human Issues, 1982, pp. 115-119).

2119
Cornelius, Wayne A.
America in the era of Limits: Nativists Reactions to the 'new' Immigration. La Jolla, Center for U.S.-Mexican Studies, University of California, San Diego, 1982, 31p. (RR 3).

2120
Cornelius, Wayne A., et al.
Mexican Immigrants and Southern California: a Summary of Current Knowledge. La Jolla, CA, Center for U.S.-Mexican Studies (Research Report Series), University of California, San Diego, 1982, 36p.

2121
Cornelius, Wayne A., et al., eds.
Mexican Immigrants and Southern California: a Summary of Current Knowledge. La Jolla, Center for U.S.-Mexican Studies, University of California, San Diego, 1982, 99p. (RR 36).

2122
Dixon, Marlene, & Jonas, S., eds.
The new Nomads; From Immigrant Labor to Transnational Working Class. San Francisco, Synthesis Publications, 1982, 165p.

2123
Flores, Estevan T.
Post-Bracero Undocumented Mexican Immigration to the United States and Political Recomposition. Austin, TX, 1982, 243p. (Ph.D. Dissertation, University of Texas at Austin)

2124
Morris, M. D., & Mayo, A.
Curbing Illegal Immigration; a Staff Paper. Washington, The Brookings Institution, 1982, 38p.

2125
Torok, Steven J.
International Trade in Commodities and Labor: the Case of the Importation of Mexican Agricultural Labor and Fresh Market Winter Tomatoes Into the United States, 1964-1979. Ames, Iowa, 1982, 164p. (Ph.D. Dissertation, Iowa State University)

2126
U.S. Senate. Committee on the Judiciary. Subcommittee on Immigration and Refugee Policy
Temporary Workers; Hearing Before the Subcommittee on Immigration and Refugee Policy of the Committee on the Judiciary, U.S. Senate, 97th Congress, First Session, on a new Temporary Worker Program with Mexico, October 22, 1981. Washington, GPO, 1982, 285p. (Y4J.89/2:J-97-95).

2127
Weist, Raymond E.
"Implications of International Labor Migration for Mexican Rural Development" (In Camara, Fernando, and Kemper, Robert V., eds. *Migration Across Frontiers: Mexico and the United States.* Albany, N.Y., Institute for Meso-American Studies, State University of New York, 1982, pp. 85-97).

2128
Howell, Frances (Baseden)
"Split Labor Market: Mexican Farm Workers in the Southwest." *Sociological Inquiry* 52, Spring 1982, pp. 132-140.

2129
Jones, Richard D.
"Undocumented Migration From Mexico: Some Geographical Questions." *Annals of the Association of American Geographers* 72, March 1982, pp. 77-87.

2130
Weintraub, Sidney, & Ross, Stanley R.
"Poor United States, so Close to Mexico." *Across the Board* 19, March 1982, pp. 54-61.

2131
Emerson, R. D.
"Trade in Products and International Migration in Seasonal Labor Markets." *American Journal of Agricultural Economics* 64, May 1982, pp. 339-346.

2132
"International Trade Agricultural Labor Markets: Farm Policy as Quasi-Adjustment." *American Journal of Agricultural Economics* 64, May 1982, pp. 355-362.

2133
Cockroft, James D.
"Mexican Migration, Crisis and the Internationalization of Labor Struggle." *Contemporary Marxism,* Summer 1982, pp. 48-66.

2134
Cornelius, Wayne A.
"Interviewing Undocumented Immigrants: Methodological Reflections Based on Fieldwork in Mexico and the United States." *International Migration Review* (16: 2), Summer 1982, pp. 378-411.

2135
Mines, Richard, & de Janvry, A.
"Migration to the United States and Mexican Rural Development: a Case Study." *American Journal of Agricultural Economics* 64, August 1982, pp. 444-454.

2136
Huffman, W. E.
"International Trade in Labor vs. Commodities: U.S.-Mexican Agriculture." *American Journal of Agricultural Economics* 64, December 1982, pp. 989-998.

2137
Anzaldua Montoya, Ricardo, & Cornelius, Wayne A., eds.
The Report of the U.S. Select Commission on Immigration and Refugee Policy: a Critical Analysis. La Jolla, CA, Center for U.S.-Mexican Studies, University of California, San Diego, 1983, 34p.

2138
Arizpe, Lourdes
"The Rural Exodus in Mexico and Mexican Migration to the United States" (In Brown, Peter G., & Shue, Henry, eds. *The Border That Joins.* Totowa, N.J., Rowman and Littlefield, 1983, 264p.).

2139
Bustamante, Jorge A.
"Mexicans are Coming: From Ideology to Labor Relations." *International Migration Review* (17: 2), 1983, pp. 323-341.

2140
Grindle, Merillee S., ed.
Issues in U.S.-Mexican Agricultural Relations: a Binational Consultation. La Jolla, Center for U.S.-Mexican Studies, University of California, San Diego, 1983, 62p. (M 8).

2141
Lever-Tracy, C.
"Immigrant Workers Postwar Capitalis." *Politics and Society* (12: 2), 1983, p. 127- .

2142
Massey, Douglas S., & Schnabel, Kathleen M.
"Recent Trends in Hispanic Immigration to the United States." *International Migration Review* (17:2), 1983, pp. 212-244.

2143
Sanderson, Steven E.
Trade Aspects of the Internationalization of Mexican Agriculture: Consequences for Mexico's Food Crisis. La Jolla, Center for U.S.-Mexican Studies, University of California, San Diego, 1983, 84p. (M 10).

2144
Bean, Frank D., et al.
"The Number of Illegal Migrants of Mexican Origin in the United States: Sex Ratio-Based Estimates for 1980." *Demography* 20, February 1983, pp. 99-109.

2145
Hayakawa, S. I.
"On Immigration Law Reform." *Inter-American Economic Affairs* 36, Spring 1983, pp. 85-89.

2146
"U.S. Group Helps Migrant Laborers Build Future in Mexico." *Latin American Times,* April 23, 1983, section I, p. 1, c. 1.

2147
Bradshaw, Benjamin S., & Frisbie, W. P.
"Potential Labor Force Supply and Replacement in Mexico and the States of the Mexican Cession and Texas: 1980-2000." *International Migration Review* 17, Fall 1983, pp. 394-409.

2148
Simon, Julian L.
Nine Myths About Immigration. Washington, The Heritage Foundation, 1984, 14p.

2149
Torok, Steven J.
"The Distribution of Illegal Mexican Aliens Employed in U.S. Agriculture" (In *Proceedings of the Annual Meeting of the Rocky Mountain Council on Latin American Studies, Tucson, Arizona, February 23-25, 1984.* Las Cruces, N.M., Center for Latin American Studies, New Mexico State University, 1984).

2150
Mines, Richard, & Martin, Philip L.
"Immigrant Workers and the California Citrus Industry." *Industrial Relations* 23, Winter 1984, pp. 139-149.

C. MEXICAN-AMERICAN FARM LABOR

1. Bibliographies

2151
Pan American Union. Division of Labor and Social Information
   Mexicans in the United States; a Bibliography. Washington (Bibliographical Series, #27), 1942, 14p.

2152
Gilbert, William H.
   Mexican Americans and Mexicans in the United States Since 1945: Selected References. Washington, Legislative Reference Service, Library of Congress, 1965, 5p.

2153
California. University. University at Los Angeles. Mexican-American Study Project
   Bibliography, Prepared by the Staff. Los Angeles, 1966, 101p.

2154
California. San Fernando Valley State College. Library
   Black, Brown Bibliography. Northridge, CA, 1968? 86p.

2155
Strange, Susan, & Priest, Rhea (Pendergrass)
   Bibliography: the Mexican-American in the Migrant Labor Setting. East Lansing, Rural Manpower Center, Michigan State University, 1968, 27p. (ED 032 188).

2156
Meier, Matt S., & Rivera, Feliciano
   A Bibliography for Chicano History. San Francisco, R & E Research Associates, 1972, 96p.

2157
Gomez-Quiñones, Juan, & Nelson Cisneros, Victor B.
Selective Bibliography on Chicano Labor Materials. Los Angeles, Aztlan Publications, 1974, 29p.

2158
Saucedo, Ramedo J.
Mexican-Americans in Minnesota; an Introduction to Historical Sources. St. Paul, Minnesota Historical Society, 1977, 26p.

2159
Stark, Greg, et al.
Annotated Bibliography of Recent Research on Chicanos and Latinos in Minnesota. Minneapolis, Center for Urban and Regional Affairs, University of Minnesota (Report #CURA 80-1), 1980, 50p.

2. Circulating Materials

2160
Nebraska. Mexican-American Commission
Annual Report of the Executive Director. Lincoln [n.d.], annual.

2161
Hittell, John S.
"Mexican Land-Claims in California." *Hutchings' Illustrated California Magazine* 2, July 1857, pp. 442-448.

2162
Hayes, J.
"Farming in Pajaro Valley." *Overland Monthly* 5, 1870, p. 345.

2163
Hall, Federic (1825-1898)
The History of San Jose and Surroundings . . . San Francisco, A. L. Bancroft & Co., 1871, 537p.

2164
Blackmar, Frank W.
Spanish Colonization in the Southwest. Baltimore, Johns Hopkins University (Studies in Historical & Political Science, 8th Series, IV), 1890, 79p.

2165
Harby, Lee (Cohen)
"Texas Types and Contrasts." *Harper's Monthly* 81, July 1890, pp. 229-246.

2166

Lowery, Woodbury
The Spanish Settlements Within the Present Limits of the United States, 1513-1561. New York, Putnam's, 1901, 515p.

2167

Twitchell, Ralph E.
The Leading Facts of New Mexican History. Cedar Rapids, Iowa, Torch Press, 1911-1917, 5v.

2168

McEuen, William W.
A Survey of the Mexicans in Los Angeles. Los Angeles, 1914, 103p. (Master's Thesis, University of Southern California)

2169

Heald, Josiah H.
"Mexicans in the Southwest." *Missionary Review of the World* 42, November 1919, pp. 860-865.

2170

Interchurch World Movement of North America
The Mexican in Los Angeles: Los Angeles City Survey. New York? 1920, 20p.

2171

Bolton, Herbert E.
The Spanish Borderlands. New Haven, Yale University Press, 1921, 320p.

2172

Stowell, Jay S.
The Near Side of the Mexican Question. New York, Doran, 1921, 123p.

2173

Harris, Townes M.
The Labor Supply of Texas. Austin, TX, 1922, 115 & 3pp. (Master's Thesis, University of Texas at Austin)

2174

Hackett, Charles W.
Historical Documents Relating to New Mexico . . . Washington, Carnegie Institution of Washington, 1923-1937.

2175

Lofstedt, Christine
"The Mexican Population of Pasadena." *Journal of Applied Sociology* 7, May 1923, pp. 260-268.

2176
Sullenger, T. E.
"The Mexican Population of Omaha." *Journal of Applied Sociology* 7,
May 1924, pp. 289-293.

2177
Crawford, Polly P.
The Beginnings of Spanish Settlement of the Lower Rio Grande Valley.
Austin, TX, 1925, 165p. (Master's Thesis, University of Texas at Austin)

2178
Twitchell, Ralph E.
Old Santa Fe; the Story of New Mexico's Ancient Capital. Santa Fe,
New Mexican Pub. Corp., 1925, 488p.

2179
Gwin, Joseph B.
"Social Problems of our Mexican Population" (In National Conference
of Social Work. *Proceedings, 1926.* Chicago, 1926, pp. 327-332).

2180
Henderson, Mary V.
Minor Empresario Grants in Texas, 1825-1834. Austin, TX, 1926, 4 &
113p. (Master's Thesis, University of Texas at Austin)

2181
Cheetham, Francis T.
"The Early Settlements of Southern Colorado." *Colorado Magazine* 5,
1928, pp. 1-8.

2182
Fuller, Roden
"Occupations of the Mexican-Born Population of Texas, New Mexico
and Arizona, 1900-1920." *American Statistical Association Journal* 23,
1928, pp. 64-74.

2183
Goldthorp, Audrey G.
Castro's Colony. Austin, TX, 1928, 133p. (Master's Thesis, University
of Texas at Austin)

2184
Walker, Helen W.
*The Conflict of Cultures in First Generation Mexicans in Santa Ana,
California.* Los Angeles, 1928, 99p. (Master's Thesis, University of
Southern California)

2185
Goethe, C. M.
"Other Aspects of the Problem." *Current History* 28, August 1928, pp.
766-768.

2186

Bresette, Linna E.
Mexicans in the United States; a Report of a Brief Survey . . . Washington, National Catholic Welfare Conference, 1929? 45p.

2187

Galarza, Ernesto
"Life in the U.S. for Mexican People: Out of the Experience of a Mexican" (In National Conference of Social Work. *Proceedings, 1929.* Chicago, University of Chicago Press, 1929, pp. 399-404).   *done?*

2188

Mangold, George B., & Thompson, S. Lucile
Community Welfare in San Diego. A Survey Conducted Under the Joint Auspices of the Community Welfare Council of San Diego, San Diego County Welfare Commission, and City of San Diego. (San Diego, Printed by Dove & Robinson, 1929?), 205p.

2189

Stacey, May (Humphreys), 1837-1886
Uncle Sam's Camels (his Journal); Supplemented by the Report of Edward Fitzgerald Beale (1857-1868). Ed. by Lewis B. Lesley. Cambridge, Harvard University Press, 1929, 298p.

2190

Myers, C. M.
"The Mexican Problem in Mason City (Iowa)." *Journal of History & Politics* 27, April 1929, pp. 227-243.

2191

Gonzalez, Jovita
Social Life in Cameron, Starr and Zapata Counties. Austin, TX, 1930, 9 & 112p. (Master's Thesis, University of Texas at Austin)

2192

Lockwood, Frank C., & Page, Donald W.
Tucson, the old Pueblo. Phoenix, Manufacturing Stationers, Inc., 1930, 94p.

2193

Santiago, Hazel D.
"The Mexican Influence in Southern California." *Sociology & Sociological Research* 16, September 1931, pp. 68-74.

2194

Allen, Ruth A.
"Mexican Peon Women in Texas." *Sociology & Social Research,* November-December 1931, pp. 131-142.

2195
Howard, Donald S.
A Study of the Mexican, Mexican-American and Spanish-American Population in Pueblo, Colorado, 1929-1930. Denver, CO, 1932. (Master's Thesis, University of Denver)

2196
Lockwood, Frank C.
Pioneer Days in Arizona, From the Spanish Occupation to Statehood. New York, Macmillan, 1932, 387p.

2197
Lopez, Espiridion B.
The History of the California State Federation of Labor. Los Angeles, 1932. (Master's Thesis, University of Southern California)

2198
California. University. University at Berkeley
Cost of Living Studies, V: How Mexicans Earn and Live: a Study of the Incomes and Expenditures of 100 Mexican Families in San Diego, California. (Prepared by the Heller Committee for Research in Social Economics, University of California, and Constantine Panunzio). Berkeley (Publications in Economics, volume 13, #1), 1933, 114p.

2199
Taylor, Paul S.
American-Mexican Frontier, Nueces County, Texas. Chapel Hill, N.C., University of North Carolina Press, 1934, 337p.

2200
Heilbron, Carl H., ed.
History of San Diego County. San Diego, San Diego Press Club, 1936, 2v.

2201
Lummis, Charles F.
The Spanish Pioneers and the California Missions. New & enl. ed. Chicago, McClurg, 1936, 343p.

2202
Schrieke, B.
"Mexicans and Indians" (In his: *Alien Americans.* New York, Viking Press, 1936, pp. 46-69).

2203
California. Dept. of Industrial Relations. Division of Immigration and Housing
Testimony of Carey McWilliams, Chief of the Division of Immigration and Housing, 1939-1942. [Sacramento, 1939-42] 1v.

2204
Montiel Olvera, J., ed.
Year Book of the Latin American Population of Texas. Mexico, J. Montiel Olvera, 1939, 71 & 20pp.

2205
Tenayuca, Emma, & Brooks, Homer
"The Mexican Question in the Southwest." *Communist* 18, March 1939, pp. 257-268.

2206
Walter, Paul
"The Spanish-Speaking Community in New Mexico." *Sociology & Social Research* 24, November-December 1939, pp. 150-157.

2207
Davis, Edward E.
"Peons" (In *The White Scourge.* San Antonio, Naylor, 1940, pp. 166-175).

2208
Donnelly, Thomas C., ed.
Rocky Mountain Politics. Albuquerque, University of New Mexico Press, 1940, 304p.

2209
Hinojosa, Federico A.
El México de Afuera. San Antonio, TX, Artes Gráficas, 1940, 71p.

2210
Sanchez, George I.
Forgotten People; a Study of New Mexicans. Albuquerque, University of New Mexico Press, 1940, 98p.

2211
U.S. Works Progress Administration
The Pecan Shellers of San Antonio. The Problem of Underpaid and Unemployed Mexican Labor, by Selden C. Menefee and Orin C. Cassmore. Washington, GPO, 1940.

2212
Tetreau, Elzer D. J.
Arizona's Agricultural Population. Tucson, University of Arizona, College of Agriculture, Agricultural Experiment Station, Technical Bulletin #88, December 15, 1940, 92p.

2213
U.S. Bureau of the Census
Sixteenth Census of the United States: 1940 Population. Population of Spanish Mother Tongue: 1940. (Series P-15, #1). Washington, GPO, 1942, 3p.

2214
California. Dept. of Industrial Relations. Division of Immigration and Housing
Proposal in re Farm Labor Authority, prepared by Carey McWilliams. Los Angeles, 1942, 9p.

2215
McNaughton, Donald A.
A Social Study of Mexican and Spanish-American Wage Earners in Delta, Colorado. Boulder, CO, 1942. (Master's Thesis, University of Colorado)

2216
Johannsen, Sigurd A.
"The Social Organization of Spanish-American Villages." *Southwestern Social Science Quarterly* 23, September 1942, pp. 151-159.

2217
Harper, Allan G., et al.
Man and Resources in the Rio Grande Valley. Albuquerque, University of New Mexico Press, 1943, 156p.

2218
King, John R.
An Inquiry Into the Status of Mexican Segregation in Metropolitan Bakersfield. Claremont, CA, 1946. (Master's Thesis, Claremont Graduate School)

2219
Press, Ernest
The Mexican Population in Laramie. Laramie, 1946. (Master's Thesis, University of Wyoming)

2220
Sandoval, T. J.
A Study of Some Aspects of the Spanish-Speaking Population in Selected Communities in Wyoming. Laramie, Wyoming, 1946. (Master's Thesis, University of Wyoming)

2221
Luevansos, E. D.
"Mexican Neighbors." *Hispania* 29, August 1946, pp. 413-415.

2222
McKain, Walter C., Jr., & Miles, Sarah
"Santa Barbara County Between Two Social Orders." *California Historical Society Quarterly* 25, December 1946, pp. 311-318.

2223
Ginn, A.
Mexicans in Belvedere, California: the Social Implications. Los Angeles, 1947. (Master's thesis, University of Southern California)

2224
Walter, Paul
Population Trends of New Mexico. The People of New Mexico, by Ross Calvin. Albuquerque, Division of Research, Dept. of Government (Publication #100), University of New Mexico, 1947, 38p.

2225
Davis, J. S.
"American Agriculture; Schultz's Analysis and Policy Proposals." *Review of Economic Statistics* 29, May 1947, pp. 80-91.

2226
Hafen, Leroy R., ed.
Colorado and its People; a Narrative and Topical History of the Centennial State. New York, Lewis Historical Pub. Co., 1948, 4v.

2227
Minnesota. Governor's Human Rights Commission
Race Relations in Minnesota; Reports of the Commission. St. Paul, 1948, 4 parts in 1 volume.

2228
Wertenbaker, Green P.
America's Heartland: the Southwest. Norman, University of Oklahoma Press, 1948, 285p.

2229
Davie, M. R.
"Our Mexican Minority; Excerpt From World Immigration" (In Lee, Alfred M., & Lee, Elizabeth B., eds. *Social Problems in America; a Source Book.* New York, Holt, 1949, pp. 612-613).

2230
Mink, James V.
The Santa Inez Valley: a Regional Study in the History of Rural California. Los Angeles, 1949. (Master's Thesis, UCLA)

2231
Saunders, Lyle
The Spanish-Speaking Population of Texas; a Study of Spanish-Speaking People. Austin, University of Texas Press, 1949, 56p.

2232
Altus, William D.
"The American Mexican: the Survival of a Culture." *Journal of Social Psychology* (29: 220), May 1949, pp. 211-220.

2233
Nelson, Eastin, & Myers, Frederic
Labor Requirements and Labor Resources in the Lower Rio Grande Valley of Texas. (Inter-American Education, Occasional Papers, #VI). Austin, University of Texas, 1950, 33p.

2234
U.S. Dept. of Agriculture. Bureau of Agricultural Economics
The Agricultural Labor Force in the San Joaquin Valley, California, 1948; Characteristics, Employment, Mobility, by William H. Metzler and Afife F. Sayin. Washington, U.S. Dept. of Agriculture, Bureau of Agricultural Economics, cooperating with University of California, Institute of Industrial Relations, 1950, 73p.

2235
Wyllys, Rufus K.
Arizona: the History of a Frontier State. Phoenix, Hobson & Herr, 1950, 408p.

2236
Carter, Hugh, & Doster, Bernice
"Residence and Occupation of Naturalized Americans From Mexico." *Monthly Review* (U.S. Immigration and Naturalization Service), VIII, 1951, pp. 47-53.

2237
Flores, Raymond J.
The Socio-Economic Status Trend of the Mexican People Residing in Arizona. Tempe, AZ, 1951. (Master's Thesis, 1951)

2238
Shapiro, Harold A.
"The Pecan Shellers of San Antonio, Texas." *Southwestern Social Science Quarterly* 32, 1951-52, pp. 299-344.

2239
McWilliams, Carey
"The Forgotten Mexican" (In his, Brothers Under the Skin. Rev. ed. Boston, Little, Brown, 1951, pp. 113-139).

2240
Keleher, William A.
Turmoil in New Mexico, 1846-1868. Santa Fe, Rydal Press, 1952, 534p.

2241
Broom, Leonard, & Shevky, Eshref
"Mexicans in the United States: a Problem in Social Differentiation." *Sociology and Social Research* 36, January 1952, pp. 150-158.

2242
Ruiz, Ramón E.
"Hijos Olvidados. La Historia del Pueblo de Descendencia Mexicana en los Estados Unidos de Norteamérica." México, *América Indígena* (12: 2), April 1952, pp. 121-130.

2243
Kibbe, Pauline (Rochester)
"The Economic Plight of Mexicans" (In McDonagh, Edward. *Ethnic Relations in the United States.* New York, Appleton, 1953, pp. 189-199).

2244
Sargent, S. S.
"Class and Class Consciousness in a California Town." *Social Problems* 1, 1953, pp. 22-27.

2245
Scotford, John R.
Within These Borders: Spanish-Speaking Peoples in the USA. New York, Friendship Press, 1953, 151p.

2246
Ullman, Paul S.
An Ecological Analysis of Social Variables of Mexican-Americans in Los Angeles County. Los Angeles, 1953. (Master's Thesis, University of Southern California)

2247
Meyers, Frederic
"Employment and Relative Earnings of Spanish-Surname Persons in Texas Industries." *Southern Economic Journal* (19: 4), April 1953, pp. 494-507.

2248
Burnhill, James
"The Mexican People in the Southwest." *Political Affairs,* September 1953, pp. 43-53; December 1953, pp. 50-63.

2249
Brookshire, Marjorie
The Industrial Pattern of Mexican-American Employment in Nueces County, Texas. Austin, TX, 1954, 181p. (Ph.D. Dissertation, University of Texas at Austin)

2250
Burma, John H.
Spanish-Speaking Groups in the United States. Durham, Duke University Press, 1954, 214p.

2251
U.S. House. Committee on Agriculture *Mexican Farm Labor.* Hearings
  Before the Committee on Agriculture, House of Representatives, 83rd
Congress, 2nd Session, on H.J. Resolution 355. (Its Serial V). Washington, GPO, 1954, 239p.

2252
Brookshire, Marjorie
  "Some Notes on the Integration of Mexican-Americans Since 1929,
Nueces County, Texas." *Industrial Relations Research Association Annual Proceedings,* 1955, pp. 356-361.

2253
Kelley, Wilfrid D.
  "Settlement of the Middle Rio Grande Valley." *Journal of Geography*
54, 1955, pp. 287-399.

2254
McDonagh, Edward C.
  "Attitudes Toward Ethnic Farm Workers in Coachella Valley."
Sociology & Sociological Research 40, September 1955, pp. 10-18.

2255
Fuller, Varden
  *Domestic and Imported Workers in the Harvest Labor Market, Santa
Clara County, California, 1954.* Berkeley, University of California, Giannini Foundation of Agricultural Economics, 1956, 52p.

2256
Galarza, Ernesto
  Strangers in our Fields. Washington, Joint U.S.-Mexican Trade Union
Committee, 1956, 80p.

2257
Waldron, Gladys (Henning)
  Anti-Foreign Movements in California, 1919-1929. Los Angeles, 1956,
121p. (Master's Thesis, University of California, Berkeley)

2258
Keleher, William A.
  Violence in Lincoln County, 1869-1881; a New Mexico Item. Albuquerque, University of New Mexico Press, 1957, 390p.

2259
Day, James M.
  Jacob de Cordova: Land Merchant. Austin, TX, 1958, 145p. (Master's
Thesis, University of Texas at Austin)

2260
Gates, Paul W.
"Adjudication of Spanish Mexican Land Claims in California." *Huntington Library Quarterly* 3, May 1958, pp. 213-236.

2261
La Farge, Oliver
Santa Fe; the Autobiography of a Southwestern Town. Norman, University of Oklahoma Press, 1959, 436p.

2262
U.S. Dept. of Labor. Bureau of Labor Standards
State Committee on Seasonal Agricultural Labor, Their Organization and Programs. Washington, 1959- .

2263
Pitt, Leonard M.
Submergence of the Mexican in California, From 1846 to 1890: a History of Culture Conflict and Acculturation. Los Angeles, 1960. (Ph.D. Dissertation, UCLA)

2264
Ford, John A.
Thirty Explosive Years in Los Angeles County. San Marino, CA, Huntington Library, 1961, 232p.

2265
Knowlton, Clark
"The Spanish Americans in New Mexico." *Sociology & Social Research* 45, July 1961, pp. 448-454.

2266
Beck, Warren A.
New Mexico: a History of Four Centuries. Norman, University of Oklahoma Press, 1962, 363p.

2267
Keleher, William A.
The Fabulous Frontier; 12 New Mexico Items. Rev. ed. Albuquerque, University of New Mexico Press, 1962, 339p.

2268
Knowlton, Clark
"Patron-Peon Pattern Among the Spanish-Americans of New Mexico." *Social Forces* 41, October 1962, pp. 12-17.

2269
Leal Carrillo, Stella
Importancia Ecónomica y Social de la Población Mexicana en los Estados Unidos de Nortéamerica. México, 1963, 125p. (Thesis, National University of Mexico).

2270
Skrabanek, R. L.
A Decade of Population Change in Texas. College Station, TX, Texas Agricultural Experiment Station, Texas A & M University, 1963, 31p. (Bulletin 1000).

2271
U.S. Dept. of Agriculture. Economic Research Service
Economic, Social and Demographic Characteristics of Spanish-American Wage Workers on U.S. Farms. (Agriculture Report #27). Washington, GPO, 1963, 21p.

2272
Economic, Social and Demographic Characteristics of Spanish-American Wage Workers on U.S. Farms, by Reed E. Friend and Samuel Baum (Agricultural Economic Report, U.S. Dept. of Agriculture, Economic Research Service). Washington, GPO, March 1963, 21p. (A 93.28, #29).

2273
Friend, Reed E., & Baum, Samuel
Economic, Social, and Demographic Characteristics of Spanish-American Wage Workers on U.S. Farms. (Report AER-27, U.S. Dept. of Agriculture, Economic Research Service). March 1963, 26p. (ED 034 613).

2274
Barnes, Elinor, J.
"Arizona's People Since 1910." *Arizona Review of Business & Public Administration* 13, January 1964, pp. 3-10.

2275
Kuvlesky, William P., & Wright, David E.
Poverty in Texas: the Distribution of Low-Income Families. College Station, Texas, Texas A & M University, Dept. of Agricultural Economics and Sociology, 1965, 53p.

2276
Landolt, Robert G.
Mexican-American Workers of San Antonio. Austin, TX, 1965, 396p. (Ph.D. Dissertation, University of Texas at Austin)

2277
U.S. Dept. of Labor
Year of Transition, Seasonal Farm Labor, 1965; a Report From the Secretary of Labor. Washington, 1965, 1 volume.

2278
Faulk, Odie B.
"Ranching in Spanish Texas." *Hispanic American Historical Review* (XLV: 2), May 1965, pp. 257-266.

2279
Jones, Lamar B., & Christian, J. W.
"Some Observations on the Agricultural Labor Market." *Industrial and Labor Relations Review* 18, July 1965, pp. 522-534.

2280
Dvorin, Eugene P., & Misner, Arthur J., eds.
California Politics and Policies: Original Essays by Richard Harvey and Others. Reading, MA, Addison-Wesley, 1966, 419p.

2281
Moseley, Joseph E., comp.
The Spanish-Speaking People of the Southwest. [n.p.] Council on Spanish-American Work, 1966, 85p.

2282
Pitt, Leonard M.
The Decline of the Californios: a Social History of the Spanish-Speaking Californians, 1846-1890. Berkeley, University of California Press, 1966, 324p.

2283
Rapton, Avra
Seasonal Work Patterns of the Hired Farm Working Force of 1964. Washington, Economic Research Service, U.S. Dept. of Agriculture (Agricultural Economic Report #102); for sale by GPO, 1966, 29p.

2284
Rubel, Arthur J.
Across the Tracks; Mexican-Americans in a Texas City. Austin, Published for the Hogg Foundation for Mental Health, by the University of Texas Press, 1966, 266p.

2285
Simpson, Lesley B.
Many Mexicos. 4th ed. rev. Berkeley, University of California Press, 1966, 389p.

2286
Vassberg, David E.
The Use of Mexicans and Mexican-Americans as an Agricultural Work Force in the Lower Rio Grande Valley of Texas. Austin, TX, 1966, 110p. (Master's Thesis, University of Texas at Austin)

2287
Grebler, Leo, et al.
Mexican-American Study Project. Advance Report #2, Mexican Immigration to the United States—the Record and its Implications. (UCLA Mexican-American Study Project. Report #AR-2). January 1966, 158p. (ED 015 798).

2288
Mittelbach, Frank G., & Marshall, Grace
Mexican-American Study Project. Advance Report 5, the Burden of Poverty. (Report #AR-5). Division of Research, School of Business Administration, UCLA (Los Angeles, CA, 90024), July 1966.

2289
Galarza, Ernesto
"La Mula no Nació Arisca." *Center Diary* 14 (Center for the Study of Democratic Institutions, Santa Barbara, CA). September-October 1966, pp. 26-32.

2290
Servin, Manuel
"The Pre-World War II Mexican-American: an Interpretation." *California Historical Society Quarterly* (XLV: 4), December 1966, pp. 325-338.

2291
Fogel, Walter
Mexican-Americans in the Southwest Labor Market. Los Angeles, Graduate School of Business, UCLA, 1967, 222p.

2292
Gonzalez, Nancie L.
The Spanish Americans of New Mexico; a Distinctive Heritage. Los Angeles, Division of Research, Graduate School of Business Administration University of California, 1967, 149p.

2293
Leonard, Olen E., & Johnson, Helen W.
Low-Income Families in the Spanish-Surname Population of the Southwest. Washington, U.S. Dept. of Agriculture, Economic Research Service, 1967, 29p.

2294
U.S. Dept. of Agriculture. Economic Research Service
Low-Income Families in the Spanish-Surname Population of the Southwest, by Olen E. Leonard & Helen W. Johnson. Washington (Agricultural Economic Report #112), 1967, 29p.

2295
Warren, John Q. A.
California Ranchos and Farms, 1846-1862 . . . Edited by Paul W. Gates. Madison, State Historical Society of Wisconsin, 1967, 232p.

2296
Fallows, Marjorie
"Mexican-American Laborers: a Different Drummer?" *Massachusetts Review* 8, Winter 1967, pp. 166-176.

2297
Peñalosa, Fernando
"The Changing Mexican-American in Southern California." *Sociology & Sociological Research* 56, July 1967, pp. 405-417.

2298
Chandler, Charles R.
The Mexican American Protest Movement in Texas. New Orleans, 1968, 323p. (Ph.D. Dissertation, Tulane University)

2299
Graham, Richard, et al.
The Mexican-American Heritage: Developing Cultural Understanding. First Papers on Migrancy and Rural Poverty. An Introduction to the Education of Mexican-Americans in Rural Areas. University of Southern California (Rural-Migrant Center, Room 1002, Phillips Hall of Education, Los Angeles, CA 90007), 1968, 48p.

2300
Gregg, Andrew K.
New Mexico in the 19th Century, a Pictorial History. Albuquerque, University of New Mexico Press, 1968, 196p.

2301
Helm, June, ed.
Spanish-Speaking People in the United States: Proceedings of the 1968 Annual Spring Meeting of the American Ethnological Society (Detroit, May 3-4, 1968). Seattle, University of Washington Press, 1968, 215p.

2302
McWilliams, Carey
The Mexicans in America; a Students' Guide to Localized History. New York, Teachers College Press, 1968, 32p.

2303
Moore, Joan W.
Mexican-Americans: Problems and Prospects. Madison Institute for Research on Poverty, University of Wisconsin-Madison, 1968, 58p.

2304
U.S. Inter-Agency Committee on Mexican American Affairs
The Mexican American; a new Focus on Opportunity. Testimony Presented at the Cabinet Committee Hearings on Mexican American Affairs, El Paso, Texas, October 26-28, 1967. Washington, 1968, 253p.

2305
Seligman, Benjamin B.
"American Poverty, Rural and Urban." *Current History* 55, October 1968, pp. 193-198.

2306
Bustamante, Charles J., & Bustamante, Patricia L.
The Mexican-American and the United States. PATTY-LAR Publications, Ltd. (PO Box 4177, Mountain View, CA 94040), 1969, 63p.

2307
Choldin, Harvey, & Trout, Grafton
Mexican Americans in Transition: Migration and Employment in Michigan Cities. East Lansing, Dept. of Sociology, Michigan State University, 1969, 426 & 32pp.

2308
Erenburg, Mark
A Study of the Potential Relocation of Texas-Mexican Migratory Farm Workers to Wisconsin. Madison, 1969, 239 & 42p. (Thesis, University of Wisconsin-Madison).

2309
Galarza, Ernesto, et al.
Mexican Americans in the Southwest. Santa Barbara, CA, McNally & Loftin, 1969, 90p.

2310
Hansen, Niles M.
"The Mexican Americans' (In *Urban and Regional Dimensions of Manpower Policy.* Washington, U.S. Dept. of Labor, Manpower Administration, 1969, pp. 276-319).

2311
Minick, Roger
Delta West: the land and People of the Sacramento-San Joaquin Delta. Photos by Roger Minick. Historical Essay by Dave Bohn. Berkeley, CA, Scrimshaw Press, 1969, 31 & 124pp.

2312
The Role of the Mexican American in the History of the Southwest.
Conference Sponsored by the Inter-American Institute, Pan American College, Edinburg, Texas, November 17, 18, 1969. Edinburg, TX, Pan American College (Publication #9), 1969, 60p.

2313
Pritchett, Howard E.
"The Political Influence of the Mexican American Community in the Imperial Valley of California." *New Scholar* 1, April 1969, pp. 79-94.

2314
Santos, Everett J.
"New Weapon Against Job Discrimination." *Civil Rights Digest* (2: 3), Summer 1969, pp. 35-38.

2315

Knowlton, Clark

"Changing Spanish-American Villages of Northern New Mexico."
Sociology & Social Research 53, July 1969, pp. 455-474.

2316

Schmidt, F. H.

"Job Caste in the Southwest." *Industrial Relations* 9, October 1969,
pp. 100-110.

2317

Grebler, Leo, et al.

The Mexican-American People, the Nation's Second Largest Minority.
New York, Free Press, 1970, 777p.

2318

Lamb, Ruth (Stanton)

Mexican Americans: Sons of the Southwest. Claremont, CA, Ocelot
Press, 1970, 198p.

2319

Mexican Fact Finding Committee

Mexicans in California. San Francisco, R & E Research Associates,
1970, 214p. (Reprint of the 1928 edition).

2320

Silva, José L.

*A Professional Report on the Feasibility of Rural and Community
Development of the Colonies in Hidalgo County, Based on a 1969 Survey.*
Austin, TX, 1970, 70p.

2321

Wagoner, Jay J.

Arizona Territory, 1863-1912: a Political History. Tucson, University
of Arizona Press, 1970, 587p.

2322

Casavantes, Edward

"Pride and Prejudice: a Mexican-American Dilemma." *Civil Rights
Digest* (3: 1), Winter 1970, pp. 22-27.

2323

Gomez Quiñones, Juan

"Plan de San Diego Reviewed." *Aztlan* (I: 1), Spring 1970, pp.
124-132.

2324

Gomez-Quiñones, Juan, & Weber, Debra A.

" 'Down the Valley Wild': Epilogue, Prologue, Media-Res Still; the
Strikes of the '30's." *Aztlan* I, Spring 1970, pp. 119-123.

2325
Marcella, Gabriel
"Spanish-Mexican Contributions to the Southwest." *Journal of Mexican American History* (I: 1), Fall 1970, pp. 1-15.

2326
Nostrand, Richard L.
"Hispanic American Borderland: Delimitation of an American Culture Region." *Annals of the Association of American Geographers* 60, December 1970, pp. 638-661.

2327
Blawis, Patricia (Bell)
Tijerina and the Land Grants; Mexican-Americans in the Struggle for Their Heritage. New York, International Publishers, 1971, 191p.

2328
Ellis, Richard N., comp.
New Mexico, Past and Present: a Historical Reader. Albuquerque, University of New Mexico Press, 1971, 250p.

2329
Frakes, George E., & Solberg, Curtis B., comps.
Minorities in California History. New York, Random House, 1971, 280p.

2330
Illinois. Spanish-Speaking People's Study Commission
Report to the 77th General Assembly of the State of Illinois. [Springfield] 1971, 26 & 11pp.

2331
Morefield, Richard H.
The Mexican Adaptation in American California, 1846-1875. San Francisco, R & E Research Associates, 1971, 106p.

2332
Scott, Robin F.
The Mexican-American in the Los Angeles Area, 1920-1950: From Acquiescence to Activity. Los Angeles, 1971, 387p. (Ph.D. Dissertation, University of Southern California)

2333
Solache, Saul
The Impact of Urban Development in the Antelope Valley on its Mexican-American Residents. Los Angeles, 1971. (Master's Thesis, UCLA)

2334
Castillo, M. G.
"Are the Spanish-Speaking Just Another Immigrant Group?" *Integrated Education* 9, January 1971, pp. 45-49.

2335
Almaguer, Tomás
"Toward the Study of Chicano Colonialism." *Aztlan* (2: 1), Spring 1971, pp. 7-22.

2336
Borrego, John G., et al.
A Study of New Mexico Agricultural Workers. Design and Planning Assistance Center (2414 Central Ave., S.E., Albuquerque, New Mexico 87106), August 1971, 75p.

2337
Barrio, R.
"The Campesinos" (In Valdez, Luis, and Steiner, Stan, eds. *Aztlan: an Anthology of Mexican American Literature.* New York, Knopf, 1972, pp. 63-76).

2338
Blair, Philip M.
Job Description and Education; an Investment Analysis; a Case Study of Mexican-Americans in Santa Clara County, California. New York, Praeger, 1972, 250p.

2339
Broadbent, Elizabeth
The Distribution of Mexican Population in the United States. San Francisco, R & E Research Associates, 1972, 121p.

2340
Bullock, P.
"Employment Problems of the Mexican American" (In Gomez, Rudolph, comp. *The Changing Mexican-American, a Reader.* El Paso, University of Texas at El Paso, 1972, pp. 90-105).

2341
Cabeza de Baca, Fabiola
"Los Caballeros de Labor y las Gorras Blancas" (In Valdez, Luis, and Steiner, Stan, eds. *Aztlan: an Anthology of Mexican American Literature.* New York, Knopf, 1972, pp. 84-90).

2342
Gutierrez, José A.
La Raza and Revolution: the Empirical Conditions of Revolution in Four South Texas Counties. San Francisco, R & E Research Associates, 1972, 79p.

2343
Janson, Donald
"Many Farm Labor Offices Favor Growers" (In Gomez, Rudolph, comp. *The Changing Mexican-American, a Reader*. El Paso, University of Texas at El Paso, 1972, pp. 106-115).

2344
Meier, Matt S., & Rivera, Feliciano
The Chicanos, a History of Mexican-Americans. New York, Hill & Wang, 1972, 302p.

2345
Minnesota. Governor's Human Rights Commission
The Mexican in Minnesota; a Report to Governor C. Elmer Anderson of Minnesota, by the Governor's Inter-Racial Commission. Rev. San Francisco, R & E Research Associates, 1972, 84p.

2346
Rojas, Arnold R.
"The Vaqueros" (In Valdez, Luis, and Steiner, Stan, eds. *Aztlan: an Anthology of Mexican American Literature*. New York, Knopf, 1972, 410p.).

2347
Simmen, Edward, comp.
Pain and Promise; the Chicano Today. New York, New American Library, 1972, 348p.

2348
Thompson, John M.
Manpower, Income and Utilization of Mexican-American Manpower in Lubbock, Texas, 1960-1970. Lubbock, 1972, 266p. (Dissertation: Texas Tech University).

2349
Alvarez, Salvador E.
"The Legal and Legislative Struggle of the Farmworkers 1965-1972. Part 1: The Legal Struggle. Part 2: The Legislative Struggle." *El Grito* (VI:2), Winter 1972, pp. 5-145.

2350
Martinez, Frank
"Oregon's Chicanos Fight for Equality." *Civil Rights Digest* 5, Winter 1972, pp. 17-22.

2351
Forbes, Jack D., comp.
Aztecas del Norte; the Chicanos of Aztlan. Greenwich, CT, Fawcett, 1973, 336p.

2352
Gomez, David F.
Somos Chicanos; Strangers in our own Land. Boston, Beacon Press, 1973, 204p.

2353
Gonzales, Ramón
Between two Cultures; the Life of an American-Mexican, as Told to John J. Poggie, Jr. Tucson, University of Arizona Press, 1973, 94p.

2354
Madsen, William
Mexican-Americans of South Texas. 2d ed. New York, Holt, Rinehart & Winston, 1973, 124p.

2355
Prago, Albert
Strangers in Their own Land; a History of Mexican-Americans. New York, Four Winds Press, 1973, 226p.

2356
Torres, Alexander J.
A Follow-up Study of Servo: a Project for Monolingual, Low-Income Unemployed Mexican-Americans. San Diego, 1973, 163p. (Master's Thesis, U.S. International University)

2357
Villareal, Roberto M.
Illusions of Progress, Chicano Labor Activity in Texas, 1940-1970. (Unpublished paper, accepted by Mexican Studies Center, University of Texas at Austin, 1973).

2358
Weber, David J., ed.
Foreigners in Their Native Land: Historical Roots of the Mexican-Americans. Albuquerque, University of New Mexico Press, 1973, 288p.

2359
"The Chicano Experience in the United States." *Social Science Quarterly,* March 1973, entire issue.

2360
"Chicano." *Pacific Historical Review* 42, August 1973, entire issue.

2361
Kane, Tim D.
"Structural Change and Chicano Employment in the Southwest, 1950-1970: Some Preliminary Observations." *Aztlan* 4, Fall 1973, pp. 383-398.

2362
Gecas, Viktor
"Self-Conceptions of Migrant and Settled Mexican-Americans." *Social Science Quarterly* 54, December 1973, pp. 579-595.

2363
Church Views of the Mexican-American. New York, Arno Press, 1974, 1v.

2364
Kibbe, Pauline (Rochester)
Latin Americans in Texas. New York, Arno Press, 1974, 302p. (Reprint of 1946 edition).

2365
The Mexican American and the Law. New York, Arno Press, 1974, 1v.

2366
Mexican Labor in the United States. New York, Arno Press, 1974, 1v.

2367
Navarro, Armando
El Partido de la Raza Unida in Crystal City; a Peaceful Revolution. Riverside, California, University of California, 1974, 557p. (Thesis, University of California, Riverside).

2368
The New Mexican Hispano. New York, Arno Press, 1974, 225 & 72 & 136 & 186pp.

2369
Tuck, Ruth D.
Not With the Fist. New York, Arno Press, 1974, 139p. (Reprint of the 1946 edition).

2370
Leitman, Spencer
"Exile and Union in Indiana Harbor: Los Obreros Católicos San José and *El Amigo del Hogar,* 1925-1930." *Revista Chicano-Riqueña* 2, Winter 1974, pp. 50-57.

2371
García, Mario T.
Obreros: the Mexican Workers of El Paso, 1900-1920. La Jolla, 1975, 359p. (Ph.D. Dissertation, University of California, San Diego).

2372
Mexican-Americans Tomorrow: Editorial and Economic Perspectives. Gus Tyler, editor. Albuquerque, University of New Mexico Press, 1975, 208p.

2373
Murguía, Edward
Assimilation, Colonialism and the Mexican-American People. Austin, Center for Mexican-American Studies, University of Texas at Austin, 1975, 124p.

2374
Tyler, Gus, ed.
Mexican-Americans Tomorrow: Educational and Economic Perspectives. Albuquerque, University of New Mexico Press, 1975, 208p.

2375
U.S. Indian Land Research Unit
Hispanic Villages of Northern New Mexico; a Reprint of Volume 2 of the 1935 Tewa Basin Study, With Supplementary Materials, edited . . . by Marta Weigle. Santa Fe, New Mexico, Lightning Tree, 1975, 278p.

2376
Trager, Lillian
"Agricultural Workers in a California Town: Economics, Social Networks, and Organizing for Change." *Human Organization* 34, Spring 1975, pp. 105-107.

2377
Nelson Cisneros, Victor B.
"La Clase Trabajadora en Tejas, 1920-1940." *Aztlan* 6, Summer 1975, pp. 239-265.

2378
Zamora, Emilio
"Chicano Labor Activity in Texas, 1900-1920". *Aztlan* (6: 2), Summer 1975, pp. 221-236.

2379
Miller, Michael V.
Mexican-American and Mexican National Farm Workers: a Literature Review. Paper Presented at the Annual Meeting of the Rural Sociological Society, San Francisco, California, August 1975. August 1975, 25p. (ED 111 563).

2380
Stoddard, Elwyn R.
Real, Regulated and Relative Poverty in the U.S.-Mexico Borderlands. Paper Presented at the Annual Meeting of the Rural Sociological Society, San Francisco, California, August 1975. August 1975, 42p. (ED 113 102).

2381
Hawkes, Glenn R., & Taylor, Minna
"The Power Structure in Mexican and Mexican-American Farm Labor Families." *Journal of Marriage and Family* (37: 4), November 1975, p. 807.

2382
Francis, Jessie (Hughes Davies)
An Economic and Social History of Mexican California, 1822-1846: volume I, Chiefly Economic. New York, Arno Press, 1976, 803p.

2383
Hispanic Colorado: Four Centuries History and Heritage. Edited . . . by Evelio Echevarría and José Otero. Fort Collins, CO, Centennial Publications, 1976, 206p.

2384
Moore, Joan W., & Pachon, Harry
Mexican Americans. 2d ed. Englewood Cliffs, N.J., Prentice-Hall, 1976, 173p.

2385
Nostrand, Richard L.
Los Chicanos; Geografía Histórica Regional. México, Secretaría de Educación Pública, 1976, 178p.

2386
Proceedings of the Symposium on Chicanos and Welfare, Albuquerque, New Mexico, November 19-20, 1976. Washington, National Council of La Raza, 1976, 350p. (ED 147 085).

2387
U.S. Commission on Civil Rights. Iowa State Advisory Commission
?Que Lejos Hemos Venido? How far Have we Come? Migrant Farm Labor in Iowa, 1975; a Report . . . Washington, GPO, 1976, 93p.

2388
U.S. Dept. of Agriculture. Economic Research Service
Special and Economic Characteristics of Spanish-Origin Hired Farm Workers in 1973, by Leslie Whitener Smith. Agricultural Economic Report #349. Washington, 1976, 19p.

2389
Martinson, Oscar B., et al.
"Feelings of Powerlessness and Social Isolation Among 'Large-Scale' Farm Personnel." *Rural Sociology* (41: 4), Winter 1976, pp. 452-472.

2390
Cameron, J. D., & Talavera, Esther
"An Advocacy Program for Spanish-Speaking People." *Social Case-work* (57: 7), July 1976, pp. 427-431.

2391
Haynes, Kingsley E., et al.
Colonias in the Lower Rio Grande Valley of South Texas: a Summary Report. (Lyndon B. Johnson School of Public Affairs, Policy Research Report #18). Austin, Texas, Board of Regents, University of Texas-Austin, 1977, 27p.

2392
Leobardo Arroyo, L., et al.
"Preludio al Futuro, Pasado y Presente de los Trabajadores Mexicanos al Norte del Río Bravo, 1600-1975" (In Maciel, David R., ed. *La Otra Cara de México, el Pueblo Chicano.* México, Eds. El Caballito, 1977, 369p.).

2393
Sloss-Vento, Adela
Alonso S. Perales: his Struggle for the Rights of Mexican-Americans. [San Antonio] Artes Graficas, 1977, 101p.

2394
U.S. Dept. of Labor. Bureau of Labor Statistics.
Workers of Spanish Origin; a Chartbook. (B.L.S. Bulletin 1970). Washington, GPO, 1977, 72p.

2395
Valencia, Atilano A.
Descendants of el Siglo de Oro y Aztlan. San Francisco, R & E Research Associates, 1977, 85p.

2396
Martinez, Oscar J.
The Chicanos of El Paso: a Case of Changing Colonization. May 1977, 69p. (ED 153 780).

2397
Bean, Frank D., & Curtis, Russell L., Jr.
"Familism and Marital Satisfaction Among Mexican Americans: the Effects of Family Size, Wife's Labor Force Participation, and Conjugal Power." *Journal of Marriage and Family* (39: 4), November 1977, p. 59.

2398
California, Agricultural Labor Relations Board
A Handbook on the California Agricultural Labor Relations Law. Un Folleto Sobre la ley de Relaciones del Trabajo Agrícola de California. Sacramento, 1978, 67p.

2399
Maldonado, Lionel A., & Byrne, David A.
The Social Ecology of Chicanos in Utah. Iowa City, University of Iowa, 1978, 69p.

2400
Peñuelas, Marcelino C.
Cultura Hispánica en Estados Unidos: los Chicanos. 2d ed. Madrid, Eds. Cultura Hispánica del Centro Ibero-americano de Cooperacion, 1978, 202p.

2401
U.S. Bureau of Labor Statistics
Trabajadores de Origen Hispano: Libro de Gráficos. Washington, Depto. de Trabajo de Estados Unidos, Dirección de Estadisticas de Trabajo; for sale by Sudocs, GPO, 1978, 75p.

2402
Rochin, R. I.
"Illegal Aliens in Agriculture: Some Theoretical Considerations." *Labor Law Journal* 29, March 1978, pp. 149-167.

2403
Fugita, Stephen S., & O'Brien, David J.
"Ethnic vs. Ethnic: Sizing up the Farm Workers Clash: Nisei vs. Mexican Americans; Study." *Human Behavior* 7, May 1978, p. 35.

2404
Miller, Michael V., & Maril, Robert L.
Poverty in the Lower Rio Grande Valley of Texas; Historical and Contemporary Dimensions. Report #TAES-H-3286. Paper Presented at the Annual Meeting of the Rural Sociological Society, San Francisco, California, August 1978. 1978, 90p. (ED 158 911).

2405
Kiser, George C., & Kiser, Martha (Woody), eds.
Mexican Workers in the United States: History and Political Perspectives. Albuquerque, University of New Mexico Press, 1979, 295p.

2406
Romero, Fred E.
Chicano Workers: Their Utilization and Development. Los Angeles, Chicano Studies Center, UCLA, 1979, 160p.

2407
Sunseri, Alvin R.
Seeds of Discord: New Mexico in the Aftermath of the American Conquest, 1846-1861. Chicago, Nelson-Hall, 1979, 195p.

2408
Steiner, Stan
The Mexican Americans; Report #39. London, Minority Rights Group, February 1979, 19p.

2409
Moles, J. A.
"Who Tills the Soil? Mexican-American Workers Replace the Small Farmer in California: an Example From Colusa County." *Human Organization* (38: 1), Spring 1979, pp. 20-27.

2410
Hunsaker, Alan, ed.
Tiempos Pasados (Past Times). Grass-Roots Oral History. Aztlan Community Services Inc., 718 E. Maitland St., Ontario, California, August 1979, 41p.

2411
Lonciano Gonzales, Juan, Jr.
Social Mobility Among Mexican-American Agricultural Workers in Northern California. Berkeley, CA, 1980, 597p. (Ph.D. Dissertation, University of California, Berkeley).

2412
Ortiz, Roxanne (Dunbar)
Roots of Resistance: Land Tenure in New Mexico, 1680-1980. Los Angeles, Chicano Studies Research Center, UCLA, and American Indian Studies Center, UCLA, 1980, 202p.

2413
Van de Ende, Arthur A.P.M., & Haring, Henk A.
Sunbelt Frontier and Border Economy: a Field-Work Study of El Paso. El Paso, Center for Inter-American and Border Studies, University of Texas at El Paso, 1980, 71p.

2414
Jones, Lamar B., & Rice, G. R.
"Agricultural Labor in the Southwest; the Post-Bracero Years." *Social Science Quarterly* 61, June 1980, pp. 86-94.

2415
Camarillo, Albert
"Mexican-American History Revisited and Corrected." *Center Magazine* 13, July/August 1980, pp. 40-46.

2416
Acuña, Rodolfo
Occupied America: a History of the Chicanos. 2d ed. New York, Harper & Row, 1981, 37p.

2417
García, Mario T.
Desert Immigrants: the Mexicans of El Paso, 1880-1920. New Haven, Yale University Press, 1981, 316p.

2418
Lancelle, Mark A.
The Labor Market Experiences of Hired Farm Laborers: Gender, Ethnicity, and the Influence of Human Capital. Philadelphia, 1981, 203p. (Ph.D. Dissertation, University of Pennsylvania)

2419
Officer, James E.
Arizona's Hispanic Perspective: a Research Report. [Phoenix] Arizona Academy (802 Arizona Title Bldg., Phoenix 85003), 1981, 235p.

2420
Rosenbaum, Robert J.
Mexican Resistance in the Southwest: "The Sacred Right of Self-Preservation." Austin, University of Texas Press, 1981, 241p.

2421
Runsten, David, & LeVeen, Phillip
Mechanization and Mexican Labor in California Agriculture. La Jolla, Center for U.S.-Mexican Studies, University of California, San Diego, 1981, 135p. (M 6).

2422
Sanchez, Ramiro
Frontier Odyssey; Early Life in a Texas Spanish Town. Austin, Jenkins Pub. Co., 1981, 110p.

2423
Estrada, Leobardo F., et al
"Chicanos in the United States: a History of Exploitation and Resistance." *Daedalus* 110, Spring 1981, pp. 103-131.

2424
Monroy, Douglas
"Essay on Understanding the Work Experience of Mexicans in Southern California, 1900-1939." *Aztlan* 12, Spring 1981, pp. 59-74.

2425
de Forest, M. E.
"Mexican Workers North of the Border." *Harvard Business Review* 59, May/June 1981, pp. 150-157.

2426
Foster, Douglas
"Not so Wonderful World of "Disneylandia'." *The Progressive* 45, September 1981, pp. 19-20.

2427
Galarza, Ernesto
"California, the Uncommonwealth" (In Rosaldo, Renato, et al., comps. *Chicano: the Evolution of a People.* Malabar, FL, Krieger, 1982, pp. 164-175).

2428
Gomez-Quiñones, Juan
Development of the Mexican Working Class North of the Río Bravo: Work and Culture Among Laborers and Artisans, 1600-1900. Los Angeles, Chicano Studies Research Center, UCLA, 1982, 116p.

2429
Horgan, Paul
"Life in New Mexico" (In Rosaldo, Renato, et al., comps. *Chicano: the Evolution of a People.* Malabar, FL, Krieger, 1982, pp. 63-81).

2430
Knowlton, Clark
"Recommendations for the Solution of Land Tenure Problems Among the Spanish Americans" (In Rosaldo, Renato, et al, comps. *Chicano: the Evolution of a People.* Malabar, FL, Krieger, 1982, pp. 310-315).

2431
Loomis, Charles P.
"El Cerrito, New Mexico: a Changing Village" (In Rosaldo, Renato, et al, comps. *Chicano: the Evolution of a People.* Malabar, FL, Krieger, 1982, pp. 220-231).

2432
Borjas, George J.
"The Earnings of Male Hispanic Immigrants in the United States." *Industrial and Labor Relations Review* 35, April 1982, pp. 343-353.

2433
"American as Apple pie and Tortillas." *American Demographics* 4, October 1982, p. 9.

2434
Hinojosa, Gilbert M.
A Borderlands Town in Transition: Laredo, 1755-1870. College Station, TX, Texas A & M Press, 1983, 148p.

2435
Martin, Patricia (Preciado)
Images and Conversations: Mexican Americans Recall a Southwestern Past. Tucson, University of Arizona Press, 1983, 110p.

2436
Chavez, R., & Ramirez, A.
"Employment and Aspirations, Expectations and Attitudes Among Employed and Unemployed Chicanos." *Journal of Social Psychology* 119, February 1983, pp. 143-144.

2437
Russell, C.
"The News About Hispanics." *American Demographics* 5, March 1983, pp. 14-25.

2438
Martinez, E.
"Decade of Depression." *Crime and Social Justice* 19, Summer 1983, p. 100- .

2439
Martin, Philip L.
"Labor-Intensive Agriculture." *Scientific American* 249, October 1983, pp. 54-59.

D. MIGRANT AGRICULTURAL LABOR

1. Bibliographies

2440
U.S. Dept. of Agriculture
Farm Migration, 1942-1945, an Annotated Bibliography, compiled by Eleanor H. Bernert and Gladys Bowles. Washington, September 1947, 51p.

2441
Folsom, J. C.
Migratory Agricultural Labor in the United States: an Annotated Bibliography of Selected References. Washington, U.S. Dept. of Agriculture, Library (Library List #59), 1953, 64p.

2442
U.S. Dept. of Labor. Bureau of Labor Standards
Selected References on Domestic Migratory Agricultural Workers, Their Families, Problems, and Programs, 1955-1960. Washington (Bureau of Labor Standards Bulletin #225), 1961, 38p.

2443
Consulting Services Corp.
Migrant Farm Workers in the State of Washington: a Selected, Annotated Bibliography. v. 1. Washington, Office of Economic Opportunity, 1966, 50p.

2444
Hopper, Jean
The Migratory Farm Worker: a Selected Bibliography. Philadelphia, Free Library of Philadelphia, 1967, 8p.

2445
Guy, Kent
Migrant Labor Law and Relations: Selected References, 1960-1969. Washington, Library of Congress, Congressional Reference Service, 1969, 8p.

2446
Heslet, Mary R.
Migratory Agricultural Labor: References to Federal Publications, Studies, and Reports, 1959-1968. Rev. by Helen N. Grubbs. Washington, Library of Congress, Legislative Reference Service, 1969, 12p.

2447
Warnell, Katherine S.
Migratory Agricultural Labor: References to Books, Periodicals and Films, 1959-1969. Washington, Library of Congress, Legislative Reference Service, 1969, 31p.

2448
Renton, Margaret A.
The Migratory Farm Labor Problem: a Select Bibliography. Irvine, CA, University of California at Irvine Library, Government Publications Dept. (Bibliography #10), 1975, 32p.

2449
Shaw, R. P.
Migration Theory and Fact: a Review and Bibliography of Current Literature. Philadelphia, Regional Science Research Institute, 1975, 203p.

2450
Conaway, Mary E.
Circular Migration: a Summary and Bibliography. Monticello, IL, Council of Planning Librarians, 1977, 9p. (Exchange Bibliography, #1250).

2. Circulating Materials

2451
California. Employment Development Dept. Office of Migrant Services
Annual Operational Summary, Migrant Family Housing Centers. Sacramento, Office of Migrant Services, Employment Development Dept. [n.d.] (annual).

2452
Michigan. Migrant Services Unit
Migrant Services Report. (DSS Publication). Lansing, Dept. of Social Services, Migrant Services Unit [n.d.]

2453
Migrant Attrition Prevention Program
Annual Report . . . Austin, TX [n.d.]

2454
Migrant Legal Action Program
MLAP Monthly Report. Washington [n.d.]

2455
Migrant Report. Santa Fe, New Mexico Dept. of Education [n.d.]

2456
New York (State). Interdepartmental Committee on Migrant Labor
Annual Report . . . New York (n.d.), annual.

2457
North Carolina. Migrant Education Section
Serving Migrant Families. Raleigh [n.d.] annual.

2458
Pennsylvania. Bureau of Employment Security
Pennsylvania Farm Placement Program; Report. Harrisburg, [n.d.] annual.

2459
Pennsylvania. Governor's Committee on Migratory Labor
Final Report. Harrisburg [n.d.]

2460
U.S. Dept. of Health, Education and Welfare. Departmental Committee on Migratory Labor
Program Directions in Migrant Labor of the U.S. Dept. of Health, Education and Welfare. Washington, Office of Program Analysis [n.d.]

2461
University of Southern California
Agencies and the Migrant: Theory and Reality of the Migrant Condition. Los Angeles [n.d., n.p.]

2462
Parker, C. H.
"The California Casual and his Revolt." *Quarterly Journal of Economics* 30, November 1915, pp. 110-126.

2463
"Labor Camp Inspection" (In California. Commission of Immigration and Housing. *Second Annual Report, 1916.* Sacramento, 1916, pp. 9-94).

2464
McCormick, E. B.
"Housing the Worker on the Farm" (In U.S. Dept. of Agriculture *Yearbook 1918.* Washington, 1918, pp. 347-356).

2465
U.S. Dept. of Agriculture
Finding Labor to Harvest the Food Crops, by G. I. Christie. Circular #115. Washington, August 2, 1918, 8p.

2466
Parker, C. H.
The Casual Laborer and Other Essays. New York, Harcourt, Brace & Howe, 1920, 199p.

2467
Gibbons, Charles E., & Armentrout, Clara B., et al.
Child Labor in the Sugar Beet Fields of Michigan. New York, National Child Labor Committee, 1923.

2468
U.S. Children's Bureau
Child Labor and the Work of Mothers in the Beet Fields of Colorado and Michigan. Washington, Bureau Publication #115, 1923, 122p.

2469
U.S. Dept. of Agriculture
Labor Requirements of Arkansas Crops, by A. D. McNair. Dept. Bulletin #1181. Washington, March 15, 1924, 64p.

2470
Bamford, Edwin F.
"The Mexican Casual Problem in the Southwest." *Journal of Applied Sociology,* July-August 1924, pp. 363-379.

2471
Gibbons, Charles E., & Armentrout, Clara B.
Child Labor Among Cotton Growers in Texas . . . New York, National Child Labor Committee (Publication #324), 1925, 124p.

2472

Gibbons, Charles E., & Bell, Howard M.

Children Working on Famrs in Certain Sections of the Western Slope of Colorado. New York, National Child Labor Committee, 1925, 112p.

2473

Parker, Laura (Hiller)

"Migratory Children." National Conference of Social Work. *Proceedings, 1925.* Chicago, 1925, pp. 347-353.

2474

Stewart, Charles L.

"Migration to and From our Farms." *Annals of the American Academy of Political and Social Science* 117, January 1925, pp. 52-60.

2475

U.S. Children's Bureau

Child Labor in Fruit and hop Growing Districts of the Northern Pacific Coast, by Alice Channing. Washington, GPO, 1926.

2476

Reynolds Evelyn D.

A Study of Migratory Factors Affecting Education in North Kern County. Los Angeles, 1932, 167p. (Master's Thesis, University of Southern California).

2477

Folsom, J. C.

"Farm Labour Research in the United States." Geneva, *International Labour Review* 25, May 1932, pp. 656-665.

2478

U.S. National Labor Board

Report to the National Labor Board by Special Commission on Labor Conditions in the Imperial Valley, California. Report #3325. Washington, February 1934, 14p.

2479

Taylor, Paul S.

The Migrants and California's Future; the Trek to California, the Trek in California. San Francisco, Resettlement Administration, 1935, 9p.

2480

Cross, W. T., & Cross, D. E.

Newcomers and Nomads in California. Stanford, Stanford University Press, 1937, 149p.

2481
Taylor, Paul S.
Seasonal Labor on Arizona Irrigated Farms. Tucson, University of
Arizona, 1937, 7p.

2482
Cross, W. T.
"The Poor Migrant in California." *Social Forces* 15, March 1937, pp.
423-427.

2483
Larson, Olaf F.
Beet Workers on Relief in Weld County, Colorado. Fort Collins, CO,
Colorado State Agricultural Experiment Station and Rural Section, Divi-
sion of Social Research, Federal Works Administration, May 1937, 31p.

2484
Taylor, Paul S.
"Migratory Agricultural Workers on the Pacific Coast." *American So-
ciological Review* 3, April 1938, pp. 225-232.

2485
Arizona. University. College of Agriculture. Agricultural Experiment Sta-
  tion
  "Hired Labor Requirements on Arizona Irrigated Farms", by E. D.
Tetreau. *Bulletin #160.* Tucson, May 1938, pp. 187-217.

2486
Wakefield, Richard, & Landis, P. H.
  "Types of Migratory Farm Laborers and Their Movement into the
Yakima Valley, Washington." *Rural Sociology* 3, June 1938, pp.
133-144.

2487
California. University. University at Berkeley. College of Agriculture.
  Agricultural Experiment Station
  Seasonal Labor Requirements for California Crops, by R. L. Adams.
Berkeley, July 1938, 28p.

2488
Washington (State). State College. Agricultural Experiment Station. Di-
  vision of Farm Management and Agricultural Economics
  Migratory Farm Labor and the hop Industry on the Pacific Coast, with
Special Application to Problems of the Yakima Valley, Washington, by C.
F. Reuss, et al. Bulletin #363. Pullman, WA, August 1938, 63p.

2489
U.S. Works Progress Administration
  Seasonal Employment in Agriculture, by B. J. Free. Washington, Sep-
tember 1938, 58p.

2490
Johansen, Sigurd A.
Migratory-Casual Workers in New Mexico. Santa Fe, N.M. Dept. of Agricultural Economics, New Mexico Agricultural Experiment Station . . . in Cooperation with the Division of Social Research, Works Progress Administration (Washington, D.C.), 1939, 49p.

2491
Johnson, Elizabeth
Welfare of Families of Sugar-Beet Laborers. Washington (U.S. Dept. of Labor, Children's Bureau Publication #247); GPO, 1939, 100p.

2492
U.S. Dept. of Labor. Children's Bureau
Welfare of Families of Sugar-Beet Laborers, by Elizabeth Johnson. Washington, 1939, 100p.

2493
U.S. Works Projects Administration
Migratory Cotton Pickers in Arizona, by Malcolm Brown and Orin Cassmore, under the Supervision of John N. Webb . . . Washington, GPO, 1939.

2494
Tetreau, Elzer D. J.
"Arizona's Farm Laborers" (In Arizona. University. College of Agriculture. Agricultural Experiment Station. *Bulletin #163,* May 1939, pp. 297-336).

2495
Sidel, James E.
Pick for your Supper; a Study of Child Labor Among Migrants on the Pacific Coast. New York, National Child Labor Committee, 1939, 67p. (Publication #378, June 1939).

2496
Caughey, John W.
"Current Discussion of California's Migratory Labor Problem in Some Recent Publications." *Pacific Historical Review* 8, September 1939, pp. 347-354.

2497
Roskelley, R. W.
Beet Labor Problems in Colorado. [n.p.] 1940, 12p. (Proceedings of the Western Farm Economic Association. 13th Annual Meeting).

2498
Tetreau, Elzer D. J.
"Social Aspects of Arizona's Farm Labor Problems." *Sociology & Social Research* 24, July-August 1940, pp. 550-557.

2499
Texas. State Employment Service
Origins and Problems of Texas Migratory Farm Labor. Austin, 1940, 93 & 87 & 42pp. (Prepared for Hearing in Oklahoma by U.S. House of Representatives, Special Committee Investigating Interstate Migration of Destitute Citizens).

2500
Walton, Roger M. V.
A Study of Migratory Mexican Pea-Pickers in Imperial Valley, August 1940. Los Angeles, 1941, 420p. (Master's Thesis, University of Southern California)

2501
Wood, Samuel E.
"California Migrants." *Sociology & Social Research* 24, January/February 1940, pp. 248-261.

2502
McEntire, Davis
"A Study of Migration and Resettlement in the far Western States" (In Western Farm Economic Association. *Proceedings, 1940.* Berkeley, 1941, pp. 89-94).

2503
Miller, Frank
Income Levels of Contract Beet Workers in Nebraska. Bulletin #335, Nebraska Agricultural Experiment Station, College of Agriculture, University of Nebraska. Lincoln, Nebraska, 1941, 23p.

2504
Smith, T. Lynn
"Characteristics of Migrants." *Social Science Quarterly* 21, March 1941, pp. 335-350.

2505
McWilliams, Carey
Ill Fares the Land: Migrants and Migratory Labor in the United States. Boston, Little, Brown, 1942, 419p.

2506
Thadden, J. F.
Migratory Beet Workers in Michigan. East Lansing, MI, 1942. (Master's Thesis, Michigan State College)

2507
U.S. Dept. of Agriculture. Bureau of Agricultural Economics
Backgrounds of the War Farm Labor Problem. Washington, May 1942, 183p.

2508
Loomis, Charles P.
"Wartime Migration From the Rural Spanish-Speaking Villages of New Mexico." *Rural Sociology* 7, December 1942, pp. 384-395.

2509
U.S. Senate. Special Committee to Investigate Farm Labor Conditions in the West
Investigation of Western Farm Labor Conditions: Hearings, November 23-December 3, 1942, on S. Res. 299; Part 1, Sacramento, California; Part 2, Los Angeles, California. Washington, GPO, 1943, 497p. (2pts.).

2510
Ducoff, Louis J., et al.
"Effects of the war on the Rural-Farm Population." *Social Forces* 21, May 1943, pp. 406-412.

2511
Schwartz, Harry
"Hired Farm Labor in World War II." *Journal of Farm Economy* 24, February 1943, pp. 826-844.

2512
McVoy, E. C.
"Wartime Changes in Employer-Employee Relations in Agriculture." *Rural Sociology,* December 1943, pp. 356-363.

2513
Hill, George W.
"Wartime and Postwar Farm Labor in the West" (In Western Farm Economic Association. *Agriculture in Transition From war to Peace.* Berkeley, 1944, pp. 110-125).

2514
Tetreau, Elzer D. J.
"Wartime Changes in Arizona Farm Labor." *Sociology and Social Research* 28, May 1944, pp. 384-396.

2515
McConnell, Beatrice
"Child Labor in Agriculture." *Annals of the American Academy of Political and Social Science* 236, November 1944, pp. 83-91.

2516
U.S. Dept. of Labor. Division of Labor Standards
Harvest Nomads; Bulletin #73. Washington, GPO, 1945, 24p. (L 16.3: 73).

2517

McWilliams, Carey

"The Citrus Belt" (In his, *Southern California Country: an Island on the Land.* New York, Duell, Sloane & Pearce, 1946, pp. 205-226).

2518

Schwartz, Harry

Seasonal Farm Labor in the United States, With Special Reference to Hired Workers in Fruit and Vegetable and Sugar Beet Production. New York, 1946, 172p. (Ph.D. Dissertation, Columbia University)

2519

Wilson, Jane E.

The IWW in California, With Special Reference to Migratory Labor, 1910-1913. Berkeley, CA, 1946. (Ph.D. Dissertation, University of California, Berkeley)

2520

New York (State). Dept. of Labor. Division of Industrial Relations, Women in Industry and Minimum Wage

Seasonal Labor on Fruit and Vegetable Farms, New York State, 1945. New York, March 1946, 38p.

2521

Wilcox, W. W.

"The Wartime use of Manpower on Farms." *Journal of Farm Economy* 28, August 1946, pp. 723-741.

2522

U.S. Dept. of Agriculture. Federal Extension Service

A Guide to Farm jobs Along Western Highways. (U.S. Dept. of Agriculture, PA-30). Washington, GPO, 1947, 20p.

2523

U.S. Dept. of Labor. Retraining and Reemployment Administration

Migrant Labor. Washington, GPO, 1947, 58p.

2524

U.S. Dept. of Agriculture. Extension Service

Outline of Plan to Facilitate Movement of Migrants Essential to Farm Production in Western States. Washington, January 1947, 3p.

2525

U.S. Federal Interagency Committee on Migrant Labor

Migrant Labor, a Human Problem, Report and Recommendations. Washington, U.S. Dept. of Labor, Retraining & Re-employment Administration, March 1947, 58p. (L24.2:M58)

2526
U.S. Bureau of the Census
United States Population: Labor Force Memorandum . . . 1: Employment, Characteristics of Migrants in United States, 1940 and 1945 to February 1946. Washington, May 19, 1947, 8p.

2527
Hill, George W.
Texas-Mexican Migratory Agricultural Workers in Wisconsin. Madison, Wisconsin Agricultural Experiment Station, Stencil Bulletin #6, 1948, 20p.

2528
U.S. Dept. of Agriculture. Federal Extension Service
Texas Mexicans in Sugar Beets, Vegetables, Fruits, Grains: a Report on Improved Relationships Between Migratory Farm Workers and Agricultural Employers in North Central and Great Plains States, 1943-1947. By Carl D. Davenport. Washington, 1948, 33p.

2529
Hurd, T. N.
"Helping Migratory Farm Labor." *State Government* 21, June 1948, pp. 120-122.

2530
Armstrong, John M.
A Mexican Community: a Study of the Cultural Determinants of Migration. New Haven, CT, 1949, 560p. (Ph.D. Dissertation, Yale University)

2531
New York (State). Interdepartmental Committee on Farm and Food Processing Labor
New York's Harvest Labor. Report Covering the 5-Year Period 1943-1948. Albany, 1949, 29p.

2532
Rowe, J. Z., & Kohlmeyer, J. B.
Migrant Farm Labor in Indiana. (Indiana Agricultural Experiment Station. Bulletin #543). Lafayette, 1949, 31p.

2533
Kaufman, J. J.
"Farm Labor During World War II." *Journal of Farm Economics* 31, February 1949, pp. 131-142.

2534
New York (State). College of Agriculture
Housing Seasonal Farm Workers, by K. N. Gallagher. Ithaca, N.Y., May 1949, 61p. (Cornell Extension Bulletin #755).

2535
Ducoff, Louis J.
Migratory Farm Workers in 1949. (Agricultural Information Bulletin #25). Washington, U.S. Dept. of Agriculture, Bureau of Agricultural Economics, 1950, 20p.

2536
Taylor, Milton C.
An Approach to the Migratory Labor Problem Through Legislation. Madison, Governor's Commission on Human Rights, 1950, 44p.

2537
U.S. President's Commission on Migratory Labor
Migratory Labor in American Agriculture: Stenographic Report of Proceedings . . . Ward & Paul, Official Reporters. Washington, 1950, 26 volumes.

2538
U.S. Dept. of Agriculture. Bureau of Agricultural Economics
The Agricultural Labor Force in the San Joaquin Valley, California, 1948. Characteristics, Employment, Mobility, by W. H. Metzler and A. F. Sayin. Washington, February 1950, 73p.

2539
Wisconsin. Governor's Commission on Human Rights
Migratory Agricultural Workers in Wisconsin: a Problem in Human Rights. Madison, June 1950, 48p.

2540
U.S. Dept. of Labor. Bureau of Labor Standards
Suggested Recommendations of the Dept. of Labor to President's Commission on Migratory Labor. Washington, October 1950, 17p. (L 16.2: M58/3)

2541
Colorado. Governor's Survey Committee on Migrant Labor
Report [n.p.], 1951, unpaged.

2542
National Child Labor Committee
Migrant Farm Labor in Colorado, by Howard E. Thomas and Florence Taylor. New York, 1951, 117p.

2543
Thomas, Howard E., & Taylor, Florence
Migrant Farm Labor in Colorado; a Study of Migratory Families. New York, National Child Labor Committee, 1951, 116p.

2544
U.S. President
Migratory Labor in American Agriculture. Report of President's Commission on Migratory Labor, 1951. (Pr 33.14: Ag 8). Washington, GPO, 1951, 188p.

2545
U.S. President's Commission on Migratory Labor
Migratory Labor in American Agriculture; Report. Washington, GPO, 1951, 188p.

2546
"President's Commission on Migratory Labor in American Agriculture." *Land Economics* 27, August 1951, pp. 249-251.

2547
Ducoff, Louis J.
"Migratory Farm Workers: a Problem in Migration Analysis." *Rural Sociology* 16, September 1951, pp. 217-224.

2548
Fisher, Lloyd H.
"Harvest Labor Market in California." *Quarterly Journal of Economics* 65, November 1951, pp. 463-491.

2549
U.S. President's Committee on Migratory Labor
Recommendations. Washington, U.S. Dept. of Labor, Bureau of Labor Standards, 1952, 18p.

2550
U.S. Senate. Committee on Labor and Public Welfare
Migratory Labor Committee Act of 1952; Report to Accompany S. 3300, a Bill to Establish a Federal Committee on Migratory Labor. (82nd Congress, Second Session. Senate Report #1696). Washington, GPO, 1952, 15p.

2551
U.S. Senate. Committee on Labor and Public Welfare. Subcommittee on Labor and Labor-Management Relations
Migratory Labor; Hearings, February 5-March 28, 1952, on Migratory Labor, 82nd Congress, Second Session. Washington, 1952, 1089p. (2 parts).

2552
Hopper, M. L., & Cantor, Marjorie
Migrant Farm Workers in New York State. New York, Consumers League of New York, 1953, 111p.

2553
Nelson, Lowry
Migratory Workers; the Mobile Tenth of American Agriculture. Prepared for the NPA Agriculture Committee on National Policy. Washington, National Planning Association, 1953, 33p.

2554
New York (State). Legislature. Joint Committee on Migrant Labor
Report. Albany, Williams Press, 1953, 39p. (New York State. Legislature. Legislative Document 1953, #49).

2555
Lyon, Richard M.
The Legal Status of American and Mexican Migratory Farm Labor; an Analysis of United States Farm Labor Legislation, Policy and Administration. Ithaca, N.Y., 1954, 655p. (Ph.D. Dissertation, Cornell University)

2556
New Jersey. Dept. of Labor and Industry. Bureau of Migrant Labor
Ten Migrant Milestones in New Jersey. Trenton, 1954, 22p.

2557
Michigan. Study Commission on Migratory Labor
Migrants in Michigan; a Handbook on Migratory, Seasonal, Agricultural Workers in Michigan. Lansing, September 1954, 37p.

2558
Douglass, J. H.
"The Migrant and the Community" (In National Conference of Social Work. *Minority Groups: Segregation and Integration. Papers Presented at the 82nd Annual Forum.* New York, Columbia University Press, 1955, pp. 23-36).

2559
League for Industrial Democracy
Down on the Farm: the Plight of Agricultural Labor. New York, 1955, 14p.

2560
Maxwell, Grace
"Youth Programs for Migrants" (In National Conference on Social Welfare. *Minority Groups: Segregation and Integration.* New York, Columbia University Press, 1955, pp. 48-57).

2561
U.S. President's Committee on Migratory Labor
Meeting, October 17, 1955. Washington, 1955, 79p.

2562
U.S. President's Committee on Migratory Labor
State Migratory Labor Committees; Their Purpose and Organization.
Washington, U.S. Dept. of Labor, President's Committee on Migratory
Labor, 1955, 6p.

2563
Wyckoff, F. R.
"The Citizen's Role in Community Planning for Services to Migrants"
(In National Conference of Social Work. *Group Work and Community Or-
ganization, 1955; Papers Presented at the 82nd Annual Forum.* New
York, Columbia University Press, 1955, pp. 44-55).

2564
Bailey, Wilfred C.
"Problems in Relocating the People of Zapata, Texas." *Texas Journal
of Science* 7, March 1955, pp. 20-37.

2565
Texas. Legislative Council
Transportation of Migrant Labor in Texas. (Staff Research Report
#54-4). Austin, 1956, 82 & xxxxii pp.

2566
U.S. Dept. of Labor. Bureau of Employment Security. Farm Placement
Service
*Service to Agricultural Migrants: What Some Communities are Doing,
July 1, 1955, to June 30, 1956.* (2nd Series, GAL. 348). Washington,
1956, 20p.

2567
U.S. House. Committee on Interstate & Foreign Commerce
Transportation of Migrant Farm Workers; Hearing Before a Subcom-
mittee, May 18, 1956, on H.R. 9836 and S. 3391, to Provide for the Regu-
lation of the Interstate Transportation of Migrant Farm Workers, 84th
Congress, Second Session. Washington, 1956, 54p.

2568
U.S. President's Committee on Migratory Labor
Report to the President on Domestic Migratory Labor. First- , Wash-
ington, September 1956- .

2569
U.S. Dept. of Agriculture. Farm Placement Service
*This is how 12 Camps for Migratory Workers in Agriculture are Oper-
ated by Growers, Associations, Counties.* (BES #F-171). Washington,
1957, 57p.

2570

Oregon. Bureau of Labor
  Report: Vamonos pal Norte; Let's go North: a Social Profile of the Spanish-Speaking Migratory Farm Laborer. Salem, 1958? 26p.

2571

Oregon. Bureau of Labor
  "We Talk to the Migrants . . ." *Preliminary Report to the Governor's Inter-Agency Committee on Agricultural Labor and to the Legislative Interim Committee on Migratory Labor.* Salem, 1958, 75p.

2572

U.S. Dept. of Labor
  Report on Operations of the Domestic Migratory Labor Program. Washington, 1958, 12p.

2573

Buckley, Louis F.
  "The Migrant Worker Today." *Review of Social Economy* 16, March 1958, pp. 36-43.

2574

Irwin, T.
  "Our Miserable Million." *Coronet* 44, September 1958, pp. 92-97.

2575

Oregon. Legislature. Interim Committee on Migratory Labor
  Migratory Labor in Oregon. Portland, October 15, 1958, 72p.

2576

Current, Tom, & Martinez Infante, Mark
  . . . And Migrant Problems Demand Attention; Final Report. Salem, Oregon, Bureau of Labor, 1959, 218p.

2577

Mid-American Conference on Migratory Labor, St. Louis, 1959
  Mid-American Conference on Migratory Labor. [n.p.] 1959? 49p.

2578

Oregon. Bureau of Labor
  . . . and Migrant Problems Demand Attention; the Final Report of the 1958-59 Migrant Farm Labor Studies in Oregon Including Material From the Preliminary Report of the Bureau of Labor (July 1959) entitled "We Talked to the Migrants . . ." Salem, 1959, 218p.

2579

U.S. Dept. of Labor. Bureau of Labor Standards
  State Committees on Seasonal Agricultural Labor, Their Organization and Programs. Washington, 1959-   .

2580
U.S. Dept. of Labor. Bureau of Labor Standards
State Migratory Labor Committees, Their Organization and Problems.
Prepared by Gwen Geach . . . Washington, 1959, 74p.

2581
Brooks, Melvin S.
The Social Problems of Migrant Farm Laborers; Effect of Migrant Farm Labor on the Education of Children. Carbondale, IL, Dept. of Sociology, Southern Illinois University, 1960, 242p.

2582
Jorgenson, Janet M., et al.
Migratory Agricultural Workers in the United States. Grinnell, Iowa, Grinnell College, 1960, 81p.

2583
Larson, Olaf F., & Sharp, Emmit F.
Migratory Farm Workers in the Atlantic Coast Stream. Ithaca, N.Y., State College of Agriculture (Cornell University Agricultural Experiment Station, Bulletin 948-949), 1960, 2v.

2584
Metzler, William, & Sargent, Frederic O.
Migratory Farmworkers in the Midcontinent Stream. Washington, U.S. Dept. of Agriculture, in cooperation with Texas Agricultural Experiment Station, 1960, 62p.

2585
U.S. Senate. Committee on Labor and Public Welfare
Migratory Labor. Hearings Before the Subcommittee on Migratory Labor of the Committee on Labor and Public Welfare, U.S. Senate, 88th Congress, First (Second) Session, on S. 1085 . . . Washington, GPO, 1960-61, 2 parts.

2586
Western Interstate Conference on Migratory Labor, Phoenix, Arizona, 1960
Proceedings. San Francisco, Council of State Governments, Western Office, 1960, 53p.

2587
McQuery, Elton K.
Western Interstate Conference on Migratory Labor, Phoenix, April 10-13, 1960. April 13, 1960, 59p. (ED 013 125).

2588
Lee, E. S., & Lee, A. S.
"Internal Migration Statistics for the United States." *American Statistical Association Journal* 55, December 1960, pp. 664-697.

2589
Perry, Josef H.
Economic Characteristics of Texas Intrastate Migrants, 1935-1940.
Austin, TX, 1961, 126 & 2pp. (Master's Thesis, University of Texas at Austin)

2590
Shotwell, Louisa (Rossiter)
The Harvesters; the Story of the Migrant People. Garden City, N.Y., Doubleday, 1961, 242p.

2591
U.S. Senate. Committee on Labor and Public Welfare. Subcommittee on Migratory Labor
Migratory Labor; Hearings, August 7, 1959-July 11, 1960, on S. 1085 and other Bills Relating to Migratory Labor. 86th Congress, First and Second Sessions. Washington, 1961, 2 parts.

2592
U.S. Senate. Committee on Labor and Public Welfare. Subcommittee on Migratory Labor
Migratory Labor; Hearings, volume 1, April 12-13, 1961, on S. 1123, S. 1224, S. 1125, S. 1126, S. 1130, and S. 1132, Bills Relating to Migratory Labor. 87th Congress, First Session. Washington, 1961, 458p.

2593
Tomasek, Robert D.
"The Migrant Problem and Pressure Group Politics." *Journal of Politics* 23, May 1961, pp. 295-319.

2594
Conference on Families Who Follow the Crops
Report and Recommendations. Sacramento, CA, Governor's Advisory Committee on Children and Youth, Subcommittee on the Migrant Child, 1962- .

2595
Raushenbush, Elizabeth (Brandeis)
The Migrant Labor Problem in Wisconsin, an Essay. Madison, Governor's Commission on Human Rights, 1962, 52p.

2596
U.S. Senate. Committee on Rules and Administration
Study of Migrant Labor; Report to Accompany S. Res. 273. (87th Congress, Second Session. Senate Report #1159). Washington, GPO, 1962, 13p.

2597
Karracker, Cyrus H.
Agricultural Seasonal Laborers of Colorado and California Philadelphia? Pennsylvania Citizens Committee on Migrant Labor, November 1962.

2598
Colorado. General Assembly. Legislative Council
Migratory Labor in Colorado, Report. Denver (Research Publication #72), December 1962, 255p.

2599
Florida. Legislative Council
Migrant Farm Labor in Florida . . . Tallahassee, 1963, 63 & 14pp.

2600
U.S. Dept. of Agriculture. Federal Extension Service
Cooperative Extension Service Work with low Income Families: Migrants. (U.S. Federal Extension Service, ESC-549). Washington, 1963, 16p.

2601
U.S. Senate. Committee on Banking and Currency
Housing for Domestic Farm Labor. Hearing Before a Subcommittee of the Committee on Banking and Currency, U.S. Senate, 88th Congress, First Session, on S. 981, a Bill to Amend Title V of the Housing Act of 1949 to Assist in the Provision of Housing for Domestic Farm Labor, October 15, 1963. Washington, GPO, 1963, 74p.

2602
U.S. Senate. Committee on Labor and Public Welfare
Migratory Labor Bills, Hearings Before Subcommittee on Migratory Labor, 88th Congress, First Session, on S. 521, and Other Bills, April 10-24, 1963. Washington, 1963, 313p. (Y4.L 11/2: L11/6/963).

2603
U.S. Senate. Committee on Labor and Public Welfare
National Advisory Council on Migratory Labor; Report, Together with Minority Views, to Accompany S. 525. (88th Congress, First Session. Senate Report #203). Washington, GPO, 1963, 10p.

2604
U.S. Senate. Reports
National Advisory Council on Migratory Labor. Report Together With Minority Views from Committee on Labor and Public Welfare to Accompany S. 525, May 27, 1963. Washington, 1963, 10p.

2605
Anderson, Henry P.
A Harvest of Loneliness, an Inquiry into a Social Problem. Berkeley, Citizens for Farm, 1964, 733p.

2606
Raushenbush, Elizabeth (Brandeis)
A Study of Migratory Workers in Cucumber Harvesting, Washara County, Wisconsin, 1964. Madison (University of Wisconsin) [n.d.] 88p.

2607
U.S. Dept. of Agriculture. Economic Research Service
Domestic and Migratory Farm Workers: Personal and Economic Characteristics (Agricultural Economic Report #120). Washington, GPO, 1964.

2608
U.S. Senate. Committee on Labor and Public Welfare
Voluntary Farm Employment Service. Hearings Before the Subcommittee on Migratory Labor of the Committee on Labor and Public Welfare, U.S. Senate, 88th Congress, First Session, on S. 527 . . . Washington, GPO, 1964, 288p.

2609
Vogel, Melvin O.
Seasonal Labor in Santa Barbara County Agriculture: an Estimation of Future Demand. Santa Barbara, CA, 1964. Master's Thesis, University of California, Santa Barbara

2610
Miller, Herman P.
What is Poverty—who are the Poor? Los Angeles, Institute of Government & Public Affairs (MR-31), UCLA, 1965, 110p. ("A Working Paper Prepared for the UCLA Seminar on Poverty, Spring, 1965")

2611
National Advisory Committee on Farm Labor
Poverty on the Land in a Land of Plenty. New York, 1965, 64p.

2612
Oklahoma. Employment Security Commission
A Study of Migrant Workers in Southwest Oklahoma. Oklahoma City, 1965.

2613
Tinney, Milton W.
A Study of Migrant Workers in Southwest Oklahoma. July 1965, 85p. (ED 020 028).

2614

Coles, Robert

The Migrant Farmer: a Psychiatric Study. Southern Regional Council, 5 Forsyth St., N.W., Atlanta, Georgia, September 1965, 17p.

2615

Migratory Workers in the United States. October 1965, 10p. (ED 014 602).

2616

Colorado. Special Health Services Division

State Migrant Plan for Public Health Services. Denver, 1966, 16p.

2617

Migrant Labor Conference Proceedings [Madison, Wisconsin], December 4, 1964. Madison, Governor's Commission on Human Rights, 1966, 29p.

2618

Miller, Herman P., ed.

Poverty, American Style. Belmont, CA, Wadsworth Pub. Co., 1966, 304p.

2619

Ohio. Governor's Committee on Migrant Labor

Migratory Labor in Ohio Agriculture, a Report. Edited by Sally Bingham. Columbus, 1966, 45p.

2620

Rodriguez-Cano, Felipe

An Analysis of the Mexican-American Migrant Labor Force in the Stockbridge Area. East Lansing, MI, 1966, 97p. (Master's Thesis, Michigan State University). (ED 026 167).

2621

"The Migrant Worker" (In Samora, Julian, ed. *La Raza, Forgotten Americans.* Notre Dame, Indiana, University of Notre Dame Press, 1966, pp. 63-94).

2622

Texas. Bureau of Labor Statistics

Report on Migratory Labor Movement and Licensed Texas Labor Agents. Austin, 1966-   (annual).

2623

Ulibarri, Horacio

"Social and Attitudinal Characteristics of Spanish-Speaking Migrant and ex-Migrant Workers in the Southwest." *Sociology & Social Research* 50, April 1966, pp. 361-370.

2624

Domestic Agricultural Migrants in the United States, Counties in Which an Estimated 100 or More Seasonal Agricultural Workers Migrated into the Area of Work During the Peak Season in 1965. August 1966, 18p. (ED 014 609).

2625

Hill, Herbert

"No Harvest for the Reaper: the Story of the Migratory Agricultural Worker in the United States." (In Dentler, Robert A., ed. *Major American Social Problems.* Chicago, Rand McNally, 1967, pp. 264-295).

2626

Hill Palomares, Uvaldo

A Study of the Role of Mobility in the Acculturation Process of Rural Migrant and non-Migrant Disadvantaged Mexican Americans in the Coachella Valley. Los Angeles, 1967, 297p. (Ph.D. dissertation, University of Southern California).

2627

Illinois. Commission on Children. Committee on Agricultural Migrant Workers

County Profile of Agricultural Migrant Workers in Illinois; a Report. Springfield, 1967, 96p.

2628

Konvitz, Milton B.

Civil Rights in Immigration. Ithaca, N.Y., Cornell University Press, 1967, 216p.

2629

Reuel, Myrtle R.

Where Hannibal Led us. New York, Vantage Press, 1967, 295p.

2630

Texas. Good Neighbor Commission

Texas Migrant Labor: the 1967 Migration. Austin, 1967-   (annual).

2631

U.S. Dept. of Agriculture. Economic Research Service

Domestic Migratory Farmworkers; Personal and Economic Characteristics, by Avra Rapton. Washington (Agricultural Economic Report #121), GPO, 1967, 32p.

2632

U.S. Senate. Executive Reports

Migratory Farm Labor Problem in United States; 1967 Report of Committee on Labor and Public Welfare, made by its Subcommittee on Migratory Labor, Pursuant to S. Res. 188 (90th Congress, First Session), Together with Individual Views; March 15, 1967. Washington, 1967, 73p.

2633
U.S. Senate. Reports
Study of Migratory Labor. Report from Committee on Rules and Administration to Accompany S. Res. 44, February 8, 1967. Washington, 1967, 7p.

2634
Washington (State). Dept. of Health
Geographic and Temporary Distribution of Migrant Agricultural Workers and Their Families in Washington; Preliminary Forecasts by Semi-month for Major Migrant-Using Areas, 1968 Harvest Season. Prepared by Paul T. Holm . . . Olympia, Washington State Dept. of Health, Migrant Health Project, 1967, 30p.

2635
Erenburg, Mark
State and Federal Rights of Migrant Farm Workers: an Appraisal. The Governor's Commission on Human Rights (902 State Office Bldg., 1 West Wilson St., Madison, WI 53702), February 1, 1967, 22p.

2636
Givens, R. A.
"Report on Migratory Farm Labor." *Labor Law Journal* 18, April 1967, pp. 246-248.

2637
Mittelbach, Frank G., & Short, James
"Rural Poverty in the West; Status and Implications." *University of Kansas Law Review* (15: 4), May 1967, pp. 453-467.

2638
Shriver, Sargent
"Rural Poverty; the Problem and the Challenge." *University of Kansas Law Review* (15: 4), May 1967, pp. 401-408.

2639
First Western Region Conference of OEO Migrant Projects, Woodburn, Oregon, June 7-9, 1967. Edited by Ralph H. Cake, Jr., et al. June 1967, 35p. (ED 068 208).

2640
American Friends Service Committee. Pacific Southwest Region
Final Report of the Farm Workers Opportunity Project. Pasadena, CA, July 1967, 130p.

2641
Friedland, William H., & Nelkin, Dorothy
"Migrant Labor: a Form of Intermittent Social Organization." *Industrial & Labor Relations Research* 13, November 1967, pp. 3-14.

2642
Abeytia, Hector, et al.
Agencies and the Migrant: Theory and Reality of the Migrant Condition. First Papers on Migrancy and Rural Poverty; an Introduction to the Education of Mexican-Americans in Rural Areas. University of Southern California (Rural-Migrant Center, Room 1002, Phillips Hall of Education, Los Angeles, CA 90007), 1968, 33p.

2643
Draper, Anne, & Draper, Hal
The Dirt on California; Agribusiness and the University. Berkeley, CA, Independent Socialist Clubs of America, 1968, 32p.

2644
Leonard, Olen E.
Changes in the Spanish-Speaking Labor Force of Saginaw County, Michigan. State College, Mississippi, Mississippi State University, Social Science Research Center, 1968, 44p.

2645
Michigan. Civil Rights Commission
Report and Recommendations on the Status of Migratory Farm Labor in Michigan. Detroit? 1968, 24p.

2646
Ohio. Governor's Committee on Migrant Labor
Migratory Labor in Ohio Agriculture; Report. Edited by Sarah R. Dalbey. Columbus, 1968, 64p.

2647
Oregon. State University, Corvallis
Seasonal Agricultural Labor in Oregon; Task Force Report. Salem, 1968, various pagings.

2648
Robinson, Howard F., et al.
Employment Adjustments in two Growing Labor Markets (Economic Research Report #7). Raleigh, N.C., Dept. of Economics, North Carolina State University, 1968, 95p.

2649
Shannon, Lyle W.
"The Study of Migrants as Members of Social Systems" (In Helm, June, ed. *Spanish-Speaking People in the United States.* Seattle, University of Washington Press, 1968, pp. 34-64).

2650
Wey, Herbert
Coordination of Programs for Migrants. Working Paper for National Meeting on Migrant Problems. 1968, 17p. (ED 017 356).

2651
Wisconsin. Governor's Committee on Migratory Labor
Report for 1966 and 1967 with a Summary of Earlier Developments, by Elizabeth Brandeis Raushenbush, Chairman. Madison, Equal Rights Div., Dept. of Industry, Labor and Human Relations, 1968, 53p.

2652
"Migrant Farm Labor in Upstate New York." *Columbia Journal of Law & Social Problems* 4, March 1968, pp. 1-49.

2653
Rendon, Armando
"How Much Longer . . . the Long Road?" *Civil Rights Digest,* Summer 1968, pp. 34-44.

2654
Brann, Richard R.
"Housing of Migrant Agricultural Workers." *Texas Law Review* (46: 6), July 1968, pp. 933-949.

2655
Nelson, Kerry D.
Migrants in Utah. August 1968, 14p. (ED 033 802).

2656
Good, Paul
Breaking new Ground. Rural Advancement Fund of the National Sharecroppers Fund, Inc. (112 East 19th St., New York, N.Y. 10003), 1969, 16p.

2657
Junkin, William I., and Faser, Patricia F.
Louisiana's Children of the Fields. (Report Number Bulletin-1148, Louisiana State Dept. of Education, Baton Rouge). 1969, 16p. (ED 038 201).

2658
New Jersey. Senate. Special Committee on Migrant Labor
Report, December 3, 1969. Trenton, N.J., 1969, 53 & 2pp.

2659
New York (State). Interdepartmental Committee on Migrant Labor
Director, New York State Services for Migrant and Seasonal Farm Workers. Albany, 1969, 50p.

2660
U.S. Office of Education
Directory of Consultants on Migrant Education; National and State Lists for Migrant Education Programs Under Title I, Elementary and Secondary Education Act, Public Law 89-10, as Amended. Washington, 1969, 87p.

2661
Friedland, William H.
"Labor Waste in New York: Rural Exploitation and Migrant Workers." *Trans-Action* 6, February 1969, pp. 48-53.

2662
Texas Labor Mobility, Experimental and Demonstration Project. Final Report. (Report #P-6717, U.S. Dept. of Labor, Manpower Administration). April 1969, 191p. (ED 032 972).

2663
Reuel, Myrtle R.
"A Preview of the Migrant as a Rehab Client." *Rehabilitation Record* (10: 6), November-December 1969, pp. 1-9.

2664
Kuntz, Karen E.
"New York Minimum Wage Act for Migrant Workers." *Prospectus* (3: 1), December 1969, pp. 249-256.

2665
Nelkin, Dorothy
"Response to Marginality: the Case of Migrant Farm Workers." London, *British Journal of Sociology* 20, December 1969, pp. 375-389.

2666
An Assessment of the Experimental and Demonstration Interstate Program for South Texas Migrants. December 1, 1969, 216p. (ED 044 199).

2667
Brody, Eugene B., ed.
Behavior in new Environments: an Adaptation of Migrant Populations. Beverly Hills, CA, Sage, 1970, 479p.

2668
California. Farm Workers Health Service
Health for the Harvesters: Decade of Hope, 1960-1970; a ten-year Report. Sacramento, 1970, 32p.

2669
Coles, Robert
Uprooted Children; the Early Life of Migrant Farm Workers. Pittsburgh, University of Pittsburgh Press, 1970, 142p.

2670
Colorado. Legislative Council
Migrant Labor Problems in the 1970's; Staff Report to the Colorado General Assembly. Denver, 1970.

2671
London, Joan, & Anderson, Henry
So Shall ye Reap. New York, Crowell, 1970, 208p.

2672
Nelkin, Dorothy
On the Season: Aspects of the Migrant Labor System (ILR Paperback #8). Ithaca, N.Y., Cornell University, New York State School of Industrial and Labor Relations, 1970, 85p.

2673
Texas. Inter-Agency Task Force on Migrant Labor
Special Report. Prepared for Governor Preston Smith by the Good Neighbor Commission of Texas. Austin 1970, 227p.

2674
U.S. Senate. Committee on Labor and Public Welfare
Migrant and Seasonal Farmworker Powerlessness; Hearings Before Subcommittee on Migratory Labor, 91st Congress, First and Second Sessions. *Part 1: Who are the Migrants?* June 9-10, 1969. Washington, GPO, 1970, 331p. (Y4.L 11/2: M58/8/pt. 1).

2675
U.S. Senate. Committee on Labor and Public Welfare
Migrant and Seasonal Farmworker Powerlessness; Hearings Before Subcommittee on Migratory Labor, 91st Congress, First and Second Sessions. *Part 2: Migrant Subculture,* July 28, 1970, pp. 333-548. *Part 3-A: Efforts to Organize,* July 15, 1970, pp. 549-870. Washington, GPO, 1970. (Y4.L 11/2: M58/8/pt. [numbers]).

2676
U.S. Senate. Committee on Labor and Public Welfare
Migrant and Seasonal Farmworker Powerlessness; Hearings Before Subcommittee on Migratory Labor, 91st Congress, First Session. Part 3-B: Efforts to Organize, July 16 and 17, 1969. Washington, GPO 1970, pp. 871-1181. (Y4.L 11/2: M58/8/pt 3-B).

2677
U.S. Senate. Committee on Labor and Public Welfare
Problems of Migrant Workers, Hearing, 91st Congress, 2nd Session, November 24, 1969. Washington, GPO, 1970, 6p. (Y4.L 11/2: M58/9).

2678
Migrant Research Project. Manpower Evaluation and Development Institute, (1329-18th St., N.W., Washington, D.C. 20036), January 31, 1970, 42p.

2679

Bryce, Herrington J.

"Alternative Policies for Increasing the Earnings of Migratory Farm Workers." *Public Policy* (18: 3), Spring 1970, pp. 413-428.

2680

Nelkin, Dorothy

"Unpredictability and Life Style in a Migrant Labor Camp." *Social Problems* 17, Spring 1970, pp. 472-487.

2681

Snyder, Eldon E., & Perry, Joseph B., Jr.

"Farm Employment Attitudes Toward Mexican-American Migrant Workers." *Rural Sociology* (35: 2), June 1970, pp. 244-252.

2682

U.S. Senate. Select Committee on Nutrition and Human Needs

Problems of Migrant Workers; Hearings, 91st Congress, 2nd Session. Part 3: National Nutrition Survey, April 27, 1970; Food Programs at Local Level, June 2, 1970; Progress Report, U.S. Dept. of Agriculture, June 19, 1970. Washington, pp. 763-901. (Y4.N 95: N 95/970/pt. 3).

2683

New Jersey. Dept. of Labor and Industry. Division of Labor Standards

Seasonal Farm Labor; Study. Trenton, N.J., August 1970, 44p.

2684

Hansen, Niles C., & Gruben, William C.

The Influence of Relative Wages and Assisted Migration on Local Preferences: a Study of Mexican-Americans in South Texas. Austin, Center for Economic Development, University of Texas at Austin, September 1970, 25p.

2685

Colorado. Legislative Council

Migrant Labor Problems in the 1970's: Staff Report to the Colorado General Assembly (Research Publication #157). Denver, November 1970, 60p.

2686

Erenburg, Mark

"Migratory Labor: a Review of Labor Market Problems" (In Somers, Gerald G., ed. *Proceedings of the 23rd Annual Winter Meeting, Industrial Relations Association.* Madison, WI, 1971, pp. 12-32).

2687

Ferster, Lucian E.

Cultural and Economic Mediation Among Spanish-Speaking Migrant Farm Workers in Dade County, Florida. (Master's Thesis, University of Miami, Coral Gables, Florida, 1970). 1971, 119p. (ED 080 219).

2688
Friedland, William, H., & Nelkin, Dorothy
  Migrant Agricultural Workers in America's Northeast. New York, Holt, Rinehart & Winston, 1971, 281p.

2689
Friends, Society of. American Friends Service Committee
  Child Labor in Agriculture, Summer, 1970: a Special Report. Philadelphia, 1971, 110p.

2690
Goodpaster, G. S.
  "Institutional Persistence and the Paradox of Reform: the Case of Migrant Farm Labor" (In Orleans, Peter A., & Ellis, William R., eds. *Race, Change and Urban Society.* Beverly Hills, Sage Publications, 1971, pp. 339-372).

2691
Helping Migrant and Seasonal Farm Worker Families. Annual Report, 1971, Migrant Action Program, Mason City, Iowa. 1971, 73p. (ED 060 994).

2692
McWilliams, Carey
  Factories in the Field; the Story of Migratory Farm Labor in California. Santa Barbara, Peregrine Publishers, 1971, 335p.

2693
Ohio. Agricultural Research and Development Center. Dept. of Agricultural Economics and Rural Sociology
  Migrant Farm Workers in Northwestern Ohio, by James D. Howell, et al. Wooster, Ohio, 1971, 26p. (Research Bulletin #1049).

2694
Perry, Joseph B., Jr., & Snyder, Eldon E.
  "Opinions of Farm Employers Toward Welfare Assistance for Mexican American Migrant Workers." *Sociological and Social Research* 55, January 1971, pp. 161-169.

2695
Illinois. Spanish Speaking People's Study Commission
  Report to the 77th General Assembly of the State of Illinois. Chicago, February 1971, 20 & 11pp.

2696
Berger, Samuel R.
  "Profiteering With Poverty." *New South: A Quarterly Review of Southern Affairs* 26, Spring 1971, pp. 52-63.

2697

Harper, Dean H.

The Relationship of Migrant Workers' Attitudes and Behavior to Their Work Environment. Final Report. (Number PB-199 772). National Technical Information Service, Springfield, VA 22151, April 26, 1971, 42p.

2698

Sherman, Lawrence J., & Levy, Joan L.

"Free Access to Migratory Labor Camps." *American Bar Association Journal* (57: 5), May 1971, pp. 434-437.

2699

Mintz, Warren

A Search for a Successful Agricultural Migrant: an Account of 5 Fruit Harvests on the West Coast of the United States. (Number PB-207 121). National Technical Information Service, Springfield, VA 2215, October 1971, 266p.

2700

Blevins, Audie L., Jr.

"Socioeconomic Differences Between Migrants and non-Migrants." *Rural Sociology* (36: 4), December 1971, pp. 509-520.

2701

Ewald, Thomas R.

Court Action for Migrants. Washington, Migrant Legal Aid Action Program, 1972, 145p.

2702

Hathway, Marion

The Migratory Worker and Family Life. New York, Reprinted by Arno Press from 1934 edition, 1972, 240p.

2703

Interstate Migrant Human Development Project. Laredo, Texas, Texas Migrant Council, Inc., 1972, 14p. (ED 097 107).

2704

Lassey, William, R., & Navratil, Gerald

The Agricultural Workforce and Rural Development: Plight of the Migrant Worker. Bozeman, Montana, Agricultural Experiment Station (Research Report #23), 1972, 32p.

2705

"The Migrations" (In Valdez, Luis, and Steiner, Stan, eds. *Aztlan: an Anthology of Mexican American Literature,* chapter 5, New York, Knopf, 1972, pp. 127-144).

2706
Miller, Paul B.
To House the Migrant. Geneseo, N.Y., New York State Migrant Center, State University College of Arts & Science, 1972, 84 & 16pp.

2707
Oregon. Migrant Housing Task Force
Report of Migrant Housing Task Force to Governor Tom McCall. Salem, 1972, 56p.

2708
U.S. Senate. Committee on Labor & Public Welfare. Subcommittee on Migratory Labor
Farmworkers in Rural America, 1971-1972: parts 3A-3C, January 11-13, 1972, on Land Ownership, Use and Distribution. 92nd Congress, second session. Washington, 1972, 3 parts.

2709
Martinez, Frank
"Oregon's Chicanos Fight for Equality." *Civil Rights Digest* 5, Winter 1972, pp. 17-22.

2710
O'Connell, Michael
"Migrant Farmers in New York?" *Civil Rights Digest* 5, Winter 1972, pp. 11-16.

2711
U.S. Dept. of Agriculture. Economic Research Service
Direct and Contract Hiring of Seasonal Farm Labor, by Walter E. Sellers, Jr. Statistical Bulletin #478). Washington, February 1972, 24p.

2712
Brody, David
"Labor of the Great Depression: the Interpretive Prospects." *Labor History* (13: 2), Spring 1972, pp. 231-244.

2713
Friedland, William H., & Nelkin, Dorothy
"Technological Trends and the Organization of Migrant Farm Workers." *Social Problems* 19, Spring 1972, pp. 509-521.

2714
Dempsey, Terrence M.
Variations in Value Orientations Among Four Ethnic Subgroups of Migratory Agricultural Workers. Coral Gables, Florida, 1973, 192p. (Ph.D. Dissertation, University of Miami)

2715
Fisher, J. D.
A Historical Study of the Migrant in California. San Francisco, R & E Research Associates, 1973, 63p.

2716
Moreno, Dorinda
La Mujer: en pie de Lucha, y la Hora es ya. México, Espina del Norte Publicaciones, 1973, 301p.

2717
Reuel, Myrtle R.
Territorial Boundaries of Rural Poverty: Profiles of Exploitation. Bulletin Office, Box 231, Michigan State University, East Lansing, Michigan 48824, 1973, 75p.

2718
Taoka, Ronald W., & Mason, Tom R.
It's Time to Stay (a Story About Settling); the Four-Year History of the Migrant Settlement Project and the Process Model of Settlement. Denver, Foundation for Urban and Neighborhood Development, 1973, 302p.

2719
U.S. Comptroller General
Impact of Federal Programs to Improve the Living Conditions of Migrant and Other Seasonal Workers. Report to the Congress. Washington, U.S. General Accounting Office, 1973, 124p.

2720
U.S. Senate. Committee on Labor & Public Welfare. Subcommittee on Migratory Labor
Farmworkers in Rural America, 1971-1972: Hearings, part 1, July 22-September 22, 1971, on Farmworkers in Rural Poverty. 92nd Congress, first and second sessions. Washington, 1973, 297p.

2721
Vega, Jaime I., ed., et al.
National Migrant Information Clearinghouse, Juarez-Lincoln Center, Annual Report, 1972-73. 1973, 73p. (ED 082 912).

2722
Pratt, Mildred
"Effect of Mechanization on Migrant Farm Workers." *Social Casework* (54: 2), February 1973, pp. 105-113.

2723
Carlson, Alvar W.
"Seasonal Farm Labor in the San Luis Valley." *Annals of the Association of American Geographers* 63, March 1973, pp. 97-108.

2724
Adelman, Lester C., & Durant, Bill E.
"Who are These men?" A Study of the Tramps of Downtown Stockton (and the Agencies That Serve Them). Research Monograph #10. Davis, University of California, Davis, Dept. of Applied Behavioral Sciences, April 1973, 43p. (ED 094 904).

2725
Gutierrez, Elizabeth, & Lujan, Herman D.
The Kansas Migrant Survey: an Interpretive Profile of the Mexican-American Migrant Family. May 1973, 75p. (ED 104 419).

2726
Bauman, John F.
"Forgotten Americans: the Migrant and Indian Poor." *Current History* 64, June 1973, pp. 264-267.

2727
Zonligt, Martin J.
Migrant and Seasonal Farmworker Powerlessness: the Need for a Survival Information Center. October 31, 1973, 62p. (ED 086 427).

2728
Hawkes, Glenn R., et al.
Patterns of Living in California's Migrant Labor Families. Research Monograph #12. Davis, University of California, Davis, Dept. of Applied Behavioral Sciences, August 1973, 33p. (ED 107 359).

2729
Beale, C. L.
"Migration Patterns of Minorities in the United States." *American Journal of Agricultural Economics* (55: 5), December 1973, pp. 938-946.

2730
Gecas, Viktor
"Self Conceptions of Migrant and Settled Mexican-Americans." *Social Science Quarterly* (54: 3), December 1973, pp. 579-595.

2731
Applen, Allen G.
Migratory Harvest Labor in the Midwestern Wheat Belt, 1870-1940. Manhattan, Kansas, 1974, 215p. (Ph.D. Dissertation, Kansas State University)

2732
Conference on Migrant Farm Workers. 1st, Columbia, S.C., 1974
Proceedings. First Annual Conference on Migrant Farm Workers, October 10, 1974, Wade Hampton Hotel, Columbia, S.C.; under the Sponsorship of the South Carolina Migrant Farmworkers Commission. [Columbia, the Commission, 1974?] 21p.

2733
Follman, Joseph F.
Migratory Workers, Provision and Financing of Health Care. Chicago, Health Insurance Association of America, 1974, 43p.

2734
Genesee/Finger Lakes Regional Planning Board
Migrant Shelter: a Housing Dilemma. Rochester, N.Y., 1974, 102p.

2735
Londhe, Suresh R., & Hurst, Robert L.
Situational Study of Migrant Farmworkers in South Carolina . . . Orangeburg, South Carolina State College, 1974 (Research Bulletin #3), 1974, 36p.

2736
National Migrant Information Clearinghouse
Migrant Programs in the Southwestern States: Arizona, Colorado, Kansas, Nevada, New Mexico, and Utah. Austin, Juarez-Lincoln Center, 1974, 173p.

2737
Rosedale, Donald, & Mamer, John
Labor Management for Seasonal Farm Workers; a Case Study. Berkeley, University of California, Cooperative Extension-Agricultural Experiment Station (Information Series in Agricultural Economics, #74-1), 1974, 39p.

2738
U.S. Commission on Civil Rights. Indiana Advisory Committee
Indiana Migrants: Blighted Hopes, Slighted Rights: a Report. . . Chicago, Midwest Regional Office, U.S. Commission on Civil Rights, 1974, 82p.

2739
U.S. Senate. Committee on Labor and Public Welfare.
Subcommittee on Employment, Poverty and Migratory Labor *Farm Labor Contractor Registration Act Amendments, 1974.* Hearings, 93rd Congress, Second Session, on S. 2070 . . . S. 3202 . . . and Related Bills. February 8, 1974, Fresno, California; April 8 and 9, 1974, Washington. Washington, GPO, 1974, 268p.

2740
Ellenbrook, David, & Enoch, J. R.
The Migrant Worker in Socio-historical Perspective. Paper Presented at the Rural Sociological Section, Annual Meeting of the Southern Association of Agricultural Scientists, Memphis, Tennessee, February 1974. February 1974, 14p. (ED 094 910).

2741
Vega, Jaime I., ed., et al.
Migrant Programs in Wisconsin and Ohio. National Farmworkers Information Clearinghouse, 715 E. First St., Austin, Texas, May 1974, 214p.

2742
Iden, G.
"Factors Affecting Earnings of Southern Migrants." *Industrial Relations* 13, May 1974, pp. 177-189.

2743
Migrant Programs in the Northwestern States—Idaho, Montana, Nebraska, North Dakota, South Dakota, Oregon, Washington, Wyoming. Juarez-Lincoln Center, National Migrant Information Clearinghouse (3001 S. Congress, Austin, Texas, 78704), November 1974, 169p.

2744
Migrant Programs in the Southwestern States—Arizona, Colorado, Kansas, Nevada, New Mexico and Utah. Juarez-Lincoln Center, National Migrant Information Clearinghouse (3001 S. Congress, Austin, Texas, 78704), November 1974, 191p.

2745
Provinzano, James
Settling out and Settling in. Paper Presented at the American Anthropological Association Annual Meeting, November 23, 1974. November 23, 1974, 12p. (ED 138 412).

2746
Croutch, Albert
Housing Migratory Agricultural Workers in California, 1913-1958. San Francisco, R & E Research Associates, 1975, 92p.

2747
Directory of Services for Migrant Families. Springfield, IL, Migrant Education Section, Illinois Office of Education, 1975-   .

2748
Sciara, Frank J.
Attitudes of Indiana Townspeople Towards Migrants. 1975, 9p. (ED 122 992).

2749
U.S. Rehabilitation Services Administration. Office of Human Development
Handicapped Migrant Farm Workers: Characteristics of Disabled Migratory and Seasonal Agricultural Workers and Their Families, Impact of the State/Federal Vocational Rehabilitation Program, and Strategies for

Expanding Services, by Michael E. Cortes. DHEW Publication number (OHD), 75-25084. Washington, U.S. Dept. of Health, Education and Welfare, 1975, 131p.

2750
Monk, Phillip M., & Medina, Dennis
Residence Projections of Mexican-American Youth From the Border Area of South Texas: a Study of Change Over Time. Paper Presented at the Annual Meeting of the Southwestern Sociological Association, Dallas, Texas, April 9, 1976. Report Numbers: TAES-H-2811; U.S. Dept. of Agriculture (DSRS)-S-81, in Cooperation with Cooperative State Research Service, Washington, D.C., April 9, 1975, 48p.

2751
Proceedings: Annual Conference on Migrant Farm Workers. 26th, October 1, 1975, Columbia, South Carolina. Columbia, S.C., Migrant Farmworkers Commission, October 1, 1975, 47p. (ED 145 981).

2752
Bissell, Kathryn A.
The Migratory Farmworker; a Multi-disciplinary Module. Washington, Institute for Multidisciplinary Graduate Research, Graduate Section, Catholic University of America, 1976, 130p.

2753
David, Benjamin G.
A Predictive Model for Migrant Farmworker Movement in the United States. Paper Presented at the Operations Research Society of America Meeting, November, 1976. 1976, 30p. (ED 147 071).

2754
Dunbar, Anthony, & Kravitz, Linda
Hard Traveling: Migrant Farm Workers in America. Cambridge, MA, Ballinger Pub. Co., 1976, 159p.

2755
Friends, Society of. American Friends Service Committee. Pennsylvania Farm Labor Project
Pennsylvania Farm Labor Plan, Submitted to the Interdepartmental Council on Seasonal Farmworkers and the Pennsylvania Dept. of Community Affairs, pursuant to Contract M.E. #74-541 of June 25, 1975. Philadelphia, Pennsylvania Farm Labor Project, National Community Relations Div., American Friends Service Committee, 1976, 151 & 27pp.

2756
Hintz, Joy
Seven Families: a Two-Year In-depth Study of Incomes and Job Experience of Seven Ohio Migrant Farm Worker Families, 1974-1976. Tiffin, Ohio, Hintz, 1976, 238p.

2757
Labor Mobility and Population in Agriculture. Assembled and Published under the Sponsorship of the Iowa State University Center for Agricultural and Economic Adjustment. Westport, CT, Greenwood Press, 1976, 231p.

2758
Morain, Lloyd
The Human Cougar. Buffalo, N.Y., Prometheus Books, 1976, 175p.

2759
New Approaches to the Study of Migration. Edited by David Guillet and Douglas Uzzel, et al. Houston, William Marsh Rice University, 1976, 181p. (Rice University Studies, v. 62, #3).

2760
Texas. Governor's Office of Migrant Affairs
Migrant and Seasonal Farmworkers in Texas. Austin, 1976, 73p.

2761
U.S. General Accounting Office
How Federal Programs Affect Migrant and Seasonal Farmworkers in the Connecticut River Valley; DHEW, Dept. of Labor, Office of Economic Opportunity. Report of the Comptroller General of the United States. Washington, 1976, 48p. (B-177486).

2762
U.S. House. Select Committee to Investigate the Interstate Migration of Destitute Citizens
Interstate Migration: Report of the Select Committee . . . House of Representatives Pursuant to H. Res. 63, 491, 629 (76th Congress), and H. Res. 16 (77th Congress) . . . New York, Da Capo Press, 1976, 741p. (Reprint of the 1941 edition of the GPO, Washington, issued as Report #369, 77th Congress, First Session, House of Reps.)

2763
Bradshaw, Benjamin S.
"Potential Labor Force Supply, Replacement and Migration of Mexican-American and Other Males in the Texas-Mexico Border Region." *International Migration Review* (10: 1), Spring 1976, pp. 29-45.

2764
An Assessment of the Migrant and Seasonal Farmworker Situation in the United States. Volume I: Executive Summary and Conclusions. Washington, Inter-America Research Associates, May 28, 1976, 54p. (ED 144 769).

2765
An Assessment of the Migrant and Seasonal Farmworker Situation in the United States. Volume II: Findings. Washington, Inter-America Research Associates, May 28, 1976, 451p. (ED 144 770—not available in hard copy).

2766
Wells, Miriam J.
"Emigrants From the Migrant Stream: Environment and Incentives in Relocation." *Aztlan* 7, Summer 1976, pp. 267-290.

2767
Migrant and Seasonal Farmworkers in Texas. Migrant and Seasonal Farmworker Population Survey. Final Report. Austin, Texas Governor's Office of Migrant Affairs (Report #GOMA-76-01), July 15, 1976, 101p. (ED 191 600).

2768
Coalson, George
The Development of the Migrant Farm Labor System in Texas, 1900-1954. San Francisco, R & E Research Associates, 1977, 132p.

2769
Coles, Robert
"God Save Them, Those Children: and for Allowing Such a State of Affairs to Continue, God Save us too"; Excerpt From "Uprooted Children" (In Gross, Beatrice, & Gross, Ronald, eds. *The Children's Rights Movement; Overcoming the Oppression of Young People.* Garden City, N.Y., Anchor Press/Doubleday, 1977, pp. 118-122).

2770
Good Neighbor Commission of Texas
Texas Migrant Labor: a Special Report to the Governor and Legislature. Austin, Texas 1977, 101p. (ED 139 568).

2771
Hintz, Joy
Gallant Women of 1977: Migrant Farm Workers. Tiffin, Ohio, Heidelberg College, 1977.

2772
Lindborg, Kristina
Five Mexican-American Women in Transition: a Case Study of Migrants in the Midwest. San Francisco, R & E Research Associates, 1977, 112p.

2773
Montejano, David
Race, Labor Repression, and Capitalist Agriculture. Notes From South Texas, 1920-1930. (Working Papers Series, #102). Berkeley, Institute for the Study of Social Change, University of California, Berkeley, 1977, 56p.

2774
Texas Farmworker Information Clearinghouse
Farmworker Programs in Texas/TFIC. Revised. Austin? 1977, 169p.

2775
Texas. Good Neighbor Commission
Texas Migrant Labor: a Special Report to the Governor and Legislature. Austin, 1977, 105p.

2776
U.S. Commission on Civil Rights. Delaware Advisory Committee
The Working and Living Conditions of Mushroom Workers: a Report, Prepared by the Delaware and Pennsylvania Advisory Committee to the U.S. Commission on Civil Rights. Washington, 1977, 65p.

2777
Villareal, Oscar L.
Texas Migrant Council. Laredo, Texas Migrant Council, 1977? 12p. (ED 175 584).

2778
Where Have all the Farmworkers Gone? (The Statistical Annihilation of Hired Farmworkers). An Analysis of the Federal Effort to Define and Count Migrant and Seasonal Farmworkers. Research Report #1. Washington, Rural America, Inc., August 1977, 122p.

2779
Harris, Sara, & Allen, Robert F.
The Quiet Revolution: the Story of a Small Miracle in American Life. New York, Rawson Associates, 1978, 283p.

2780
Judson, Horace A.
Reflections of a Former Migrant. Keynote Address to the Annual Migrant Education Institute at Salisbury State College (8th, Salisbury, MD, June 1976). Baltimore, Maryland State Dept. of Education, Division of Compensatory, Urban and Supplementary Programs, 1978, 29p. (ED 196 812).

2781
Sosnick, Stephen H.
Hired Hands: Seasonal Farm Workers in the United States. Santa Barbara, McNally & Luftin West, 1978, 453p.

2782
U.S. Commission on Civil Rights. Rocky Mountain Regional Office
People who Follow the Crops . . . Washington, U.S. Commission on
Civil Right (for sale by GPO), 1978, 80p.

2783
Coles, Robert, & Coles, J. H.
Women of Crisis. New York, Delta, 1979, 304p.

2784
Deveaux, William P.
*Migrant Farm Workers: a Study Based on Gibson Winter's Concept of
Responsible Society.* Nashville, 1979, 240p. (Ph.D. Dissertation, Vanderbilt University).

2785
North Dakota. State Employment Security Bureau. Employment Service
Division
Job Service, North Dakota Annual Rural Report, 1979, by James
Schneider. Bismarck, 1979-   (annual).

2786
*Annual Operational Summary (of) Migrant Family Housing Centers, 1978
Open Season.* Sacramento, California State Dept. of Employment
Development, Migrant Services Section, March 1979, 28p. (ED 188
795).

2787
Goyette, Cherie A., et al.
*Farmworker Needs—Agency Services: a Study of Migrant and Seasonal
Farmworkers and Service Agencies in a 4-County Central Florida Area.*
April 1979, 259p. (ED 175 609).

2788
Slesinger, Doris P., & Muirragui, Eileen
Migrant Agricultural Labor in Wisconsin; a Short History. Madison,
University of Wisconsin, Institute for Research on Poverty (Report #IRP-
DP-565-79), October 1979, 26p. (ED 190 337).

2789
Mounts, G. J.
"Laws of the Land: Arizona's Agricultural Labor Relations Law."
Monthly Labor Review 102, November 1979, pp. 54-55.

2790
Ourada, Patricia K.
Migrant Workers in Idaho. [Boise, State University? 1980] 94p.

2791
Thomas-Lycklama a Nijeholt, G.
On the Road for Work; Migratory Farm Workers on the East Coast of the United States. Boston, Nijhoff, 1980, 211p.

2792
North, David S.
Non-Immigrant Workers in the United States; Current Trends and Future Implications. Washington, New TransCentury Foundation, Center for Labor & Migration Studies (for U.S. Dept. of Labor, Employment & Training Administration), May 1980, 172 & 7pp.

2793
U.S. Commission on Civil Rights. Idaho Advisory Committee
A Roof Over our Heads: Migrant and Seasonal Farmworker Housing in Idaho. Washington, September 1980, 99p.

2794
Goldfarb, Ronald L.
Migrant Farm Workers: a Caste of Despair. Ames, Iowa, Iowa State University Press, 1981, 237p.

2795
The H-2 Program and Non-Immigrants. Hearing Before the Subcommittee on Immigration and Refugee Policy of the Committee on the Judiciary, U.S. Senate, 97th Congress, First Session. Senate Document J-97-85, November 30, 1981. Washington, 1981, 378p. (ED 224 965—not available in paper copy due to small type).

2796
Margolis, Richard J.
Homes of the Brave: a Report on Migrant Farmworker Housing. Rural America, 1346 Connecticut Ave., N.W., Washington, D.C. 20036, 1981, 36p.

2797
Public Policy and the Migrant Child. A Symposium Conference—Report and Papers, New Brunswick, N.J., October 17-19, 1980. National Organization for Migrant Children (310 E. 42nd St., New York, N.Y. 10017), 1981, 149p.

2798
U.S. Senate. Committee on Labor and Human Resources. Subcommittee on Employment, Poverty and Migratory Labor
Oversight on Issues Affecting Hispanics and Migrant and Seasonal Farmworkers; Hearing Before the Subcommittee on Employment, Poverty and Migratory Labor, U.S. Senate, 96th Congress 2nd Session, on Ex-

amination on Whether and to What Extent Existing Federal Programs Effectively and Efficiently Meet the Needs of Hispanics and Migrant and Seasonal Farmworkers, Milwaukee, Wisconsin, September 6, 1980. Washington, GPO, 1981, 127p. (Y4.L11/4:H62).

2799
Annual Demographic Data for Migrant Housing Centers: 1980 Harvest Season, by Mark. R. Trabing. Sacramento, California, State Dept. of Housing & Community Development, July 1981, 20p. (ED 216 839).

2800
U.S. Dept. of Agriculture. Economic Research Service
Hired Farmworkers: Background and Trends for the '80's, by Leslie Whitener Smith and Robert Coltrane. (Rural Development Research Report, #32). Washington, September 1981, 37p.

2801
U.S. House. Committee on Banking, Finance and Urban Affairs. Subcommittee on Housing and Community Development
Migrant and Seasonal Farmworker Housing in the United States; Hearings Before the Subcommittee on Housing and Community Development, House of Representatives, 97th Congress, First Session. Washington, GPO, 1981. (Part 1: "Sept. 17, Sept. 19 (Melfa, VA), and Oct. 9, 1981 (San Antonio, TX").

2802
Laylo, Peter R., & Puente, Juan
Training, Employment and Services Opportunities for Migrant and Seasonal Farmworkers in the Midwest. Chicago, Association of Farmworker Organizations, October 16, 1981, 53p.

2803
Hoffer, Eric
"The Role of the Undesirables" (In his, *Between the Devil and the Dragon; the Best Essays and Aphorisms of Eric Hoffer.* New York, Harper & Row, 1982, pp. 74-83).

2804
Mines, Richard, & Anzaldúa, Ricardo
New Migrants vs. old Migrants: Alternative Labor Market Structures in the California Citrus Industry. La Jolla, Center for U.S.-Mexican Studies, University of California, San Diego, 1982, 118p. (M 9).

2805
Solís, Faustina
"Socioeconomic and Cultural Conditions of Migrant Workers" (In Rosaldo, Renato, et al., comps. *Chicano: the Evolution of a People.* Malabar, FL, Krieger, 1982, pp. 176-183).

2806
U.S. Senate. Committee on the Judiciary.
Subcommittee on Immigration and Refugee Policy. *Temporary Workers: Hearing* . . . 97th Congress, first session, on a new Temporary Worker Program With Mexico, October 22, 1981. Washington, GPO, 1982, 285p. 89/2:J-97-75).

2807
Reichert, Joshua S.
"Town Divided: Economic Stratification and Social Relations in a Mexican Migrant Community." *International Migration Review* 15, April 1982, pp. 411-423.

2808
Mines, Richard, et al.
"Migration to the United States and Mexican Rural Development: a Case Study." *American Journal of Agricultural Economics* 64, August 1982, pp. 444-454.

2809
Shim, K. R.
"Differential White-non White Migration Sensitivities to Income Differentials." *American Economist* 26, Fall 1982, pp. 66-68.

2810
Whitener, Leslie A.
Migrant Farmworkers and Their Attachment to Farmwork. Paper Presented at the Annual Meeting of the Rural Sociological Society, San Francisco, California, September 1-4, 1982. September 1982, 31p. (ED 221 330).

2811
Migrant Outreach Resource Center Network. San Juan, Texas, Colonias del Valle, Inc., 1983, 12p.

2812
U.S. House. Committee on Education and Labor. Subcommittee on Labor Standards
Hearing on the Migrant and Seasonal Agricultural Worker Protection Act; Hearing, September 14, 1982, on H.R. 7102. Washington, 97th Congress, 2nd Session, 1983, 177p.

2813
Terry, Jim
"Political Economy of Migrant Farm Labor." *Insurgent Sociologist* (11: 4), Spring 1983, p. 63- .

2814
Iowa Annual Evaluation Report for Migrant Programs, Fiscal Year 1982, by James F. Bottenfield. Des Moines, Iowa State Dept. of Public Instruction, March 1983, 17p.

2815
U.S. Commission on Civil Rights. Maryland Advisory Committee
Migrant Workers on Maryland's Eastern Shore. Washington, June 1983, 55p.

E. AGRICULTURAL LABOR UNIONS

1. Bibliographies

2816
Social Science Research Council. Pacific Coast Regional Commission
Agricultural Labor in the Pacific Coast States; a Bibliography and Suggestions for Research . . . [n.p.] 1938, 64p.

2817
Cameron, Colin, & Edelson, Joanne
Farm Labor Organizing: an Annotated Bibliography. Madison, WI, Institute for Research on Poverty, University of Wisconsin, 1969, 62p.

2818
Fairbanks, Helen
Collective Bargaining in Agriculture. Princeton, N.J., Princeton University (Selected References #148), 1969, 4p.

2819
Yinger, Winthrop
San Joaquin Valley Farm Workers Collection. Fresno, CA, Fresno State College Library, 1970, 11p.

2820
Mortimer, Louis R.
Unionism and Collective Bargaining for Agricultural Workers: a Selected Bibliography. Updated by Joseph Fulton. Washington, Library of Congress, Congressional Reference Service, 1974, 13p.

2821
Fodell, Beverly
Cesar Chavez and the United Farm Workers: a Selective Bibliography. Detroit, Labor History Archives, Wayne State University, January 1974, 103p.

2822
Majewski, Carolyn
Selected Bibliography; United Farm Workers, 1973-1976. Detroit, Wayne State University, Walter P. Reuther Library of Labor and Urban Affairs, 1976, 6p.

2. Circulating Materials

2823
Industrial Workers of the World. Agricultural Workers Industrial Union
Minutes of the Convention . . . Fargo, N.D.? 19-

2824
Industrial Workers of the World. Agricultural Workers Industrial Union No. 110
The Remedy for California's Misery. Chicago, 19- ? 4p.

2825
Bruère, Robert W.
Following the Trail of the IWW, a First-Hand Investigation Into Labor Troubles in the West . . . New York, New York Evening Post, 1918, 39p.

2826
Industrial Workers of the World. Agricultural Workers Industrial Union No. 400
Agricultural Workers, Attention. Organization, Solidarity, Shorter Hours, More Wages and Better Conditions. Chicago, IWW Publishing Bureau (Pamphlet . . . volume 7, #1), 1918? 4p.

2827
Industrial Workers of the World. Agricultural Workers Industrial Union
By-laws of the Agricultural Workers Industrial Union #110 of the I.W.W. Instructions to Members . . . Stationary Delegates and Branch Secretaries as Adopted by Previous Referendum and Amended by the Referendum of the Spring Convention at Sioux City, Iowa, 1921. Chicago, 1921, 64p.

2828
Industrial Workers of the World. Agricultural Workers Industrial Union
An Economic Interpretation of the job. Chicago, Dept. of Education of the Agricultural Workers Industrial Union #110 of the I.W.W. Chicago? 1922, 61p.

2829
Industrial Workers of the World
Minutes of the 18th Convention of the Agricultural Workers Industrial Union, #110, of the IWW, Held at Spokane, Washington, October 11-14, 1926. Chicago, 1926, 18p.

2830
Cross, Ira B.
A History of the Labor Movement in California. Berkeley, CA, University of California Press, 1935, 354p.

2831
Speth, Frank A.
A History of Agricultural Labor in Sonoma County, California. Berkeley, CA, 1938. (Ph.D. Dissertation, University of California, Berkeley)

2832
Sufrin, Sidney C.
"Labor Organization in Agricultural America, 1930-35." *American Journal of Sociology* 43, January 1938, pp. 544-559.

2833
Fuller, Varden
The Supply of Agricultural Labor as a Factor in the Evolution of Farm Organization in California. Berkeley, 1939, 345p. (Dissertation, University of California, Berkeley).

2834
Allen, Ruth A.
Early Chapters in the Organization of Labor in Texas. Austin, University of Texas Press, 1941, pp. 96-100.

2835
Schwartz, Harry
"Organizational Problems of Agricultural Labor Unions." *Journal of Farm Economy* 23, May 1941, pp. 456-466; November 1941, pp. 833-842.

2836
Spiegel, H. W.
"Trade Unions in Agriculture." *Rural Sociology* 6, June 1941, pp. 117-125.

2837
U.S. Bureau of Labor Statistics
Labor Unionism in American Agriculture. Bulletin #836. Washington GPO, 1945, 457p.

2838
Weintraub, Hyman
The IWW in California, 1905-1931. Los Angeles, 1947. (Ph.D. Dissertation, UCLA).

2839
Williamson, Paul G.
Labor in the California Citrus Industry. Berkeley, CA, 1947. (Ph.D. Dissertation, University of California, Berkeley)

2840
Adams, R. L.
"Impact of Unionization of Farm Workers Upon Farm Organization and Management" (In Western Farm Economic Association. *Proceedings, 1948.* Berkeley, CA, 1948, pp. 138-148).

2841
National Farm Labor Union
Agricultural Labor in 1948. Report . . . to the 15th Annual Convention . . . Cincinnati . . . 1948. Washington? 1948, 14p.

2842
Heilman, Grace E.
The Early History of the Labor Movement in Los Angeles. Philadelphia, 1949, 214p. (Ph.D. Dissertation, University of Pennsylvania)

2843
National Farm Labor Union
Constitution. Washington, 1949.

2844
National Farm Labor Union
Statement of H. L. Mitchell, President, on Amending Fair Labor Standards Act to Include Agricultural Workers. [n.p.] 1949.

2845
Morin, Alexander J.
Potential Trade Union Organization of Farm Laborers in the United States. Cambridge, MA, 1950. (Ph.D. Dissertation, Harvard University)

2846
National Agricultural Workers Union
American and Foreign Farmworkers in California; Statement to the President's Commission on Migratory Labor, by Ernesto Galarza. Washington, 1950, 30p.

2847
National Farm Labor Union, American Federation of Labor
Proceedings: 16th Convention, Fresno, California, January 13-15, 1950. Washington, 1950, 4 & 13pp.

2848
National Agricultural Workers Union
Constitution. [n.p., 1951] 13p.

2849
McWilliams, Carey
"America's Disadvantaged Minorities: Mexican-Americans." *Journal of Negro Education* 20, Summer 1951, pp. 301-309.

2850
Greer, Scott A.
The Participation of Ethnic Minorities in the Labor Unions of Los Angeles County. Los Angeles, 1952, 413p. (Ph.D. Dissertation, UCLA)

2851
Morin, Alexander J.
The Organizability of Farm Labor in the United States. Cambridge, MA, Harvard University Press, 1952, 102p.

2852
National Agricultural Workers Union. Research and Education Dept.
The Louisiana Sugar Cane Plantation Workers vs. the Sugar Corporations, U.S. Dept. of Agriculture, et al. Washington, Inter-American Educational Association, 1954, 159p.

2853
Stimson, Grace
Rise of the Labor Movement in Los Angeles. Berkeley, University of California Press, 1955, 529p.

2854
Shapiro, Harold A.
"The Labor Movement in San Antonio, Texas, 1865-1915." *Southwestern Social Science Quarterly* 36, September 1955, pp. 160-175.

2855
National Agricultural Workers Union
Datelines for a Deal. Washington, 1956, 20p.

2856
National Agricultural Workers Union
Report of the Executive Board to Officers and Delegates, 19th Convention, Memphis, Tennessee, March 30, 1957. Washington? 1957, 17p.

2857
National Agricultural Workers Union
Correspondence and Press Releases, 1958-1960. San Jose, 1958-60, 1 volume.

2858
Scruggs, Otey M.
A History of Mexican Agricultural Labor in the United States, 1942-1954. Cambridge, MA, 1958. (Ph.D. Dissertation, Harvard University)

2859
Greer, Scott A.
Last Man in; Racial Access to Union Power. Glencoe, IL, Free Press, 1959, 189p.

2860
National Agricultural Workers Union
Workers in our Fields, 1934-1959, 25th Anniversary. Washington, 1960? 38p.

2861
Holcomb, Ellen L.
Efforts to Organize the Migrant Workers by the Cannery and Agricultural Workers. Chico, CA, 1963. (Master's Thesis, Chico State College)

2862
Perry, Louis B., & Perry, Richard S.
History of the Los Angeles Labor Movement, 1911-1941. Berkeley, University of California Press, 1963, 622p.

2863
California. Legislature. Assembly. Interim Committee on Industrial Relations
Transcript of Proceedings of the Assembly Interim Subcommittee on Special Employment Problems of the Assembly Interim Committee on Industrial Relations. Hearings in Los Angeles, January 10, 1964, on the Subject of Special Employment Problems of the Mexican-American. Sacramento? 1964, 101p.

2864
Kirkendall, Richard S.
"Social Science in the Central Valley of California." *California Historical Society Quarterly* (43: 3), September 1964, pp. 195-218.

2865
Jones, Lamar B.
Mexican-American Labor Problems in Texas. Austin, University of Texas at Austin, 1965, 234p. (Ph.D. dissertation, University of Texas at Austin).

2866
Glass, Judith (Chanin)
Conditions Which Facilitate Unionization of Agricultural Workers. A Case Study of the Salinas Valley Lettuce Industry. Los Angeles, 1966, 179p. (Ph.D. Dissertation, UCLA)

2867
National Farm Workers Association
The Plan of Delano. Delano, CA, 1966, 4p.

2868
Rayback, Joseph G.
A History of American Labor. New York, Free Press, 1966, 491p.

2869
Taft, Philip
"Mayor Short and the IWW Agricultural Workers." *Labor History* 7, Spring 1966, pp. 173-177.

2870
Logsdon, G.
"Fight for Farm Labor." *Farm Journal* 90, March 1966, p. 89.

2871
Chavez, Cesar, & Rustin, Bayard
Right to Work Laws; a Trap for America's Minorities. New York, A. Philips Randolph Institute, 1967, 15p.

2872
National Advisory Committee on Farm Labor
Farm Labor Organizing, 1905-1967; a Brief History. New York, 1967, 68p.

2873
Sons of Zapata. Rio Grande City, TX, University Farm Workers Organizing Committee, AFL-CIO, 1967, 77p.

2874
Tooni, Linda (Lewis), et al.
Farm Labor Organizing, 1905-1967, a Brief History. July 1967, 72p. (ED 013 679).

2875
Kornbluh, Joyce L., ed.
Rebel Voices: an I.W.W. Anthology. Ann Arbor, University of Michigan Press, 1968, 419p.

2876
Caso, Thomas
Collective Bargaining in California Agriculture, Viable? San Francisco, 1969, 134p. (Master of Arts thesis, San Francisco State College).

2877
Rowan, Helen
The Mexican-American. Paper prepared for the U.S. Commission on Civil Rights. Available from Community Opportunity Programs in Education (4441 University Ave., San Diego, California 92105), November 1969, 36p.

2878
Nelson, Eugene
"Who is Cesar Chavez?" (In Servin, Manuel P. *The Mexican Americans: an Awakening Minority.* Beverly Hills, Glencoe Press, 1970, pp. 227-235).

2879
Cauchols, Jr., Scott, & Lianos, Theodore P.
"Some Economic Effects of Farm Labor Unionization." *University of Akron Business Review* 1, Summer 1970, pp. 45-55.

2880
Lander, Robert S.
"Unionization of the Agricultural Labor Force: an Inquiry of Job Property Rights." *Southern California Law Review* (44: 1), Fall 1970, pp. 181-217.

2881
Day, Mark
Forty Acres; Cesar Chavez and the Farm Workers. New York, Praeger, 1971, 222p.

2882
De Toledano, Ralph
Little Caesar. Washington, Anthem Books, 1971, 144p.

2883
Levenstein, Harvey A.
Labor Organizations in the United States and Mexico; a History of Their Relations. New York, Greenwood Press, 1971, 258p.

2884
Pitrone, Jeanne (Maddern)
Chavez, Man of the Migrants. New York, Alba House, 1971, 169p.

2885
"La Causa, in the Beginning" (In Valdez, Luis, and Steiner, Stan, eds. *Aztlan: an Anthology of Mexican American Literature,* chapter 7. New York, Knopf, 1972, pp. 197-226).

2886
"La Causa, La Tierra." (In Valdez, Luis, and Steiner, Stan, eds. *Aztlan: an Anthology of Mexican American Literature,* chapter 8. New York, Knopf, 1972, pp. 227-256).

2887
Daniels, Cletus
Labor Radicalism in Pacific Coast Agriculture. Seattle, 1972. (Ph.D. Dissertation, University of Washington)

2888

Solís Garza, Luis A.

"Cesar Chavez: the Chicano Messiah?" (In Simmen, Edward, ed. *Pain and Promise*. New York, New American Library, 1972, 348p.).

2889

Gomez-Quiñones, Juan

The First Steps: Chicano Labor Conflict and Organizing 1900-1920." *Aztlan* (3: 1), Spring 1972, pp. 13-49.

2890

Moore, Joan W.

"LUCHA in Agencyland: a Chicano Self-Help Organization Meets the Establishment." *Growth and Change* III, July 1972, pp. 43-50.

2891

Weber, Debra A.

"The Organization of Mexicano Agricultural Workers, the Imperial Valley and Los Angeles, 1928-1934, an Oral History Approach." *Aztlan* (3: 2), Fall 1972, p. 307- .

2892

Alvarez, S. E.

"The Legal and Legislative Struggle of the Farmworkers." (In Romano V., Octavio I., comp. *Voices: Readings From El Grito, a Journal of Contemporary Mexican-American Thought, 1967-1973*. Rev., expanded 2d ed. Berkeley, Quinto Sol Publications, 1973, 542p.).

2893

Privett, John D.

Agricultural Unionism Among Chicanos in Texas. Austin, University of Texas, Bureau of Business Research (Research Monograph #36), 1973.

2894

Lewarne, Charles P.

"On the Wobbly Train to Fresno." *Labor History* 14, Spring 1973, pp. 264-289.

2895

Reisler, Mark

"Mexican Unionization in California Agriculture, 1927-1936." *Labor History* (14: 4), Fall 1973, pp. 562-579.

2896

U.S. House. Committee on Education & Labor. Subcommittee

Agriculture Labor-Management Relations. Hearing: 93rd Congress, First Session . . . May 21, 1973. Washington, GPO, 1974, 195p. (Hearing on H.R. 881 [Title 1], 4007, 4011, 4408, 7513).

2897
Young, Jan
The Migrant Workers and Cesar Chavez. New York, Messner, 1974, 191p.

2898
Mayes, K.
"Deadlock in the Desert." *Industrial Management* 4, February 1974, pp. 35-37.

2899
Murphy, T. E.
"End to American Serfdom—the Need for Farm Labor Legislation." *Labor Law Journal* 25, February 1974, pp. 85-93.

2900
Taylor, Ronald B.
Chavez and the Farm Workers. Boston, Beacon Press, 1975, 342p.

2901
Yinger, Winthrop
Cesar Chavez: the Rhetoric of Nonviolence. Hicksville, N.Y., Exposition Press, 1975, 143p.

2902
Jamieson, Stuart M.
Labor Unionism in American Agriculture. New York, Arno Press, 1976, 457p.

2903
Levy, Jacques E.
Cesar Chavez: Autobiography of La Causa. New York, Norton, 1976, 546p.

2904
Meister, Dick, & Loftis, Anne
A Long Time Coming: The Struggle to Unionize America's Farm Workers. New York, Macmillan, 1977, 241p.

2905
Martin, Philip L.
"Harvest Mechanization and Agricultural Trade Unionism: Obreros Unidos in Wisconsin." *Labor Law Journal* 28, March 1977, pp. 166-173.

2906
Jenkins, J. C., & Perrow, Charles
"Insurgency of the Powerless: Farm Worker Movements, 1946-1972." *American Sociological Review* 42, April 1977, pp. 249-268.

2907
Rochin, R. I.
"New Perspectives on Agricultural Labor Relations in California."
Labor Law Journal 28, July 1977, pp. 395-402.

2908
Nelson-Cisneros, Victor B.
"UCAPAWA Organizing Activities in Texas, 1935-1950." *Aztlan* 9,
1978, pp. 71-84.

2909
Fuller, Varden, & Mamer, J. W.
"Constraints on California Farm Worker Unionization." *Industrial Relations* 17, May 1978, pp. 143-155.

2910
Marentes, Carlos
"El Sindicato de Trabajadores Agrícolas de Texas." México, *Revista de México Agrario* (XI: 4), October-December 1978, pp. 145-172.

2911
Yates, M. D.
"Make Whole Remedy for Employer Refusal to Bargain: Early Experience Under the California Agricultural Labor Relations Act." *Labor Law Journal* 29, October 1978, pp. 666-676.

2912
Garcia, Beatrice M.
The Effects of Conflict Upon Mexican-American Workers and Union Activists. San Francisco, 1979, 101p. (Master of Arts thesis, San Francisco State University).

2913
Walsh, Edward J., & Craypo, Charles
"Union Oligarchy and the Grass Roots; the Case of the Teamsters' Defeat in Farmworker Organizing." *Sociology & Social Research* 63, January 1979, pp. 269-293.

2914
Denney, William M.
"Participant Citizenship in a Marginal Group: Union Mobilization of California Farm Workers." *American Journal of Political Science* 23, May 1979, pp. 330-337.

2915
Segur, Winthrop H., Jr.
Representation Elections for Farm Workers: Voting Power Under Alternative Rules of Eligibility. Davis, CA, 1980, 284p. (Ph.D. Dissertation, University of California, Davis)

2916
Sanchez, Guadalupe L., & Romo, Jesús
Organizing Mexican Undocumented Farm Workers on Both Sides of the Border. La Jolla, Center for U.S.-Mexican Studies, University of California, San Diego, 1981, 12p. (RR 27).

2917
Majka, Linda C.
"Labor Militancy Among Farm Workers and the Strategy of Protest, 1900-1979." *Social Problems* 28, June 1981, pp. 533-547.

2918
Cottle, Rex L., et al.
Labor and Property Rights in California Agriculture: an Economic Analysis of the CALRA. College Station, Texas, Texas A & M University Press, 1982, 116p.

2919
Voos, Paula B. (Vogel)
Labor Union Organizing Programs, 1954-1977. Cambridge, MA, 1982, 397p. (Ph.D. Dissertation, Harvard University)

2920
Murray, Douglas L.
"The Abolition of *el Cortito,* the Short-Handled hoe: a Case Study in Social Conflict and State Policy in California Agriculture." *Social Problems* 30, October 1982, pp. 26-39.

2921
Zamora, Emilio
Mexican Labor Activity in South Texas, 1900-1920. Austin, TX, 1983, 270p. (Ph.D. Dissertation, University of Texas at Austin)

2922
Browne, W. P.
"Mobilizing and Activating Group Demands: the American Agricultural Movement." *Social Science Quarterly* 64, March 1983, pp. 19-34.

F. FARM LABOR STRIKES

1. Bibliographies

2923
Taylor, Paul S.
Material Relating to Agricultural and Maritime Strikes in California; Report and Key to Arrangements. Berkeley, University of California, Berkeley, Bancroft Library, 1975, 6p.

2. Circulating Materials

2924
Emerick, C. F.
"Analysis of Agricultural Discontent in the United States." *Political Science Quarterly* 11, 1896, pp. 434-601.

2925
Parker, Carleton H.
"The California Casual and his Revolt." *Quarterly Journal of Economics* 30, November 1915, pp. 110-126.

2926
Lowenstein, Norman
Strikes and Strike Tactics in California Agricultural History. Berkeley, CA, 1940. (Ph.D. Dissertation, University of California, Berkeley)

2927
Roskelley, R. W.
Beet Labor Problems in Colorado. Fort Collins, CO, State Agricultural College, 1940, 12p.

2928
Taylor, Paul S.
"Social Aspects of Arizona's Farm Labor Problems." *Sociology & Social Research,* July-August 1940, pp. 550-557.

2929
McWilliams, Carey
"Politics of Utopia" (In his, *Southern California Country; an Island on the Land.* New York, Duell, Sloane & Pearce, 1946, pp. 273-313).

2930
Bauers, Ulla E., Jr.
The DiGiorgio Strike. Berkeley, CA, 1949. (Ph.D. Dissertation, University of California, Berkeley)

2931
Hough, John
Agricultural Labor Relations in the Imperial Valley From 1934. Los Angeles, 1951. (Ph.D. Dissertation, University of Southern California)

2932
Chavez, Cesar
The Grape Boycott; why it has to be. [Delano, California, United Farm Workers Organizing Committee, 196-], 4p.

2933
California. Legislature. Senate. Fact-Finding Committee on Labor and Welfare
California's Farm Labor Problem: Report. Sacramento, 1961-63.

2934
Wolf, Jerome
The Imperial Valley as an Index of Agricultural Labor Relations in California. Los Angeles, 1964, 385p. (Ph.D. Dissertation, University of Southern California)

2935
Gray, James
The American Civil Liberties Union of Southern California and the Imperial Valley Agricultural Disturbances, 1930-1934. Los Angeles, 1966, 365p. (Ph.D. Dissertation, UCLA)

2936
Nelson, Eugene
Huelga: the First Hundred Days of the Great Delano Grape Strike. Delano, CA, Farm Workers Press, 1966, 122p.

2937
Cohen, Irving J.
Huelga, a Milestone in Farm Unionism. September 1966, 9p. (ED 014 598).

2938
Monfross, John
Farm Labor Difficulties in California in 1933-1934. Sacramento, CA, 1967. (Master's Thesis, Sacramento State College)

2939
United Farm Workers Organizing Committee
Sons of Zapata; a Brief Photographic History of the Farm Workers Strike in Texas. Edited by David M. Fishlow. Rio Grande City, Texas, 1967, 32p.

2940
McWilliams, Carey
The California Revolution. New York, Grossman Pubs., 1968, 240p.

2941
Miller, M. V.
"Grape Pickers in California" (In Larner, Jeremy, & Howe, Irving, eds. *Poverty: Views From the Left.* New York, Morrow, 1968, pp. 207-220).

2942

Wollenberg, Charles

"Huelga, 1928 Style: the Imperial Valley Cantaloupe Workers' Strike." *Pacific Historical Review* (38: 1), February 1969, pp. 45-58.

2943

Lewis, Jon

From This Earth: . . . of the Delano Grape Strike. San Francisco, 1970, 98p. (Master's Thesis, San Francisco State College)

2944

United Farm Workers Organizing Committee

Collective Bargaining Agreement Between the United Farm Workers Organizing Committee and the Wonder Palms Ranch. [n.p.] 1970, 12p.

2945

Lopez, Ronald W.

"The El Monte Berry Strike of 1933." *Aztlan* (I: 1), Spring 1970, pp. 101-114.

2946

Bergez, John

"The Grape Strike in Delano: a 3-Part Case Study" (In Frakes, George D., & Solberg, Curtis B., eds. *Minorities in California History.* New York, Random House, 1971, pp. 269-273).

2947

Dunne, John G.

Delano; Revised and Updated. New York, Farrar, Strauss & Giroux, 1971, 202p.

2948

McWilliams, Carey

"The Strike: for and Against." (In his, *The Strike: for and Against.* New York, Hart, 1971, pp. 194-228).

2949

Reccow, Louis

The Orange County Citrus Strikes of 1935-1936: the 'Forgotten People' in Revolt. Los Angeles, 1971, 292p. (Ph.D. Dissertation, University of Southern California)

2950

Rose, Gerald A.

"Westwood Lumber Strike." *Labor History* 13, Spring 1972, pp. 171-179.

2951

Wollenberg, Charles

"Race and Class in Rural California: El Monte Berry Strike of 1933." *California Historical Quarterly* 51, Summer 1972, pp. 155-164.

2952
California. Legislature. Assembly. Select Committee on Farm Labor Violence
An Examination of Violence in the Farm Labor Dispute, Bakersfield, California, October 1, 1973. Sacramento, 1973.

2953
California. Legislature. Assembly. Select Committee on Farm Labor Violence
An Examination of Violence in the Farm Labor Dispute, Fresno, California, Oct. 2, 1973. [Sacramento, 1973] 141p.

2954
Perez, José G.
Viva la Huelga! The Struggle of the Farm Workers. New York, Pathfinder Press, 1973, 15p.

2955
United Farm Workers
Why we Boycott? Keene, CA, 1973, 31p.

2956
Hoffman, Abraham
"El Monte Berry Pickers Strike; 1933—International Involvement in a Local Labor Dispute." *Journal of the West* XII, January 1973, pp. 71-84.

2957
Hurd, Richard W.
"Organizing the Working Poor: the California Grape Strike Experience." *Review of Radical Political Economics* 6, Spring 1974, pp. 50-75.

2958
Kushner, S.
The Long Road to Delano. New York, International Publishers, 1975, 224p.

2959
Yett, Jane M.
Farm Labor Struggles in California, 1970-1973, in Light of Reinhold Niebuhr's Concepts of Power and Justice. Berkeley, CA, 1980, 196p. (Ph.D. Dissertation, Graduate Theological Union)

2960
Thomas, R.
"The Social Organization of Industrial Agriculture." *Insurgent Sociologist* (10: 3), Winter 1981, p. 5-   .

2961
Majka, Linda C.
"Labor Militancy Among Farm Workers and the Strategy of Protest: 1900 to 1979." *Social Problems* 28, June 1981, pp. 533-547.

Appendix A: Audiovisual Materials

AGRICULTURAL LABOR

2962
Dementis, Gilbert
Resource Allocation in the Lower Rio Grande River Valley, 1940-1956.
Chicago, Dept. of Photoduplication, University of Chicago Library, 1960
(Microfilm 6640 HD).

2963
The Land (film)
National Broadcasting Company, 30 Rockefeller Plaza, New York,
N.Y. 10020. Distributor: McGraw-Hill Book Co., 1221 Avenue of the
Americas, New York, N.Y. 10020. Black and white, 54 minutes, sound,
16mm, 1962.
(ISBN 0-699-16389-7)
Audience: junior high and high school.

2964
The Land: A Report by Chet Huntley (film)
McGraw Hill Book Co., 1221 Avenue of the Americas, New York,
N.Y. 10020.
Black and white, 50 minutes, sound, 16mm, 1962.
(ISBN 0-699-16390-0).
Audience: high school to graduate school.

2965
Human Relations in Agricultural Business (filmstrip)
University of Illinois, Vocational Agriculture Service, Urbana, IL
61801 (1972).
57 frames, color, 35mm.
Credits: authors, E. E. Trotter, J. H. Herbst.

2966
Vayan Volando (film)
Production: Southwest Network, 1020 "B" St., Hayward, CA 94541
(1975).
Distributor: Instructional Media Library, University of California-Los
Angeles, Los Angeles, CA 90024.
27 minutes, color, 16mm.

IMMIGRATION OF MEXICAN AGRICULTURAL LABOR

2967
Give and Take With Mexico (film)
Frith Films, P O Box 424, Carmel Valley, CA 93924.
Color, sound, 16mm, 17 minutes, 1944.
(ISBN 0-699-11919-7).
Audience: high school to graduate school.

2968
Why Braceros? (motion picture)
Council of California Growers, 1533 Wilshire Blvd., Los Angeles,
California 90017 (1962).
Made by Wilding-Butler Division, Wilding, Inc.
19 minutes, sound, black and white, 16mm.

2969
The Imperial Valley, Part 2: Men, Machines and a Bountiful Harvest
(film)
Informational Materials, Inc., 1615 W. Burbank Blvd., Burbank, CA
91506 (1967)
(ISBN 0-699-14476-0).
21 minutes, color, sound, 16mm.

2970
From South of the Border (educational filmstrip with captions)
Educational Projections Corp., 3070 Lake Terrace, Glenview, Illinois
60025, 1972.
(Third Level Reading Program Series)
48 frames, 35mm.

2971
Rio Grande: Where Four Cultures Meet (film)
Audio-Visual Center, Media Library, State University of Iowa, Iowa
City, Iowa 52242 (1972).
Producer: Art Evans
15-1/2 minutes, color, 16mm.

2972
Borderline (motion picture, color, sound)
ITC Productions, Inc., 12711 Ventura Blvd., Studio City, California
91604, 1980.
Broadcast on TV Channel 2, Chicago, CBS-TV, April 27, 1984, 8-10
PM, Central Standard Time.

2973
We're Moving up: The Hispanic Migration (videorecording)
Films, Inc., 733 Green Bay Rd., Wilmette, IL 60091 (1980).
1 videocassette, 80 minutes, sound, in color.
Issued as U-matic inch or Beta 1/2 ", or VHS 1/2 ".

2974
Pogue, Alan
Agricultural Workers of the Rio Grande and Rio Bravo Valleys: a Port-folio. Austin, Center for Mexican-American Studies, University of Texas at Austin, 1984.
(contains twenty 11 " × 14 " photos by Alan Pogue, and essays by Professor Rolando Hinojosa Smith, Dept. of English, University of Texas at Austin, and by journalist-essayist Ruperto García).

2975
Mexico and the United States: Discord Over Immigration and Central America. Great Decision Series, Discussion Broadcast Over Radio Station WHAD, Delafield, Wisconsin, February 20, 1984, 10 PM. Recorded by Viacom-Milwaukee, 1711 W. Florist Ave., Milwaukee, WI 53209. Videotape number L-172-60 (50 minutes), sound, in color, U-matic inch.

MEXICAN-AMERICAN FARM LABOR

2976
Mexican Americans, Part I: La Mula no Nació (Two-Track 49 minutes,
 3-3/4 ips.   audio tape, monaural)
Mexican Americans, Part II: Who is the Enemy (Two-Track 40 minutes,
 3-3/4 ips.   audio tape, monaural)
Mexican Americans, Part III: The Cactus Curtain (Two-Track 45 minutes,
 3-3/4 ips.   audio tape, monaural)
Center for the Study of Democratic Institutions, P O Box 4068, Santa Barbara, CA 93103.

2977
The Proud Peoples—the Heritage and Culture of Spanish-Speaking Peoples (10 " record)
Production: American Printing House for the Blind, Instructional Materials Reference Center, P O Box 6085, Louisville, KY 40206.
Distributor: Division for Blind and Physically Handicapped, Library of Congress, 1291 Taylor St., N.W., Washington, D.C. 20542.
Written by Harold J. Alford; Narrator, Jim Walton. 8 rpm, 8 sides.

2978
What is La Raza? (videotape, 2-inch)
Distributor: Great Plains Instructional TV Library, University of Nebraska, P O Box 80669, Lincoln, Nebraska 68501.
30 minutes, color
(That's a Good Question Series)
Audience: intermediate level.

2979
Mexican-Americans (educational filmstrip, with record and cassette)
Warren Schloat Productions (Warren Schloat, Sunburst Communications, Inc., 39 Washington Avenue, Pleasantville, N.Y. 10570), 1968.
68 frames, 35mm.
(Minorities That Have Made America Great, pt. 2, Series)
Audience: intermediate—junior high school.

2980
Tijerina (video-reel).
Extension Media Center, University of California, Berkeley, 2223 Fulton St., Berkeley, CA 94720, 1968.
(ISBN 0-699-20547-4).
30 minutes, black and white, sound.

2981
Most Hated Man in New Mexico (film)
National Broadcasting Company, 30 Rockefeller Plaza, New York, N.Y. 10020.
Distributed by Films, Inc., 1144 Wilmette, Wilmette, Illinois 60091.
Color, 30 minutes, sound, 16mm, 1969.
(ISBN 0-699-19712-0).
Audience: junior high school through university.

2982
Chicano From the Southwest (motion picture)
Encyclopedia Britannica Educational Corp., 425 N. Michigan Ave., Chicago, IL 60611 (1970).
15 minutes, sound, color, 16mm. Magnetic sound track.
With teacher's guide.
Credits: collaborator, Julia Gonsalves.

2983
I am Joaquin (film)
George Ballis Associates, 1476 N. Van Ness, Fresno, California, 93728 (1970).
20 minutes, color, sound, 16mm.

2984

Los de la Raza (Those From the Nation) (educational sound filmstrip, record)
Scott Education Division, Prentice-Hall, Inc., Holyoke, MA 01040 (1970).
50 frames, 35 mm.
(American Children's Series)

2985

Salazar Family: a Look at Poverty (film)
Media Extension Center, University of California, Berkeley, Berkeley, CA 94720 (1970).
14 minutes, optical sound, black and white, 16mm.

2986

El Teatro Campesino (Farmworkers Theatre) (film)
Audio-Visual Center, Indiana University, Bloomington, Indiana 47401 (1970).
(ISBN 0-699-08712-0).
61 minutes, black and white, sound, 16mm.

2987

Chicano! (motion picture).
J. Gary Mitchell. Released by BFA Educational Media, 468 Park Ave. South, New York, N.Y. 10016 (1971).
23 minutes, sound, color, 16mm.
With study guide.

2988

Los Compadres (film)
St. Francis Productions, 1229 South Santee St., Los Angeles, CA 90015 (1971).
(ISBN 0-699-17665-4).
10 minutes, color, sound, 16mm.

2989

Mexican Americans: a Quest for Equality (film)
Anti-Defamation League of B'nai Brith, 315 Lexington Ave., New York, N.Y. 10016 (1971).
(ISBN 0-699-19075-4).
28 minutes, black and white, sound, 16mm.

2990

North From Mexico: Exploration and Heritage (motion picture)
Center for Mass Communication, Columbia University Press, 440 W.
110th St., New York, N.Y. 10025.
Released by Greenwood Press, P O Box 5007, Westport, CT 06881
(1971).
20 minutes, sound, color, 16mm.
Based on book, *North From Mexico,* by Carey McWilliams.
Credits: producer-director, Sumner Glimcher; script, Harold Flender;
consultant and narrator, Philip D. Ortego; adviser, Carey McWilliams;
photographer and editor, Warren Johnson.

2991

Somos Uno (film)
Menyah Productions (El Centro Campesino Cultural), P O Box 1278,
San Juan Bautista, CA 95045 (1971).
40 minutes, color, 16 mm.
Audience: high school.

2992

The Southwest; the Modern Southwest (educational filmstrip, with record,
cassette, script)
United Learning, 6633 W. Howard St., Niles, IL 60648 (1971).
52 frames, 35mm.
Audience: junior high school.

2993

Strangers in Their Own Land: the Chicanos (motion picture)
ABC News. Released by ABC Media Concepts, American Broadcasting Co., Inc. 1331 Ave. of the Americas, New York, N.Y. 10019
(1971).
16 minutes, sound, color, 16mm.
Credits: producer-writer, Hope Ryden; narrator Frank Reynolds.

2994

Yo Soy Chicano (I Am a Chicano) (film)
Audio-Visual Center, Indiana University, Bloomington, Indiana 47401,
1972.
(ISBN 0-699-32855-1).
59 minutes, color, sound, 16mm.

2995

The Mexican Texans—to 1865 (educational slide)
Institute of Texan Cultures, P O Box 1226, San Antonio, Texas 78294
(1973).
2 ″ × 2 ″ slide with cassette and script (also available in Spanish).
79 frames, color.
Audience: intermediate-high school.

2996

The Mexican Texans . . . to 1865 (filmstrip)
Institute of Texan Cultures, P O Box 1226, San Antonio, Texas 78294 (1973).
79 frames, color, 35mm and phonotape: single-track, 1 reel (5 "), 7-1/2 ips, 11 minutes.
Produced in cooperation with the Texas Commission on the Arts and Humanities.
Spanish version released under the title, *Los Texanos Mexicanos . . . Hasta 1865.*
Also issued as slide set.
With teacher's supplement.

2997

The Richest Land (Motion picture)
George Ballis Associates, 1476 N. Van Ness, Fresno, California 93728 (1973).
23 minutes, sound, color, 16mm.
With study manual.
Credits: production crew, George Ballis, John Ballis, Maia Sortor, Alan Eberhart, Jack Cashion, Galen Larson, Hayes Pearson.

2998

Spanish Ranching in Texas (sound filmstrip, audio tape)
Institute of Texan Cultures, P O Box 1226, San Antonio, Texas 78294 (1973).
79 frames, 35mm.
Audience: intermediate-high school.

2999

Contemporary Chicano Life Series (filmstrip)
Bilingual Educational Services, 1607 Hope St., South Pasadena, California 91030 (1975).
8 rolls: color, 35mm, and 16 cassettes.
With teacher's guides.
Sound accompaniment in English and Spanish (8 cassettes each).

3000

Magic Valley (motion picture)
Made by Cary White. Houston, White, 1976.
Lyndon B. Johnson School of Public Affairs, University of Texas at Austin, Austin, Texas 78712.
1 reel, 28 minutes, sound, color, 16mm.

3001
Sun Dried Foods (videorecording).
Self Reliance Foundation, Las Trampas, New Mexico, 1980.
1 cassette 29 minutes: sound, color, 3/4 ", U standard.
Also issued in Spanish.
Also issued as motion picture.

3002
Mexican Americans, the Invisible Minority (videorecording).
National Educational Television & Radio Center.
Audio-Visual Center, Indiana University, Bloomington, Indiana 47401 (1980?).
1 videorecording, 38 minutes; sound, color.
(Public Broadcast Lab).
Available as cassette (U standard, 3/4 " or Beta 1/2 ", or VHS 1/2 ") or reel (EIAJ 1/2 ").
Issued in 1969 as motion picture.
Credits: producer, Joseph Louw; editor, Bill Doreste.

MIGRANT AGRICULTURAL LABOR

3003
The Forgotten Families (motion picture)
U.S. Public Health Service. Made by Jack L. Copeland Productions.
Released by National Education Media, Inc., 21601 Devonshire St., Suite 300, Chatsworth, CA 91311.
1 reel, sound, color, 16mm.
Credits: producer and director, Jack L. Copeland; writer, Don Hall.

3004
Home is a Long Road (motion picture)
University of Wisconsin-Madison Bureau of Audiovisual Instruction and (Station) WHA-TV, Madison, Wisconsin. Released by University of Wisconsin Bureau of Audiovisual Instruction, Madison, WI 53706.
16 minutes, sound, black and white, 16mm.
Credits: producer and cinematographer, David Myers; director, Ray Stanley; script, Claire Prothero; narration, Karl Schmidt.

3005
Los de la Raza (filmstrip)
Made by Jam Handy School Service Center.
Scott Education Division, Prentice-Hall, Inc., Holyoke, MA 01040.
52 frames, color, 35mm, and phonodisc: 2 sides (1 side for manual projector, 1 side for automatic projector), 10 ", 33-1/3 rmp. (America's Children, #3).
Also issued with phonotape in cassette. With teacher's guide.

3006
Shelter for Migrants (filmstrip)
U.S. Dept. of Agriculture, Farm Security Administration, (Washington, D.C.), 194- ?
Made by Photo Lab.
47 frames, black and white, 35mm.

3007
Algo Para Mañana (motion picture)
U.S. Social Security Administration (Washington, D.C.), 1958. Made by Sarrell and Gage.
11 minutes, sound, black and white, 16mm.
English version released under the title, *Something for Tomorrow.*

3008
Bitter Harvest (motion picture)
(Station) KING-TV, 333 Dexter Ave., North, Seattle, Washington 98109 (1960).
28 ?minutes, sound, black and white, 16mm.

3009
Harvest of Shame (motion picture)
CBS Television. Released by McGraw-Hill Book Co., Inc., 1221 Avenue of the Americas, New York, N.Y. 10036 (1961).
54 minutes, sound, black and white, 16mm.
Issued in 2 parts.
Credits: narrator, Edward R. Murrow.

3010
Seeds of Progress (motion picture)
Dept. of Public Affairs, (Station) WCAU-TV, City Line and Monument Avenues, Bala Cynwyd, PA 19004 (1961).
54 minutes, sound, black and white, 16mm.
Credits: producer and director, George Dessart; narrator, John Facenda.

3011
The Harvesters Help Provide our Food (film)
Frank N. Stanton Films, 7934 Santa Monica Blvd., Los Angeles, CA 90046. (ISBN 0-699-12893-5).
Color, 11 minutes, sound, 16mm, 1963.
Audience: intermediate and junior high school.

3012

Thorn of Plenty (motion picture)
American Broadcasting-Paramount Theaters (American Broadcasting Co., Inc., 1330 Avenue of the Americas, New York, N.Y. 10019), 1965.
29 minutes, sound, black and white 16mm. (ABC Scope).
Telecast on the ABC-TV Documentary Show, *ABC Scope.*
Credits: producer, director and writer, Harry Rasky; photographer, Tex Ziegler; Film editors, Marvis Lenauer, Edward Lempa.

3013

A Group of Farm Workers Who Face a Dilemma. A Town Plans a Clinic (Two-Track Audio Tape, Monaural)
H. Wilson Corp., 555 W. Taft Drive, South Holland, Illinois 60473 (1968).
3-3/4 ips (At Issue—The Quality of Life Series).
Audience: intermediate-high school.

3014

What Harvest for the Reaper? (motion picture)
National Educational Television. Released by Indiana University Audiovisual Center (Bloomington, Indiana), 1968.
59 minutes, sound, black and white, 16mm (NET Journal).
Credits: producer, Morton Silverstein; editor, Laurence Soloman.

3015

The Forgotten Families (motion picture)
U.S. Community Health Services Administration, 1969.
Released by National Audiovisual Center, U.S. National Archives and Records Service, Washington, D.C. 20409.
29 minutes, sound, color, 16mm.

3016

Migrant (motion picture)
NBC (made by NBC News). Released by NBC Educational Enterprises, 30 Rockefeller Plaza, New York, N.Y. 10020 (1970).
53 minutes, sound, color, 16mm.
Credits: producer and director, Martin Carr; writers, Marilyn Nissenson, Martin Carr; narrator, Chet Huntley.

3017

Fruits, Vegetables and People (filmstrip)
United Method Communications, 810 Twelfth Ave. South, Nashville, Tennessee 37203 (1971).
33-1/3 rpm, 20 minutes.
With script and guide.

3018

Children of the Fields (film)
Production: Xerox Films, 245 Long Hill Rd., Middletown, CT 06457 (1973).
Distributor; Instructional Media Library, University of California-Los Angeles, Los Angeles, CA 90024.
25 minutes, color, 16mm.
Audience: junior high school-high school.

3019

Angel and Big Joe (film)
Informational Materials, Inc., 1615 Burbank Blvd., Burbank, CA 91506.
27 minutes, color, sound, 16mm, 1975.
(Learning to be Human Series)
Audience: junior and senior high school.

3020

Yellow Trail From Texas (videorecording 3/4 ")
BBC-TV.
Distributor: Time-Life Multimedia, 1271 Avenue of the Americas, New York, N.Y. 10020 (1978, made 1975).
1 cassette, 50 minutes; sound, color, U-standard.
With discussion guide.
Also issued in 1/2 " Beta cassette and as motion picture.

3021

Victor (motion picture)
La Mesa, California, Chocolate Sandwich Productions, 1979.
1 reel, 11 minutes, sound, color, 16mm.

3022

The Migrants—1980: Parts 1 and 2 (film)
Production: NBC Educational Enterprises, 30 Rockefeller Plaza, New York, N.Y. 10020 (1980)
Distribution: Audio-Visual Services, Pennsylvania State University, Special Services Bldg., University Park, PA 16802.
50 minutes, sound, color, 16mm.
Audience: Junior high school-adult.

3023

We're Moving Up! The Hispanic Migration (videocassette)
Films, Inc., 733 Green Bay Rd., Wilmette, IL 60091 (1980)
80 minutes.

AGRICULTURAL LABOR UNIONS

3024
Birth of a Union (film)
   Audio-Visual Center, Indiana University, Bloomington, Indiana 47401
   (1967)
   26 minutes, black and white, 16mm.

3025
Bargaining Power (film)
   University of Nebraska, Bureau of Audiovisual Instruction, 421 Nebraska Hall, Lincoln, Nebraska, 68508.
   color, 28 minutes, sound, 16mm., 1969.
   (Eleventh Round Series). (ISBN 0-699-02299-1).

3026
Cesar Chavez (educational sound filmstrip, record)
   AVI Associates, 825 Third Ave., New York, N.Y. 10022 (1970).
   55 frames, 35 mm.
   (American Leaders of the 20th Century Series)

3027
Nosotros Venceremos (We Shall Overcome). (motion picture)
   United Farm Workers Organizing Committee (El Centro Campesino
   Cultural), Box 1278, San Juan Bautista, California 95045 (1971).
   Made by Jon Lewis Ventures.
   11 minutes, sound, black and white, 16mm.
   Originally released in Spanish.

3028
California Conflict: Migrant Farm Workers (filmstrip)
   Society for Visual Education, Inc., 1345 Diversey Pkwy., Chicago, IL
   60614 (1972).
   94 frames, color, 35mm, and phonodisc: 1 side, 12 ", 33-1/3 rpm, 18
   minutes.
   (Focus on America—The Pacific States).
   Also issued with phonotape in cassette.
   With teacher's guide.
   Credits: consultant, Irving Siigle; photographers, Jeanne Porterfield,
   Lisa Chickering.

3029
Viva La Causa (motion picture)
   United Church Board for Homeland Ministries, 287 Park Avenue, So.,
   New York, N.Y. 10010 (1972).
   26 minutes, sound, color, 16mm.

3030
Viva La Causa: the Migrant Labor Movement (filmstrip).
Denoyer-Geppert Audio-Visuals. Released by Denoyer-Geppert Co., 355 Lexington Ave., New York, N.Y. 10017 (1972).
200 frames, color, 35mm. and phonodisc: 2 sides, 12 ", 33-1/3 rpm, 32 minutes.
Also issued with phonotape in cassette.
With teacher's guide.

3031
Si se Puede (motion picture)
National Farm Workers Service Center, United Farm Workers of America, La Paz, Keene, California 93531 (1973).
45 minutes, sound, color, 16mm.
Spanish version also issued.

3032
Cesar Chavez, Leader of the Downtrodden (filmstrip, audio tape)
AVI Associates, 825 Third Ave., New York, N.Y. 10022 (1974)
62 frames, 35 mm.
(American Leaders of the 20th Century Series)

3033
The Green Rising, 1910-1977 (FILM 80/24) University of Cali-
Z   fornia, Berkeley,
Bancroft Library.
A Supplement to the Southern Tenant Farmers Union Papers. 17 reels (Positive Microfilm), Including Materials on Mexican Farm Laborers.
FILM   *A Guide to the Collection Prepared by the Manufacturing*
80/24   *Corporation of America.*
Z
Key

FARM LABOR STRIKES

3034
Huelga! (motion picture)
King Screen Productions, Division of King Broadcasting Co., 320 Aurora Avenue N., Seattle, Washington 98109.
52 minutes, sound, color, 16mm.
Credits: producer and writer, Mark Harris; director, Skeets McGrew; narrator, Paul Herlinger; photographers, Richard Pearce, John Haney; editor, Dick Gilbert.

3035

Decision at Delano (motion picture)
Cathedral Films, 1967. Made by Jack L. Copeland Productions (National Educational Media, Inc., 21601 Devonshire St., Suite 300, Chatsworth, California 91311), 1967.
26 minutes, sound, color, 35mm.
Cartridge film (super 8mm), also issued.
With study guide.

3036

Pilgrimage (Delano to Sacramento) (film, record)
Multi-Media Productions, P O Box 5097, Stanford, CA 94305 (1967).
10 minutes, color, 16 mm.

3037

Mexican-Americans (filmstrip)
Warren Schloat Productions (Warren Schloat, Sunburst Communications, Inc., 39 Washington Ave., Pleasantville, N.Y., 10570), 1968.
68 frames, color, 35mm. and phonodisc: 1 side, 12″, 33-1/3rpm, 15 minutes, microgroove.
(Minorities Have Made America Great, set #2).
With teacher's guide and script.
Credits: producer, B. Martinsons; writers, B. Martinsons, S. Glassner.

3038

Delano Grape Strike (motion picture)
Thorne Films, Inc., 1229 University Ave., Boulder, Colorado 80302 (1971).
4 minutes, silent, color, super 8mm.
(8mm. Documents Project, #319). Loop film in cartridge.
With film notes on cartridge case.
Credits: producer, James C. Schott.

3039

Cesar Chavez—the California Grape Boycott (audio tape cassette, monaural)
CBC Learning Systems, Box 500, Terminal A, Toronto, Ontario, Canada (1972)
60 minutes, 1-7/8 ips.

3040

Why We Boycott (film)
United Farmworkers: Informational Materials, 1615 W. Burbank Blvd., Burbank, CA 91506 (1973)
(ISBN 0-699-32197-2).
20 minutes, color, sound, 16mm.

3041

Boycott (motion picture)
Super Market Institute (in care of Food Marketing Institute, 1750 "K" St., N.W., Suite 700, Washington, D.C. 20006), 1974.
Made by Donald Manelli and Associates.
21 minutes, sound, color, 16mm.

3042

Struggle of the Texas Farmworkers March (film)
(University of California, Berkeley, Bancroft Library).
Texas Farmworkers Union, San Antonio, Texas (1977)

3043

"Cesar Chavez" segment (In *Sixty Minutes*. Television Program, CBS-Television. Sunday, December 25, 1983, Milwaukee, Wisconsin, TV Channel 6, 6-7 PM).

Appendix B:
Archival and Manuscript Materials

AGRICULTURAL LABOR

3044

San Diego Mission (Manuscript Materials).
Inventario de Misión de San Diego de Alcalá, 1777-1784, 43p. Berkeley, Bancroft Library (Cowan Collection, Manuscript, MSS C-C 237).

3045

Tiburcio Vasquez, José, 1795-   ca. 1862.
Papers, 1839-1865.   ca. 200 items.
Mexican Soldier, Farmer and Merchandiser, of San Mateo, California . . . Correspondence . . . Accounts (1839-40) of Mission Dolores . . . and Material From his Rancho de los Pilarcitos.
Unpublished Finding aid in the Repository.
Probably Gift of Harry C. Peterson, Sacramento, California, 1938.

3046

Federal Writers' Project, Oakland, California.
Source Materials Gathered by Federal Writers' Project on Migratory Labor, District #8, ca. 1936-1937. (Chiefly Abstracts Clippings, etc., From Various Publications Concerning Agricultural Labor . . . in California . . . 1849-1939 . . . Bancroft Library, University of California, Berkeley (36 cartons and 3 card file boxes), C-R 2.

3047

McElroy, John J.
(Manuscript Materials).
Papers Relating to his Work as State Supervisor, Emergency Farm Labor, for the California Cooperative Extension Work in Agriculture and Home Economics, 1946-1947. Portfolio. (Includes . . . circulars issued by the California Farm Production Council. They Relate Primarily to the postwar Farm Labor Situation . . . Berkeley, Bancroft Library, University of California, Berkeley, 76/106.

c

3048
Graham, Edwin S., 1831-1899.
Papers, 1825-1917.   ca. 2 ft.
In University of Texas-Austin Library, Texas Archives.
In Part, Transcripts.
Land Agent and Businessman. Correspondence (1857-95), Diaries (1870-72), Reminiscences, Daybooks, Account Books . . . Sale of Land . . . Articles Dealing With Peter's Colony Lands in Young County, Texas, and with Graham's Attempt to Encourage Immigration to this Area . . .
Unpublished Guide in the Library.
Gift of Graham's son, E. S. Graham, 1942.

3049
U.S. National Archives
Preliminary Inventory of the Records of the Office of Labor of the War Food Administration (Record Group 224). Compiled by Harold T. Pinkett. (National Archives Publication #53-17. Preliminary Inventories, #51). Washington, 1953, 18p.

3050
Nutting, Franklin P., 1876-
(Manuscript Materials).
An Interview with Franklin P. Nutting, Berkeley, California, 1955, 7 & 93pp. (Raisin Growing in the San Joaquin Valley . . . Litigation Involving the Sun Maid Growers Corp.). Berkeley, Bancroft Library, University of California, Berkeley, C-D 4015.

3051
Mexican-American Project, 1968-70.   42 items.
In California State University, Fullerton, Library.
Transcripts of Tape-Recorded Interviews Relating to Various Facets of Mexican-American Life. Topics Include the Experience of "Wetbacks", the Bracero Program, Repatriation Program During the 1930's, Farm Labor Strife, Mexican Revolution, and Chicano.
Index in the Repository.

3052
Lugo, Jose del Carmen
Vida de un Ranchero, a History of San Bernardino Valley, by Jose del Carmen Lugo as told to Thomas Savage, 1877. Translation by Helen Pruitt Beattie. [Bloomington, California] 1971, 41p. (San Bernardino County Museum Association *Quarterly,* volume 8, #2).

3053
Taylor, Paul S., 1895-
(Manuscript Materials).

California Social Scientist; Education; Field Research and Family. Berkeley, California, 1973, 26 & 342pp. (Photocopy of Typed Tapescript of Tape-Recorded Interviews Conducted 1970 . . . for the Regional Oral History Office, Bancroft Library, University of California, Berkeley. Photographs, Including . . . Study of Mexican Agricultural Laborers; Association with Dorothea Lange in California Emergency Relief Administration, Working with Migratory Labor). Berkeley, Bancroft Library, University of California, Berkeley (74/164

c

v.1)

IMMIGRATION OF MEXICAN AGRICULTURAL LABOR

3054

U.S. Dept. of State

Records of the Department of State Relating to Internal Affairs of Mexico, 1910-1929 (Decimal Files). Washington, U.S. National Archives and Records Service (M274). See: "Economic Matters" for the following microfilm roll numbers:

162. 812.5034-812.504/235.
163. 812.504/236-555.
164. 812.504/556-760.
165. 812.504/761-930.
166. 812.504/931-1077.
167. 812.5041-812.51/55.

(Note the above-listed items are available in microfilm from National Archives and Records Service, General Services Administration, Washington, D.C. 20408).

3055

U.S. National Archives and Records Service

Record Group 85: Immigration and Naturalization Service, Subject Correspondence, 1906-40.

File Description: Material Related to Admission Illiterate Laborers, Mexican, 1917-19.

Case File Numbers: 54261/202A-B-C-D-E-F.

Box Number: 243.

3056

U.S. National Archives and Records Service

Record Group 85: Immigration and Naturalization Service, Subject Correspondence, 1906-40.

File Description: Contract Laborers Admission, 1918, Mexican.

Case File Number: 54261/202.

Box Number: 241.

3057

U.S. National Archives and Records Service

Record Group 85: Immigration and Naturalization Service, Subject Correspondence, 1906-40.

File Description: Material Related to Admission Illiterate Laborers, Mexicans, 1919.

Case File Numbers: 54261/202G-H-I.

Box Number: 244.

3058

U.S. National Archives and Records Service

Record Group 59: Correspondence on the Deportation of Aliens, 1922-27. (Entry 906). 1 foot.

Correspondence of the Department of State with Foreign Missions, the Dept. of Labor, and U.S. Foreign Service Officers, Concerning the Deportation of Undesirable Aliens From the United States. Much of the Correspondence Relates to Obtaining From Foreign Governments the Passports Needed for Deportation. For Lists of the Papers in this Series, see Entry 898. Most of this File has been Disposed of; Only Records Consisting of Precedent Cases and Policy Materials have been Retained. Arranged According to a Decimal Classification Scheme by Country and Thereunder Alphabetically by Name of Deportee.

3059

U.S. National Archives and Records Service

Record Group 59: Correspondence Regarding Immigration. 1910-39. (Entry 897). 120 feet.

Correspondence of the Visa Division and predecessor organizations with other Government Agencies, U.S. Consular and Diplomatic Officer . . . Foreign Governments, Regarding the Administration of U.S. Immigration Laws. Lists of the Papers in this File are Described in Entry 898. The subjects covered . . . include statistics, laws and regulations, certification of alien manifests, fees . . . complaints, inspections . . . deportations . . . Arranged by subject under Decimal File Numbers 150.00-151.997 and thereunder chronologically or by name of alien.

3060

U.S. National Archives and Records Service

Record Group 59: List of Papers ("Purport lists") Regarding Immigration. 1910-39 (Entry 898). 6 feet.

List of Papers in the Series Described in Entries 897 and 906. Each List Entry gives the subject of the Paper, its File Number and Date, the Names of Sender and Recipient, and a Summary of its Contents. Arranged by Decimal File Number and Thereunder Chronologically or by Name of Alien.

MEXICAN-AMERICAN FARM LABOR

3061
Corbett, J. Knox, born 1861.
Papers, 1880-1884. 1 box.
In Arizona Pioneers' Historical Society Collections, Tucson, Arizona.
Businessman and Mayor of Tucson, Arizona. Correspondence Relating to
. . . Description of Tucson, Arizona and its Mexican Population and an
Account Book.

3062
Mahony, Thomas F.
Problem of the Mexican Wage Earner [Denver, CO, 1930] 7p.
(Address by the Chairman of the Mexican Welfare Committee of the Colo-
rado State Council, Knights of Columbus, Delivered at the Catholic Con-
ference on Industrial Problems, Denver, Colorado, May 12, 1930).

3063
Galarza, Ernesto, 1905-
(Manuscript Materials).
*The Burning Light: Action and Organizing in the Mexican Community in
California.* Berkeley, California, 1982, 6 & 152pp. Manuscript: Photocopy of 3 of his Talks Relating to Mexican Americans and to his Labor Organizing Activities and Photocopy of Typed Transcripts of Interviews
Conducted 1977-1978 and 1981 . . . Berkeley, Regional Oral History Office, Bancroft Library, University of California, Berkeley, 83/15
c
v. 1.

MIGRANT AGRICULTURAL LABOR

3064
Wood, Irving W.
(Manuscript Materials).
Correspondence and Papers, 1934-1937. Re: Establishment of Camps
for Migratory Laborers, mainly in the Marysville Area . . . Also includes
some materials re . . . Mexican Laborers in the Imperial Valley in 1934.
Berkeley, University of California, Berkeley, (1 box and oversize portfolio), 77/111.
c

3065
U.S. Works Progress Administration. Federal Writers Project
*Monographs Prepared for A Documentary History of Migratory Farm
Labor.* (Oakland, CA ? 1938), 1 box.

17 monographs (type-script), many of them with emendations by Raymond P. Barry, editor. (With these: Wage Chart by Crops: State of California 1865-1938). Bancroft Library, University of California, Berkeley: 72/187.

c

3066
U.S. Works Progress Administration. Federal Writers Project
Source Material Gathered by Federal Writers' Project on Migratory Labor, District no. 8, ca. 1936-1939. (36 cartons & 3 card file boxes). Bancroft Library, University of California, Berkeley: C-R 2, Group 6 (carton 39, file NF 169)
————— —————. *Index and Key to Arrangement.* (Material at Edwards Field).

3067
Clements, George P., 1867-1958.
Papers, 1925-45. 33 ft.
In UCLA Library (118).
Agricultural Economist and Physician. Correspondence . . . Including Material Relating to . . . South California Agriculture. Mexican and Other Migrant Labor . . .
Unpublished Inventory in the Library.

3068
U.S. National Archives
Preliminary Inventory of the Records of the President's Commission on Migratory Labor (Record Group 220), comp. by Hardee Allen. Washington, 1955, 7p. (Publication No. 56-4. Preliminary inventories, no 86).

3069
California Federation for Civic Unity.
(Manuscript Materials).
Records, 1945-1956. Correspondence, Organizational Papers Including Minutes of Meetings and Accounts; Papers Relating to Conferences and Miscellaneous Pamphlets. Materials Relating to Racial Discrimination and Segregation; Immigration; Employment and Practices . . . Many Letters from California Legislators and Congressmen. Berkeley, Bancroft Library, University of California, Berkeley (6 boxes & 3 cartons), C-A.
274

3070
Garrod, Ralph V.
(Manuscript Materials).
Miscellaneous Papers, 1958-1959. Portfolio. Includes his Statement Prepared for the California Industrial Welfare Commission on Fruit Growing in the Saratoga Area and Labor Problems Pertaining Thereto . . . Berkeley, Bancroft Library, University of California, Berkeley, C-G
246.

3071
Illinois Commission on Employment of Youth.
Records, 1934-1962.   7 ft.
In University of Illinois, Chicago Circle Campus Library.
Correspondence . . . Relating to . . . Migratory Labor in Illinois and Minnesota. (Unpublished Guide in the Library).
Gift of the Commission, 1966.

3072
California Migrant Ministry.
Records, 1939-68.   14 ft.
In Wayne State University, Archives of Labor History and Urban Affairs, Detroit.
Correspondence . . . Relating to Braceros, the Delano Grape Strike, Boycotts, Labor Organizing Among Farm Workers, National and State Legislation for Farm Workers, Rural Housing, Poverty and Worker-Priest Programs . . .
Unpublished Finding Aid in the Repository.
Information on Literary Rights Available in the Repository.
Acquired from California Migrant Ministry.

3073
Camp, Wofford B., 1894-
Cotton, Irrigation and the AAA. Berkeley, California, 1971, 30 & 4 & 4pp. (Treats Agricultural Labor, Farm Labor Strikes, Among Other Topics, Including his Speeches, Clippings, Press Releases, Reprints of Articles and Other Documents on his Career). Berkeley, Bancroft Library, University of California, Berkeley (2 boxes), 71/250.

3074
Barry, Raymond P.
(Manuscript Materials).
Papers, ca. 1942-1973. Includes his Annotated Bibliography of Housing, Relief and Health Care for Migratory Farm Labor in California, 1866-1939; Scrapbooks of Clippings on Migratory Farm Labor in California, 1942-1973; and Notes. Berkeley, Bancroft Library, University of California, Berkeley, 75/67.
c

3075
McWilliams, Carey, 1905-
(Manuscript Materials).
Honorable in all Things. Los Angeles, 1982, 522 p.
Manuscript. Photocopy of Typed Transcript of Tape-Recorded Interview Conducted 1978 by Joel Gardner for Oral History Program, UCLA. Comments on . . . political activism and Involvement with Social Protest Groups in California; Work as Commissioner of California Division of

Immigration and Housing . . . Berkeley, Bancroft Library, University of California, Berkeley, 82/109.

c

AGRICULTURAL LABOR UNIONS

3076
U.S. Works Progress Administration. Federal Writers Project
Unionization of Agricultural Labor in California.
Oakland ? CA, 193- ? 23p. (Master negative available (Box 898: 9).
Bancroft Library, University of California, Berkeley. Acq: 6937708x
03/29/83 C.

3077
U.S. Works Progress Administration. Federal Writers Project
Unionization of Migratory Labor, 1903-1930. Oakland ? CA, 193- ?
23p. (Master negative available, Box 898:7).
Bancroft Library, University of California, Berkeley. Acq: 69138679
02/17/83 C.

3078
Mahony, Thomas F., 1873-1957.
Papers, 1925-1950. ca. 3 ft.
Newspaper Correspondent of Longmont, Colorado, Active in Improving the Condition of Mexican and Other Laborers in Colorado . . . Correspondence . . . Statements From Workers and Photos of Workers Relating to Colorado Labor.
Open to Investigators Under Restrictions by the Repository.

3079
Michigan AFL-CIO Collection, 1939-58.   103 ft.
In Wayne State University, Archives of Labor History and Urban Affairs, Detroit.
Correspondence . . . Farm Labor and Farmers' Unions . . .
Unpublished Inventory in the Repository. Information on Literary Rights Available. Deposit, 1963.

3080
Mexican-American Farm Workers' Movement Records, 1951-69.
(Manuscript Materials)   ca. 7 ft.
Newspaper Clippings, Some Concerning Migrant Labor in Texas and the Valley Farmers Strike 1966-68, handbills . . . relating to the United Farm Workers' Organizing Committee, Local 2, Rio Grande City, Texas, Formerly the National Farm Workers' Association, Local 2. (Unpublished Guides and Inventories in the Repository).
Information on Literary Rights Available in the Repository.
Permanent Deposit by the Texas AFL-CIO, 1968.

3081
Velasco, Victorio Acosta, 1903-1968.
  Papers, 1920-69.   ca. 11 ft.
  In University of Washington Library, Seattle.
  Journalist, of Seattle, Washington. Correspondence . . . Relating to
. . . Farm Laborers Union . . .
  Unpublished Inventory in the Repository.
  Access to Some Case-Files Restricted.
  Information on Literary Rights Available in the Repository.
  Gift of Mrs. Velasco, 1970.

3082
Tarrant County Central Labor Council, Fort Worth, Texas
  Records, 1957-71.   ca 7 ft.
  In University of Texas at Arlington, Texas Labor Archives.
  Correspondence, minutes, financial records . . . on the Council's civic
and political activities, and records (1966-70) on the Farm Workers'
Movement—Texas and California . . .
  Unpublished Guides and Inventories in the Repository.
  Information on Literary Rights Available in the Repository. Permanent
Deposit by the Council.

3083
Food, Tobacco, Agricultural and Allied Workers Union of America.
  Records, 1938-47.   ca. 350 items.
  In University of Texas-Arlington Library, Division of Archives and
Manuscripts.
  In Part, Photocopies Made in 1972 of Originals Owned by Dr. Ray Mar-
shall, Austin, Texas.
  Correspondence . . . Anti-Labor Legislation, and Particularly the 1938
Strike of the Pecan Workers Union of San Antonio, Local 172.
  Unpublished Guides, Inventories, and Partial Calendar in the Library.
  Information on Literary Rights Available in the Library.
  Gift of George P. Lambert, Dallas, Texas, 1968. Loaned for Copying
by Dr. Ray Marshall, Austin, Texas, 1972.

3084
Draper, Anne, 1916-1973.
  Papers, 1959-71.   ca. 20 ft.
  Ca. 16,000 items. In Stanford University Library, California.
  Labor Leader, of California . . . Correspondence . . . Chiefly Relating
to Farm Labor and its Organization in California . . . Agricultural Work-
ers Organizing Committee, National Agricultural Workers Union, United
Farm Workers Union, Delano Grape Strike, DiGiorgio Strikes, Cesar
Chavez, Ernesto Galarza and H. L. Mitchell . . .
  Information on Library Rights Available in the Library.
  Gift of Mr. and Mrs. Draper, 1973.

rkers of the World.
)07-1955.   (MS 66-1519).
_____ _____. Addition, 1905-72.   ca. 76 ft.
In Wayne State University, Walter P. Reuther Library, Archives of Labor & Union Affairs, Detroit.
. . . General Executive Board Minute Book (1906-11), and Other Minutes (1917-39) . . . Regional I.W.W. Branches . . . Los Angeles, California (1937-65) . . . Oakland, California . . .
Unpublished Guide in the Repository.
Deposited by the I.W.W., 1973.

3086
Texas AFL-CIO.
Records, 1928-73.   ca. 125 ft.
In University of Texas-Arlington Library, Dept. of Special Collections.
Correspondence . . . Mexican-American Affairs Committee . . . AFL-CIO . . .
Unpublished Finding aid in the Repository.
Access Restricted in Part.
Information on Literary Rights Available in the Repository.
Permanent Deposit by Texas AFL-CIO, 1971-75.

3087
New Democratic Coalition of Ohio.
Records, 1969-76.   2 ft. (MSS-566)
In Ohio Historical Society Collections (Columbus).
Correspondence . . . Minutes . . . Protests, United Farm Workers.
Unpublished Inventory in the Repository.
Gift of James Dougherty, Member of the Executive Committee, 1976.

3088
Texas Farmworkers Union. *Collected Materials, 1966-1980.*
(Manuscript Materials).
Contents: 3 " in one box; form letters, news clippings, brochures, broadsides, press releases; buttons; bumper stickers; printed reports and articles; photograph records; 35mm. film. (Mx Am/Mss/021, in Mexican-American Archives, Benson Latin American Collection, University of Texas-Austin).

FARM LABOR STRIKES

3089
Maloy, Fred
Diary. October 23-27, 2933? 30p. A. Manuscript.

Record of Mexican Agricultural Laborers' Strike in Tulare and Cor-
coran, California, by a Member of an Unspecified Union. Berkeley, Bancroft Library, University of California, Berkeley, 68/105.

c

3090

Taylor, Paul S., 1895-

(Manuscript Materials).

*Materials Relating to Agricultural and Maritime Strikes in California,
1933-1942.* Berkeley, Bancroft Library, University of California,
Berkeley, C-R (3 cartons).

3

3091

Rose, Gerald A.

The Brentwood Plan for Agricultural Labor; a Study in Suppression.
Berkeley, California, 1962, 46 & 10 pp.

(Manuscript Materials).

Copy of Seminar Paper, Prepared for Dr. Clarke Chambers, University
of California, Concerning Agricultural Strike in Contra Costa County,
1934, and Adoption of Brentwood Plan for Registering Farm Laborers.
Berkeley, Bancroft Library, University of California, Berkeley, C-R.

123

3092

Cohen, David, 1945-

Papers, 1961-67. ca. 2 ft.

In Wayne State University, Archives of Labor History and Urban Affairs, Detroit.

Labor Leader and Labor Program Specialist at the Institute of Labor and
Industrial Relations, Wayne State University. Correspondence . . . Relating to the United Farm Workers Organizing Committee Grape Strike
and Boycott (1965-67) . . . Correspondence with Cesar Chavez.

Unpublished Finding aid in the Repository.

Information on Literary Rights Available in the Repository.

Acquired From Mr. Cohen, 1967.

3093

De Shettler, Irwin, 1906-

Papers, 1933-68. 52 ft.

In Wayne State University, Archives of Labor History and Urban Affairs, Detroit.

Labor Leader. Correspondence . . . Organization of Mexican Farm
Workers in California (1953-68); . . . DiGiorgio Grape Strike (1966-
67); . . .

Unpublished Finding aid in the Repository.

Information on Literary Rights Available in the Repository.

Deposited by Mr. De Shettler, 1968.

3094
Haughton, Ronald Waring, 1916-
Papers, 1946-69.   ca. 3 ft.
In Wayne State University, Archives of Labor History and Urban Affairs, Detroit.
Educator and Labor Arbitrator . . . Correspondence . . . Concerning the Arbitration Between the United Farm Workers Organizing Committee and the DiGiorgio Corporation (1964-69) . . .
Unpublished Finding aid in the Repository.
Information on Literary Rights Available in the Repository.
Acquired From Mr. Haughton, 1961, 1970.

3095
National Campaign for Agricultural Democracy.
Records, 1967-70.   ca. 15 ft.
In Wayne State University, Archives of Labor History and Urban Affairs, Detroit.
Correspondence . . . to Extend Coverage of National Labor Relations Act to Farm Workers . . . Includes Material on Legislation, Boycott of California Table Grapes . . . Alien Strike-Breakers, Green Card Issue . . .
Unpublished Finding Aid in the Repository.
Information on Literary Rights Available in the Repository.

3096
Galarza, Ernesto, 1905-
Papers, 1940-72.   38 ft.   (ca. 23,000 items).
In Stanford University Libraries, California.
In Part, Photocopies (Positive), and Mimeographs.
Sociologist and Labor Leader, of Los Angeles, California.
Correspondence . . . Relating to Farm Workers, Bracero Program, Migrant Labor, DiGiorgio Company Strikes . . . Delano, California Grape Strike With Cesar Chavez and National Farm Workers Association . . . History of Mexican-American Minority in the United States . . .
Unpublished Guide in the Library.
Information on Literary Rights Available in the Repository.
Gift of Dr. Galarza, 1971.

Appendix C: Directory

JOURNALS AND MAGAZINES

3097

Agenda; a Journal of Hispanic Issues. National Council of La Raza, 1725 "I" Street, NW, Washington, DC 20006 (1972- quarterly).

3098

Aztlan; International Journal of Chicano Studies Research. Chicano Studies Research Center, Campbell Hall 3122, University of California at Los Angeles, Los Angeles, CA 90024 (1970- semiannual).

3099

California History. California Historical Society, 2090 Jackson Street, San Francisco, CA 94109 (1922- quarterly).

3100

Con Safos: Reflections of Life in the Barrio. Box 31004, Los Angeles, CA 90031 (1968- quarterly).

3101

Grito del Sol; a Chicano Quarterly. Box 9275, Berkeley, CA 94709 (1976- quarterly).

3102

IRCD Bulletin. Institute for Urban and Minority Education, Teachers College, Columbia University, 525 W. 120th Street (Box 40), New York, N.Y. 10027.

3103

El Malcriado, the Voice of the Farm Worker. United Farm Workers of America, La Paz, Keene, CA 93531 (1968- bimonthly).

3104

New Mexico Historical Review. In care of University of New Mexico, Buena Vista 1013, Albuquerque, New Mexico 87131 (1926- quarterly).

3105

Southwestern Historical Quarterly. Texas State Historical Association, Richardson Hall 2-306, University Station, Austin, Texas 78712 (1897-quarterly).

3106
Southwestern Studies, Monographs. Texas Western Press, University of Texas at El Paso, El Paso, Texas 79968 (1963- quarterly).

BULLETINS AND NEWSPAPERS

3107
Alta California. San Francisco, 1849-1955.

3108
California. Monterey, 1846-

3109
California Farm Labor Report: Employment Estimates by County. California State Employment Development Dept., Sacramento, CA 95814 (semi-monthly).

3110
California Labor Supply and Demand, and *California Labor Market Bulletin* (monthly), both available from California State Employment Development Dept., Sacramento, CA 95814.

3111
El Chicano. Colton, CA, weekly.

3112
Diario del Hogar. México, D.F., 1900-1912.

3113
Diario Oficial. México, D.F., 1900-1912.

3114
Farm Labor. Citizens for Farm Labor, PO Box 1173, Berkeley, CA 94701.

3115
Farm Labor. Crop Reporting Board, U.S. Dept. of Agriculture, 14th Street & Independence Ave., S.W., Washington, D.C. 20250 (1936- quarterly).

3116
El Farolero. Long Beach, CA, monthly.

3117
Labor Press. Los Angeles, 1916-

3118
Labor Journal. Bakersfield, CA, 1903-

3119
Los Angeles Times. Los Angeles, 1881-

3120
The New Mexico Independent. Albuquerque, weekly.

3121
Oakland Tribune. Oakland, CA, 1903-

3122
La Opinión. Los Angeles, daily.

3123
Oxnard Courier. Oxnard, CA, 1903-

3124
Regeneración. Los Angeles, 1910-18.

3125
Sacramento Bee. Sacramento, 1857-

3126
San Diego Labor Leader. San Diego, 1906-

3127
San Diego Union. San Diego, 1868-

3128
San Francisco Chronicle. San Francisco, 1865-

Appendix D: Directory

1. AGRICULTURAL AND GROWERS' ASSOCIATIONS AND ORGANIZATIONS

3129
Apricot Producers of California, 1762 Holmes Street, Livermore, CA 94550

3130
California Artichoke Advisory Board, P O Box 747, Castroville, CA 95012

3131
California Avocado Commission, 17620 Fitch St., Irvine, CA 92714

3132
California Iceberg Lettuce Commission, P O Box 3354, Monterey, CA 93940

3133
California Fig Institute, P O Box 709, Fresno, CA 93712

3134
California Table Grape Commission, P O Box 5498, Fresno, CA 93755

3135
Cling Peach Advisory Board, P O Box 7111, San Francisco, CA 94120

3136
Great Plains Agricultural Council, 205 Pilley Hall, University of Nebraska, Lincoln, NE 68583

3137
Hop Growers of America, 504 N. Naches Avenue, Suite 5, Yakima, WA 98901

3138
Lemon Administrative Committee, 117 West 9th Street, Room 905, Los Angeles, CA 90015

3139
National Association of State Departments of Agriculture, 1616 H Street, NW, Washington, DC 20006

3140
Northwest Horticultural Council, P O Box 570, Yakima, WA 98907

3141
Plains Cotton Growers, P O Box 3640, Lubbock, TX 79452

3142
Sunkist Growers Association, 14130 Riverside Drive, Sherman Oaks, CA 91423

3143
Valley Fig Association, P O Box 1987, Fresno, CA 93718

3144
Washington State Apple Commission, P O Box 18, Wenatchee, WA 98801

2. ASSOCIATIONS CONCERNED WITH IMMIGRANTS IN GENERAL

3145
American Immigration Lawyers Association, 1000 Sixteenth Street, NW, Suite 501, Washington, DC 20036

3146
Citizens' Committee for Immigration Reform, 1424 Sixteenth Street, NW, 4th floor, Washington, DC 20036

3147
Immigrant History Society, in care of Professor Carlton Qualey, Minnesota Historical Society, 690 Cedar Street, St. Paul, MN 55101

3148
National Center for Immigrants Rights, 1544 West 8th Street, Los Angeles, CA 90017

3149
National Lawyers Guild, Immigration Project, 14 Beacon Street, Suite 407, Boston, MA 02108

3150
National Migrant Information Clearinghouse, Juarez-Lincoln Center, 3001 South Congress, Austin, TX 78704

3151
The Population Council, 1 Dag Hammarskjöld Plaza, New York, NY 10017

3. ASSOCIATIONS CONCERNED
WITH MEXICAN-AMERICANS

3152
Chicano Federation of San Diego County, Inc., 920 E St., San Diego, CA 92101

3153
Comisión Femenil Mexicana Nacional, 379 South Loma Drive, Los Angeles, CA 90017

3154
League of United Latin American Citizens, 4445 Fruitridge Road, Sacramento, CA 95820

3155
Mexican-American Legal Defense and Educational Fund, 28 Geary Street, San Francisco, CA 94108

3156
Mexican-American Opportunity Foundation, 670 Monterey Pass Road, Monterey Park, CA 91754

3157
Mexican Women's National Association, 1201 Sixteenth Street, NW, Washington, DC 20036

4. ASSOCIATIONS CONCERNED
WITH MIGRANT AGRICULTURAL WORKERS

3158
East Coast Migrant Health Project, 1234 Massachusetts Ave., NW, Washington, DC 20005
3158-A
Farm Worker Justice Funds, Inc., 2001 "S" Street, NW, Washington, DC 20009

3159
Migrant Legal Action Program, 806 Fifteenth Street, NW, Suite 600, Washington, DC 20005

3160
Migrant Outreach Resources Center Network, Colonias del Valle, Inc., San Juan, TX 78589

3161

Migrant Services Section, California State Dept. of Employment Development, 8000 Capitol Mall, Sacramento, CA 95814

3162

National Association of Farmworker Organizations, 1316 Tenth Street, NW, Washington, DC 20001

3163

National Committee on the Education of Migrant Children, National Child Labor Committee, 1501 Broadway, Room 1111, New York, N.Y. 10036

3164

National Conference of Catholic Bishops, U.S. Catholic Conference, Section for Hispanic Affairs, 1312 Massachusetts Avenue, NW, Washington, DC 20005

3165

National Farm Worker Ministry, 111-A Fairmount Avenue, Oakland, CA 94611

3166

National Migrant Information Clearinghouse, 3001 South Congress Street, Austin, TX 78704

3167

Pennsylvania Farm Labor Project, National Community Relations Division, American Friends Service Committee, 1501 Cherry Street, Philadelphia, PA 19102

3168

Rural Housing Alliance, 1346 Connecticut Avenue, NW, Suite 500, Washington, DC 20036

3169

Texas Farmworker Information Clearinghouse, 715 E. First Street, Austin, TX 78701

3170

Texas Governor's Office of Migrant Affairs, Executive Office of the Governor, Sam Houston Building, 7th floor, Austin, TX 78701

3171

Texas Good Neighbor Commission, Sam Houston Building, 201 E. 14th Street, Austin, TX 78701

3172

United Church Board for Homeland Ministries, 132 West 31st Street, New York, NY 10001

3173
U.S.-Mexico Border Health Association Secretariat, Coaches Coronado Tower, 6004 North Mesa Street, El Paso, TX 79912

5. RESEARCH CENTERS: GENERAL (WHICH HAVE TREATED THE TOPICS)

3174
Agricultural History Center, University of California, Davis, Davis, CA 95616

3175
Archives of Labor and Urban Affairs, Wayne State University, Walter P. Reuther Library, Detroit, MI 48202

3176
Bureau of Economic Research, University of Colorado-Boulder, Box 257, Boulder, CO 80309

3177
Center for Agricultural and Rural Development, Iowa State University, Ames, Iowa 50011
3177-A. Center for Labor and Migration Studies, New Transcentury Foundation, 1789 Columbia Rd., NW, Washington, D.C. 20009

3178
Center for the Study of Human Resources, 107 West 27th Street, University of Texas at Austin, Austin, TX 78712

3179
Center for the Study of Man in Contemporary Society, University of Notre Dame, Notre Dame, IN 46556
3179-A
Farm Labor Research Committee, 1901 "L" Street, NW, Washington, DC 20036

3180
Florida Atlantic University, Institute of Behavioral Research, College of Social Sciences, Boca Raton, FL 33431

3181
Institute for Research on Poverty, Social Science Building, Room 3412, University of Wisconsin-Madison, Madison, WI 53706

3182
Institute of Industrial Relations, University of California, Berkeley, 2521 Channing Way, Berkeley, CA 94720

3183
Population Research Center, University of Texas at Austin, Austin, TX 78712

3184
Population Research Center, University of Chicago, 1126 East 59th Street, Chicago, IL 60637

3185
Population Research Laboratory, University of Southern California, University Park, Los Angeles, CA 90007

6. RESEARCH AND INFORMATION CENTERS: MEXICAN IMMIGRATION

3186
Center for Inter-American and Border Studies, University of Texas at El Paso, El Paso, TX 79968

3187
Research Institute on Immigration and Ethnic Studies, 955 L'Enfant Plaza, SW, Washington, DC 20560
3187-A U.S.-Mexico Border Program, American Friends Service Committee, 1501 Cherry St., Philadelphia, PA 19102

3188
Center for Migration Studies, 209 Flagg Place, Staten Island, N.Y. 10304

3189
Center for U.S.-Mexican Studies, Q-057, University of California, San Diego, La Jolla, CA 92093

3190
Colegio de México, Programa de Estudios Estadounidenses, Camino al Ajusco, Mexico 20, D.F., México

3191
International Population Program, Cornell University, Uris Hall, Ithaca, NY 14853

3192
Centro de Estudios Fronterizos, El Colegio de México, Camino al Ajusco #20, Colonia Pedregal de Santa Teresa, Mexico 20, D.F., Mexico

3193
Centro de Estudios Fronterizos del Norte de México, Blvd. Abelardo Rodriguez 21, Zona del Río, Tijuana, B.C., Mexico

3194

Centro de Investigacion y Docencia Económicas, A.C., Carretera México—Toluca Km. 16.5, México 10, D.F., Mexico

3195

Institut d'Etudes Méxicaines, Université de Perpignan, Chemin de la Paiso Vella, 66000 Perpignan, France

3196

Institut des Hautes Etudes de l'Amérique Latine (I.H.E.A.D.), 28 Rue Saint Guillaume, 75007 Paris, France

3197

Centro de Estudios Económicos y Demográficos, El Colegio de México, Camino al Ajusco #20, Colonia Pedregal de Santa Teresa, Mexico 20, D.F., Mexico

3198

Escuela de Economia, Universidad Autónoma de Baja California, Ejido Tampico—Ciudad Universitaria, Tijuana, B.C., Mexico

3199

Mexico-U.S. Border Research Program, University of Texas at Austin, Austin, Texas 78712

3200

Centro de Información y Estudios Migratorios, Calle 2a., #1935-B, Despacho 110, Tijuana, B.C., Mexico

3201

Instituto de Investigaciones Económicas, Universidad Autónoma de Baja California, Tijuana, B.C., Mexico

3202

Centro de Información para Asuntos Migratorios y Fronterizos, American Friends Service Committee, Ignacio Mariscal #132, Mexico 1, D.F., Mexico

3203

Centro de Estudios Económicos y Sociales del Tercer Mundo, A.C., Cor. Porfirio Díaz #50, San Jeronimo Lidice, Mexico 20, D.F., Mexico

7. RESEARCH CENTERS: MEXICAN-AMERICANS

3204

Chicano Studies Research Center, University of California, Los Angeles, 405 Hilgard Avenue, Los Angeles, CA 90024

3205
Center for Iberian and Latin American Studies, University of California, San Diego, History Dept., C-004, La Jolla, CA 92093

3206
Center for Mexican-American Studies, Student Services Building, 4.120, University of Texas at Austin, Austin, TX 78712

3207
Mexican-American Studies and Research Center, Modern Languages Building, Room 209, University of Arizona, Tucson, AZ 85721

3208
Mexican-American Studies Program, University of Houston, 3801 Cullen Boulevard, Houston, TX 77004

3209
Stanford Center for Chicano Research, P O Box 9341, Stanford University, Stanford, CA 94305

3209-A
Arizona Farm Workers Union, 12221 Grand Avenue, El Mirage, Arizona 85335

8. UNIONS AND FARM LABOR ORGANIZATIONS

3210
Citizens for Farm Labor, P O Box 1173, Berkeley, CA 94701

3211
Farm Labor Organizing Committee (FLOC), 714-1/2 South St. Clair Street, Toledo, Ohio 43609 (Baldemar Velazquez, President)

3212
Farm Labor Research Committee, 1901 "L" Street, NW, Washington, DC 20036

3213
United Farm Workers of America, La Paz, Keene, CA 93531 (Cesar Chavez, President)

9. UNITED STATES GOVERNMENT AGENCIES, COMMISSIONS AND DEPARTMENTS

3214
Dept. of Agriculture, Fourteenth Street & Independence Ave., SW, Washington, DC 20250

3215

Dept. of Health and Human Services, 200 Independence Avenue, SW, Washington, DC 20201

3216

Dept. of Interior, C Street between 18th and 19th Streets, NW, Washington, DC 20240

3217

Dept. of Justice, Constitution Avenue & 10th Street, NW, Washington, DC 20530

3218

Dept. of Labor (OSHA), 200 Constitution Avenue, NW, Washington, DC 20210

3219

Employment Opportunity Commission, 2401 E Street, NW, Washington, DC 20506

3220

Immigration and Naturalization Service, 425 I Street, NW, Washington, DC 20536

3221

International Boundary and Water Commission, United States and Mexico, Executive Center, 4110 Rio Bravo, El Paso, TX 79902

10. STATE OF CALIFORNIA AGENCIES, DEPARTMENTS AND PROGRAMS

3222

Agricultural Labor Relations Board, 915 Capitol Mall, Sacramento, CA 95814

3223

Employment Development Dept., Capitol Mall, Sacramento, CA 95814

3224

Rural Legal Assistance Program, in care of California Industrial Relations Dept., 1006 Fourth Street, Sacramento, CA 95814

Author Index

Abeytia, Hector, et al., 2642
Abrams, E., 2056
Acuña, Rodolfo, 722,2416
Adair, Doug, 1277
Adamic, Louis, 1228
Adams, J., 541
Adams, Leonard P., 1571
Adams, R. L., 1468,1470,2840
Adelman, Lester C., 2724
Adler, Stephen, 965
Agricultural Workers Health & Medical
  Association, 1003,1011
Aguirre, J. D., 749
Ahearn, D. J., Jr., 1507
Airman, D., 187
Alaniz, Y., 597
Alba, Francisco, 2028
Albig, John W., 1757
Alexander, N., 630
Alexander, R. J., 323
Allen, Gary, 1271
Allen, Gina, 571
Allen, Robert F., 2779
Allen, Ruth A., 779,1481,2194,2834
Allen, Steve, 900
Allwell, Patrick J., 1723
Almaguer, Tomás, 2335
Alston, Lee J., 1662
Althoff, P., 1660
Altus, William D., 2232
Alvarado, Ernestine M., 1699
Alvarez, José, 1944
Alvarez, Salvador E., 2349,2892
Alvarez Dávalos, Rafael, 294
American Friends Service Committee,
  2640
American GI Forum of Texas, 1844
Amidon, Beulah, 808
Anderson, Henry, 1898,1920,2605,2671

Anzaldua, Ricardo, 2804
Anzaldua Montoya, Ricardo, ed., 2137
Applen, Allen G., 2731
Arias, Armando A., 2086,2087
Arias, Pedro, 1309
Arias, R., 627
Arizona. University College of
  Agriculture, 2485
Arizpe, Lourdes, 2138
Armentrout, Clara B., 2467,2471
Armstrong, John M., 2530
Armstrong, Richard, 1645
Arrington, Leonard J., 1556
Atwater, Ernesta E., 1787
Austin, Danforth W., 395
Austin, Mary H., 221,669
Avery, D., 1146,1384
Baca, Raynaldo, 2109
Bach, Robert L., 2029
Baer, Joshua, 451
Bailey, F., Jr., 1037
Bailey, Linwood K., 48
Bailey, Wilfred C., 2564
Baird, Peter, 2046
Baker, C. C., 1465
Baker, Verne A., 311
Ball, C. D., 1022
Ballis, George, 67,714
Bamford, Edwin F., 1710,2470
Banco Nacional de Comercio Exterior,
  324
Bank, J., 1066,1076,1078
Banks, E. H., 798
Barger, W. K., 1208
Barker, Eugene O., 1462
Barker, Frederick F., 1941
Barnes, Elinor J., 2274
Barr, E. L., 1292
Barrio, R., 2337

Book Title Index

(Note: this Index contains entries for print-format materials of a non-serial type, such as monographs, text and reference books, pamphlets, government publications of all types of jurisdictions from local to national, conference papers and proceedings, masters' theses and doctoral dissertations.)

Farmworker Need—Agency Services: a Study of Migrant and Seasonal Farmworkers and Service . . . , 2787

Farmworker Programs in Texas/TFIC, 2774

Farmworkers in Rural America, 1971-1972: Hearings: parts 4A-4B, June 19 & 20, 1972, on the Role . . . , 1615

Farmworkers in Rural America, 1971-1972: Hearings, part 1, July 22-September, 1971, on Farmworkers . . . , 2720

Farmworkers in Rural America, 1971-1972: parts 3A-3C, January 11-13, 1972, on Land Ownership, Use . . . 2708

Field Study in Mexico of the Mexican Repatriation Movement, 1772

Field Workers in California Cotton, 1515

Fields of Bondage; the Mexican Contract Labor System in Industrialized Agriculture, 1920

Final Report, 2459

Final Report, 1945, 1508

Final Report of the Farm Workers Opportunity Project, 1949

Final Report of the Farm Workers Opportunity Project, 2640

Finding Labor to Harvest the Food Crops, 2465

First Western Region Conference of OEO Migrant Projects, Woodburn, Oregon, June 7-9, 1967, 2639

Five Mexican-American Women in Transition: a Case Study of Migrants in the Midwest, 2772

Flores y Dolares: the Mexican Migrant to Half-Moon Bay, California, 2017

Follow-up Study of Servo: a Project for Monolingual, Low-Income Unemployed Mexican-Americans, 2356

Following the Trail of the IWW, a First-Hand Investigation Into Labor Trouble in the West . . . , 2825

For Land's Sake; the Autobiography of a Carefree Arizonian, 83

Foreigners in Their Native Land: Historical Roots of the Mexican-Americans, 2358

Forgotten Legions; Sheep in the Rio Grande Plain of Texas, 1592

Forgotten People; a Study of New Mexicans, 2210

Forty Acres; Cesar Chavez and the Farm Workers, 2881

Free Press Interview with Cesar Chavez, 1049

From Over the Border, a Study of the Mexicans in the United States, 1711

From This Earth . . . of the Delano Grape Strike, 2943

Frontier Odyssey; Early Life in a Texas Spanish Town, 2422

Future of Mexican Immigrants in California; a new Perspective for Public Policy, 2089

Gallant Women of 1977: Migrant Farm Workers, 2771

Geographic Differentials of Agricultural Wages in the United States, 1543

Geographic and Temporary Distribution of Migrant Agricultural Workers and Their Families in . . . , 2634

Golden Door: International Migration, Mexico and the United States, 2049

Good Neighbor Policy and Mexicans in Texas, 1791

Grape Boycott; why it has to be, 2932

Great American Land Bubble: the Amazing Story of Land Grabbing, Speculations and Booms From . . . , 20

Green Card Labor and the Delano Grape Strike: a Study of Postbracero Mexican National Farm . . . , 1951

Green Card Workers in Farm Labor Disputes; a Study of Postbracero Mexican National Farm Workers . . . , 1966

Role of the Mexican American in the History of the Southwest, 2312
Romance of the Ranchos, 27
Roof Over our Heads: Migrant and Seasonal Farmworker Housing in Idaho, 2793
Roots of Resistance: Land Tenure in New Mexico, 1680-1980, 2412
Roots of the Farm Labor Problem: Changing Technology, Changing Capital use,
     Changing Labor Needs, 1560
Rural Employment and Services Report, 1453
Rural Employment Report, 1460
Rural Manpower Report, 1456
Saddle in the Sky, 31
San Joaquin Valley Farm Workers Collection, 2819
Santa Fe; the Autobiography of a Southwestern Town, 2261
Santa Inez Valley: a Regional Study in the History of Rural California, 2230
Search for a Successful Agricultural Migrant: an Account of 6 Fruit Harvest on the
     West Coast of . . ., 2699
Seasonal Agricultural Labor in Oregon; Task Force Report, 2647
Seasonal Agricultural Laborers From Mexico, 1718
Seasonal Employment in Agriculture, 2489
Seasonal Farm Labor in the United States, With Special Reference to Hired Workers
     in Fruit and . . ., 2518
Seasonal Farm Labor: Study, 2683
Seasonal Labor in Santa Barbara County Agriculture: an Estimation of Future
     Demand, 2609
Seasonal Labor on Arizona Irrigated Farms, 2481
Seasonal Labor on Fruit and Vegetable Farms, New York State, 1945, 2520
Seasonal Labor Requirements for California Crops, 2487
Seasonal Work Patterns of the Hired Farm Working Force of 1964, 2283
Seeds of Discord: New Mexico in the Aftermath of the American Conquest, 1846-1861,
     2407
Selected Bibliography; United Farm Workers, 1973-1976, 2822
Selected Readings on Mexico, 1878
Selected References on Domestic Migratory Agricultural Workers, Their Families,
     Problems, and . . ., 2442
Selected References on the Labor Importation Program Between Mexico and the
     United States, 1675
Selected Research Bibliography on Mexican Immigration to the United States, 1680
Selective Bibliography of California Labor History, 1442
Selective Bibliography on Chicano Labor Materials, 2157
Service to Agricultural Migrants; What Some Communities are Doing, July 1, 1955,
     to June 30, 1956, 2566
Serving Migrant Families, 2457
Settling out and Settlin in, 2745
Seven Families: a Two-Year In-depth Study of Incomes and Job Experience of Seven
     Ohio Migrant Farm . . ., 2756
Short-run Effects of the Termination of Public Law 78 on the California Farm Labor
     Market for 1965 . . ., 1593
Short-run Socioeconomic Effects of the Termination of Public Law 78 on the
     California Farm Labor . . ., 1960
Situational Study of Migrant Farmworkers in South Carolina, 2735

Strangers in the Land; Patterns of American Nativism, 1860-1925, 1861
Strangers in Their own Land; a History of Mexican-Americans, 2355
Strangers in our Fields, 1869
Strangers in our Fields, 2256
Statement of H. L. Mitchell, President, on Amending Fair Labor Standards Act to
  Include . . ., 2844
Story of the Mexican-Americans; the men and the Land, 722
Strikes and Strike Tactics in California Agricultural History, 2926
Structure of Labor Markets; Wages and Labor Mobility in Theory and Practice, 1608
Study of Interpersonal Relations Among Managers and Employees of Fruit and Vegetable
  Farms with . . ., 1582
Study of Mexicans and Spanish Americans in the United States, 177
Study of Migrant Labor; Report to Accompany S. Res. 273 . . . , 2596
Study of Migrant Workers in Southwest Oklahoma, 2612
Study of Migrant Workers in Southwest Oklahoma, 2613
Study of Migratory Factors Affecting Education in North Kern County, 2476
Study of Migratory Labor, 2633
Study of Migratory Mexican Pea-Pickers in Imperial Valley, August 1940, 2500
Study of Migratory Workers in Cucumber Harvesting, Washara County, Wisconsin,
  1964, 2606
Study of New Mexico Agricultural Workers, 2336
Study of Some Aspects of the Spanish-Speaking Population in Selected Communities
  in Wyoming, 2220
Study of the Mexican, Mexican-American and Spanish-American Population in Pueblo,
  Colorado . . ., 2195
Study of the Mexican Population of Imperial Valley, California, 1714
Study of the Potential Relocation of Texas-Mexican Migratory Farm Workers to
  Wisconsin, 2308
Study of the Role of Mobility in the Acculturation Process of Rural Migrant and
  non-Migrant . . ., 2626
Study of the Social Attitudes of Adult Mexican Immigrants in Los Angeles and
  Vicinity, 1978
Study of 281 Farm Labor Families of South Texas, 1502
Submergence of the Mexican in California, From 1846 to 1890; a History of Culture
  Conflict and . . ., 2263
Suggested Recommendations of the Dept. of Labor to President's Commission on
  Migratory Labor, 2540
Sunbelt Frontier and Border Economy: a Field-Work Study of El Paso, 2413
Supply of Agricultural Labor as a Factor in the Evolution of Farm Organization in
  California, 2833
Survey of Agricultural Labor Conditions in Placer County, California, 1492
Survey of Farm Placement in Texas, 1936 and 1937, 1495
Survey of the Mexicans in Los Angeles, 2168
Survey of the Problems of the Migratory Mexicans, 1838
Sweatshops in the Sun: Child Labor on the Farm, 1619
Tabulation of Facts on Conditions Existent in Hicks' Mexican Camp, 1787
Tales of Americans on Trek, 792
Technological Change and Farm Labor use, Kern County, California, 1961, 1556
Temporary International Labor Migration, 2105

Periodical Article Title Index

Abatti Produce, Inc. to Halt Farming Operations Over Labor . . ., 1431
Abolition of el Cortito, the Short-Handled hoe: a Case . . ., 2920
Across the Border: Southern California Citrus Growers see . . ., 247
Across the River to the Farm, 571
Actos: Teatro Campesino, a Theatrical Part of the United . . ., 1031
Adjudication of Spanish Mexican Land Claims in California, 2260
Administering our Immigration Laws, 1824
Admission of Agricultural Workers into the United States, 1817
Admission of Alien Farm Workers into United States, 245
Advocacy Program for Spanish-Speaking People, 2390
Affluence Amid Poverty, 933
AFL and Mexican Immigration in the 1920's: an Experiment . . ., 1955
AFL vs. Wetback Labor, 306
AFL-CIO and United Farm Workers Peace Treaty due, 1114
AFL-CIO Backs Bosses' Anti-Immigrant . . ., 600
AFL-CIO Goes After Farm Workers, 1022
AFL-CIO Organizers go After Farm Labor, 1246
After Tijerina: La Raza, the Land and the Hippies, 80
Agrarian Revolt in California, 1214
Agribusiness Gets the Upper Hand, 156
Agricultural Distribution of Immigrants, 1685
Agricultural Distribution of Immigrants, 1686
Agricultural Employment: has the Decline Ended?, 141
Agricultural History of the Lower Rio Grande Valley Region, 1483
Agricultural History of the Lower Rio Grandee Valley Region, 1776
Agricultural Labor Problem, 1570
Agricultural Labor Relations Laws in Four States, 1117
Agricultural Labor-Contractor System in California, 1010
Agricultural Laborers in the United States, 1464
Agricultural Minimum Wage: a Preliminary Look, 66
Agricultural Research and Social Conflict, 1161
Agricultural Workers Strike, 1239
Agricultural Workers in California, 1546
Agricultural Workers in a California Town: Economics . . ., 2376
Agricultural Workers in the Class Structure, 1616
Agriculture and the Minimum Wage, 1589
Aiding Illegal Aliens, 422
Alatorre Column on U.S. INS Guest Worker Program With Mexico, 584
Alienation, Work Structure, and the Quality of Life: Can . . ., 1661
Aliens in the Fields: the Green Card Commuter Under the . . ., 1963
Aliens, Jobs and Immigration Policy, 2037

Title Index to Appendix A: Audiovisual Materials

Agricultural Workers of the Rio Grande and Rio Bravo Valleys: A Portfolio, 2974
Algo Para Manana (motion picture), 3007
Angel and Big Joe (film), 3019
Bargaining Power (film), 3025
Birth of a Union (film), 3024
Bitter Harvest (motion picture), 3008
Borderline (motion picture, color, sound), 2972
Boycott (motion picture), 3041
California Conflict: Migration Farm Workers (filmstrip), 3028
Los Compadres (film), 2988
Cesar Chavez (educational sound filmstrip, record), 3026
Cesar Chavez, Leader of the Downtrodden (filmstrip, audio tape), 3032
Cesar Chavez segment (In Sixty Minutes . . .), 3043
Cesar Chavez—the California Grape Boycott (audio tape cassette, monaural), 3039
Chicano! (motion picture), 2987
Chicano From the Southwest (motion picture), 2982
Children of the Fields (film), 3018
Contemporary Chicano Life Series (filmstrip), 2999
Decision at Delano (motion picture), 3035
Delano Grape Strike (motion picture), 3038
The Forgotten Families (motion picture), 3003
The Forgotten Families (motion picture), 3015
From South of the Border (educational filmstrip with captions), 2970
Fruits, Vegetables and People (filmstrip), 3017
Give and Take With Mexico (film), 2967
The Green Rising, 1910-1977 (FILM 80/24), 3033
A Group of Farm Workers Who Face a Dilemma. A Town Plans a Clinic (Two-Track Audio-Tape, Monaural), 3013
Harvest of Shame (motion picture), 3009
The Harvesters Help Provide our Food (film), 3011
Home is a Long Road (motion picture), 3004
Huelga! (motion picture), 3034
Human Relations in Agricultural Business (filmstrip), 2965
I am Joaquin (film), 2983
The Imperial Valley, Part 2: Men, Machines and a Bountiful Harvest (film), 2969
The Land (film), 2963
The Land: A Report by Chet Huntley (film), 2964
Los de la Raza (filmstrip), 3005
Los de la Raza (Those From the Nation) (educational sound filmstrip, record), 2984

Author Index to Appendix B:
Archival and Manuscript Materials